Family Therapy Basics

Third Edition

Mark Worden, Ph.D.
Fairfield University

THOMSON

BROOKS/COLE

Australia • Canada • Mexico • Singapore • Spain
United Kingdom • United States

THOMSON

BROOKS/COLE

Executive Editor: Lisa Gebo
Acquisitions Editor: Julie Martinez
Assistant Editor: Shelley Gesicki
Editorial Assistant: Mike Taylor
Technology Project Manager: Barry Connolley
Marketing Manager: Caroline Concilla
Marketing Assistant: Mary Ho
Advertising Project Manager: Tami Strang
Project Manager, Editorial Production:
Stephanie Zunich
Print/Media Buyer: Vena Dyer
Permissions Editor: Sue Ewing

Production Service: Jon Dertien, BookComp, Inc.
Text Designer: Jeanne Calabrese
Art Editor: Fred Schoerner
Copy Editor: Maria denBoer
Illustrator: Fred Schoerner
Cover Designer: Cloyce Wall
Compositor: BookComp, Inc.
Printer: Webcom Limited

For more information about our products, contact us at:
Thomson Learning Academic Resource Center
1–800–423–0563
For permission to use material from this text,
contact us by: **Phone:** 1–800–730–2214
Fax: 1–800–730–2215
Web: http://www.thomsonrights.com

Library of Congress Control Number: 2002104364

ISBN 0-534-51971-7

Brooks/Cole—Thomson Learning
511 Forest Lodge Road
Pacific Grove, CA 93950
USA

Asia
Thomson Learning
5 Shenton Way #01–01
UIC Building
Singapore 068808

Australia
Nelson Thomson Learning
102 Dodds Street
South Melbourne, Victoria 3205
Australia

Canada
Nelson Thomson Learning
1120 Birchmount Road
Toronto, Ontario M1K 5G4
Canada

Europe/Middle East/Africa
Thomson Learning
High Holborn House
50/51 Bedford Row
London WC1R 4LR
United Kingdom

Latin America
Thomson Learning
Seneca, 53
Colonia Polanco
11560 Mexico D.F.
Mexico

Spain
Paraninfo Thomson Learning
Calle/Magallanes, 25
28015 Madrid
Spain

Contents

Preface

"The theories make sense to me, but what do I do for an entire session with a live family?" lamented a beginning therapist facing his first family session. That statement, first uttered to me in supervision, captured the dilemma and anxiety of the beginning family therapist. About to complete a master's degree, the trainee was well versed in a variety of family therapy theories. He could distinguish strategic from structural approaches. He was facile in discussing differentiation and triangles. Family boundaries and coalitions made exquisite sense to him, but he had been awed at workshops where wizard-like masters made magical leaps of intuition, and he doubted whether he could ever do the same. And now, faced with his first interview, he felt a great gap between what he had learned in textbooks and what he was actually going to do in this upcoming session.

Paying closer attention to the questions supervisees were asking, I felt many of them could be summarized by a simple question, "What do I do next?" This is not a request for a conceptual discussion but a very pragmatic, down-to-earth, action-oriented question. Time after time it occurred to me that beginning family therapists—and even though my memory fades, I still remember my own terror in my first few sessions—experience great difficulty translating theories into action. They lack a good map to help them navigate the choppy waters of a family therapy session.

This book, therefore, addresses the needs of the beginning clinician by providing a process or "nuts-and-bolts"-oriented introduction to family therapy—a reference book of sorts for actually conducting family interviews. A thorough discussion of theoretical models, however, is left to other texts as a professor or supervisor deems appropriate. Instead, the book provides the student or trainee with practical guidelines for conducting family interviews (and, I hope, will relieve much of the anxiety of actually working with families), emphasizes common clinical problems, and serves as a springboard for theoretical and clinical discussions. To aid the reader, conceptual terms are boldfaced in the text and are defined in glossaries at the ends of chapters.

To accomplish its purpose, the book divides the treatment process into phases: the first interview, engagement, change and resistance, change techniques, and termination. The chapters include steps in conducting a first interview, establishing therapeutic boundaries and the therapist's use of self, the identification of family dysfunctional patterns, a discussion of the models for change and the role of resistance in change, techniques for promoting change, and termination within a developmental perspective.

Most chapters are divided into a conceptual discussion of a particular aspect or phase of treatment, the case presentation, and treatment notes. The treatment notes represent the therapist's internal dialogue: "Should I (the therapist) push for all family members to attend the next session?" "Should I let the father continue to dominate the session?" "How do I engage the adolescent?"—and so forth. These notes pose therapeutic questions but also offer practical here-and-now answers.

A single family—Donna and Peter Martin, his teenage daughter from a previous marriage, and her two children from her first marriage—is followed through the entire treatment process. As a result, the case presentation provides a continuing focus for the discussion of clinical problems and their solutions. The text further emphasizes the therapeutic choice points that occur during a therapy session. With this presentation, a balance is struck between providing the reader with a conceptual understanding of the family treatment process and offering a variety of potential therapeutic interventions.

This third edition builds and expands on the first two by adding a new chapter on assessment. Increasingly the field of family therapy swings back and forth between social constructionism and its emphasis on a family's unique narrative and a desire to build an empirical research base. The new chapter explores three empirical models of family assessment and applies these models to the Martin family. In keeping with the tone of the first two editions, the pros and cons of employing each model are highlighted.

I would like to thank the manuscript reviewers, who offered helpful suggestions for improving the text: Dr. Charles Seidel, Mansfield University; Siobhan McEnaney Hayes, Chestnut Hill College; Dr. Carol Pistole, Purdue University; Dr. Joshua Kirven, University of Central Florida; Dr. Roland Worthington, The College of New Jersey; Dr. Craig Abrahamson, James Madison University; Dr. Elyce A. Cron, Oakland University; Dr. Peggy H. Smith, California State University at San Francisco; Dr. Riley Venable, Texas Southern University; Dr. Jackie Halstead, Abilene Christian University. I found their comments most thoughtful and constructive.

Mark Worden

About the Author

Mark Worden, Ph.D., is a professor of psychology at Fairfield University, Fairfield, Connecticut, and has been a practicing clinical psychologist for over 25 years. He specializes in Marriage and Family Therapy, Adolescents, and Health Psychology. He is the author of *Adolescents and Their Family: An Introduction to Assessment and Intervention* (1991, The Haworth Press); *The Gender Dance in Couples Therapy* (1998, Brooks/Cole); and *Family Therapy Basics* (1st edition 1994; 2nd edition 1998).

1

The Movement to Systems and Social Construction

"You are lying!" yells 16-year-old Randy.

"No, I am not, and do not talk to me in that tone!" strikes back Randy's father, Mr. James. A sneer forms on Randy's face while Mr. James glares threateningly at his son.

The mother sits anxiously, fearing an escalation; Randy's 11-year-old sister, Susan, nervously shifts in her chair; next to Mrs. James sits 8-year-old Alice, sucking her thumb.

At this point, the battle lines are drawn; the spectators are seated and the moment freezes in what seems an interminable time. As the room fills with raw hostility, a thought passes through the therapist's mind: "Is it too late to see them each individually or to refer them individually to other therapists? In fact, why don't I suggest individual sessions with the son? That will certainly take the tension out of the room, and besides, that's what the parents came in for anyway: to fix their son!"

In retrospect, family therapy looked much more fulfilling and far less problematic to the therapist in the textbooks.

The therapist's reaction is common for someone beginning to work with families. In contrast to individual psychotherapy, in which the therapist-client dyad is much more predictable, therapist-family interactions can occur at a fast and furious pace, sometimes seeming to spin out of control. At other times, family exchanges are guarded, suspicious, and infrequent, with each member unwilling to volunteer any information; silence often dominates these sessions. Nevertheless, what becomes clear to a beginning family therapist is that adding more family members to the counseling session multiplies individual dynamics and increases the clinical data dramatically.

In the case of the James family, the father-son conflict would erupt with the least provocation and had the power to rivet everyone's attention. Any topic mentioned could provoke a father-son face-off and demand that the therapist focus on them. In reaction to the emotional power of arguments and the wealth of clinical data in the room, beginning family therapists tend to fall back on familiar turf. They narrow the clinical focus to the individual dynamics: What is the son's fury all about? Why does the father need control over such trivial matters?

The questions of causality and change swirl in the therapist's head. For example, the family would function better if the father were less controlling or if the son could release his fear of dependency and stop confronting his father. With this in mind, the therapist would begin to focus on changing one or both individuals. More often the case, the therapist would attempt to negotiate a settlement between the two.

Unfortunately, each session is strikingly like the previous one: A topic is brought up, the son complains, the father argues back, and the downward spiral of conflict begins. Caught in this cycle of futility, the therapist frequently applies more of the same by trying to get the father to be less controlling and the son to accept some of the father's limits. To accomplish this, the therapist solicits a compromise:

> **Therapist:** Now, Mr. James, if you will just allow a later curfew and if your son will just abide by these reasonable limits, then you two might not fight so much.

The therapist soon discovers, however, that what appears to be a reasonable intervention in the office—at least the father and son are sitting quietly at the end of the session—dissolves within a week's time after one or both of these family members violate the agreement. At this point the therapist is faced with a nagging question: "*Now* what do I do? The father will not back down from trying to control his son, and the son appears compelled to continually challenge the father's rules."

To answer the "now what" question, the therapist, rather than trying to change individual behavior, shifts perspective (or **epistemology**) and focuses on the family system. In doing so, the therapist moves to another level of conceptualization. Specifically, this epistemological shift occurs on three key dimensions:

1. transition from individual to systems dynamics
2. shift from linear to circular causality
3. distinction between content and process dynamics

Family Perspective Dimensions

Individual Versus Systems Dynamics

The power and pull of focusing on individual dynamics in therapy are reinforced by the wealth and depth of existing individual personality theories, the findings of developmental psychology concentrating on the individual, individually oriented psychiatric diagnostic categories, and one's personal idiosyncratic experiences.

Beginning first with Freudian, intrapsychic, psychodynamic theory, you have probably been introduced to a variety of personality theories in undergraduate and graduate courses. These theories center on the individual's experience on both the conscious and unconscious levels: intrapersonal experiences. Likewise, developmental psychology courses address the stages of individual development. True, some attention is paid to the interaction with others (social development), but the centerpiece is the individual responding to internal demands. In addition, current psychiatric diagnostic categories, based on the medical model, demand an individual perspective. Disorders exist and reside within the person. Finally, we are all most familiar with our own phenomenological experience in the world. Individual perspective is certainly a valid commodity because we all have it all the time.

What, then, is a family systems viewpoint all about? What does it add to our conceptualization of clinical problems and our desire to help our clients?

Briefly, when therapists move from the individual system to the family system level of analysis, they can see a family not merely as a collection of individuals but as a whole that is greater than the sum of its parts. Consequently, they can understand individual behavior within the context of the whole. The family becomes an entity of analysis in and of itself—an entity that seeks stability (**morphostasis or homeostasis**) in the face of environmental vagaries; at other times, however, it must change its structure (**morphogenesis**) to adapt better to internal and external demands. In other words, just as we can perceive a person as a developing entity responding to both internal and external forces and also seeking a sense of stability and continuity, we can observe the family behaving in a similar fashion.

More to the point, a systems perspective offers a way to conceptualize the wealth of data gathered in a family session as well as provide a foundation on which to plan and implement interventions. Individual behavior, therefore, no longer occurs in isolation but is embedded within the broader family context. Consequently, an individual family member's problematic or symptomatic behavior is seen as an outcome of family interactions and not as the result of individual dynamics. From a systems perspective, the therapist distinguishes between the forest (family dynamics) and the trees (individual dynamics). Rather than staying on the conceptual plane, however, we can apply systems concepts to the James family.

Because of failing grades and unexcused absences, Randy, 16 years of age, was referred by the school psychologist. He was judged by school personnel as being "at risk" of dropping out of school or even of potential involvement with the juvenile justice system. Both parents readily agreed to counseling because they had increasingly felt that Randy's behavior was outside their control. The family consisted of Mr. James (43 years of age), Mrs. James (42 years of age), Randy (16 years of age), Susan (11 years of age), and Alice (8 years of age).

From all accounts, the family had experienced few problems until Randy began high school. Mr. and Mrs. James felt that at the time he began to pull away from the family and to test his parents' authority continually. Arguments began over clothes, friends, curfew, and the like. From Randy's perspective, all he wanted was "a little freedom" to make his own decisions.

Simplified, the family pattern was for Randy to violate one of his parents' rules. His father would then confront him. This encounter would lead to an argument that would quickly escalate into a screaming match between the two. At that point, Mrs. James would enter the skirmish in an attempt to "calm them down before someone got hurt." More often than not, she would pull Randy away from his father and attempt to soothe her son. As for the two younger sisters, Susan would be in her room listening to every angry word; Alice would seek her mother out to nurture and to be nurtured.

From a systems perspective, the emergence of adolescence in one or more of the children, particularly the oldest child, is **feedback** (a circular message) within a family that change is required. Specifically, a transformation of the parent-child relationship needs to occur that will permit greater autonomy for the blossoming young adult while still maintaining a sense of connection among the family members (Worden, 1991). In the James family, the **rules** (overtly or covertly agreed-to relationship patterns that organize the system) guiding the parent-child relationship had been established when the children were younger; they were clearly ill-suited for a parent-adolescent relationship. Concretely, the means of disciplining and guiding an 8-year-old are different from the parental practices effective with a 16-year-old. The James family, moreover, was experiencing great difficulty changing or transforming (morphogenesis) the parent-child relationship into a parent-adolescent one. Mr. James's position was that a child was always a child as long as he or she continued to live under the parents' roof.

Moreover, within the family, both the rules and **roles** (individually prescribed patterns of behavior) were rigid. Children were to be seen and not heard, a rule Mr. James enforced with an iron hand. He was clearly the autocrat in the family and had a dogmatic idea of right and wrong; consequently, Randy's rebellious behavior was intolerable to him. Mr. James was the judge and sergeant-at-arms attempting to bring order to his home. Mrs. James was the peacekeeper. Randy was the victim or rebel, depending on one's point of view. Susan was the innocent bystander caught in conflict she had no hand in creating or controlling. Alice was the lost child wanting to be nurtured.

The family's **boundaries** (emotional barriers that protect and enhance the integrity of individuals, subsystems, and families) were relatively impermeable to the outside environment: "I don't care what other kids are allowed to do; as long as you live under *my* roof, you will follow *my* rules." At the same time, these boundaries were internally diffuse. That is, the family's **subsystem boundaries** were poorly defined. Family members were not permitted a sense of individuality, which was sacrificed for the greater whole. For example, Randy was not allowed to spend very much time alone in his room. What was normal adolescent developmental behavior, sitting in his room with the radio blasting, was viewed by his parents as a rejection of the family.

Clinically, when viewed from a systems perspective, Randy's "rebellious" behavior is placed within the family context and, thus, the definition of the problem broadens. The question of "What is wrong with Randy?" shifts to "What is the function, purpose, or meaning of Randy's behavior within the family dynamics?" Several initial systems hypotheses might be tried:

1. Randy's behavior reflects the family's inability to transform a parent-child relationship into a parent-adolescent one.

2. Randy's behavior is the steam valve on the family's boiling kettle; his blowups release built-up pressures, such as marital problems.

3. Randy's behavior is an outgrowth of the parents' inability to set reasonable, consistent, and fair limits.

[handwritten margin note: To develop hypothesis question function, purpose or meaning of ___ behavior within the family dynamic.]

4. Randy and his father are fighting over Mrs. James's attention.
5. Randy is fighting his father in defense of what he perceives to be his mother's oppression by the father.

Furthermore, when viewed from a systems perspective, the level of intervention also shifts. Individual therapy with Randy is complemented or replaced by family therapy. Embedded in the family's interactional patterns, Randy's behavior changes as the family changes. Thus, modifying the **family system** (the family's structure or organization and its interactional patterns) becomes the focus of treatment.

Linear Versus Circular Causality

Just as the movement to a systems model changes the definition of the problem, the shift in perspective also changes one's view of causality—from linear to circular. With linear causality, event A causes event B; the dominoes are in a straight line and fall in sequence. Applying this line of reasoning to the James family, the following would be hypothesized:

1. If Randy would only obey his parents and stop his rebellious behavior, everything would be fine in the family.
2. If Randy were only granted more freedom, his rebellious behavior would stop.
3. If Mr. James would stop being so intrusive with his son, Randy would be less angry and more likely to comply with his parents' wishes.
4. If the father-son relationship could be improved, Randy's behavior would change.
5. If Mrs. James would only consistently support her husband in his battles with their son, Randy would receive a united message from his parents and obey.

The choice of any of the above lines of reasoning will strongly determine the therapist's behavior. For example, if Randy's behavior is seen as the cause of the family's disruption, individual therapy is the treatment of choice. Even if family therapy is employed, the therapist's response might still be strongly influenced by linear assumptions. For instance, if the father is seen as the "cause" of Randy's behavior, using the family session to influence Mr. James to change becomes the therapist's overt or covert agenda.

Circular causality, on the other hand, places individual behavior within a network of **circular feedback loops** (an individual family member's behavior affects other family members, which in turn affects the individual); everyone's behavior impacts everyone else's. Thus, the cause and effect of linear causality becomes purely arbitrary; one individual's behavior is in reaction to the behavior of others but also influences others' behavior. To say, therefore, that one person causes another's behavior misses the power of the circular pattern of interactions; rather, person A affects B and C as much as B and C affect A in mutual reciprocal interactions.

Returning to the James family, Randy was reacting to his father's seemingly inappropriate restrictions, but Mr. James was restricting because his son was out of control. Mrs. James was trying to be fair to both her husband and her son, but her behavior only served to make both of them more angry because she appeared to be supporting one against the other. In turn, both Randy and his father became increasingly angry toward one another and toward Mrs. James. Consequently, Mr. James had to prove to his wife how out of control Randy was, and Randy, in turn, had to show his mother how unfair his father was. Finally, Susan vicariously absorbed the conflict and was potentially destined to act out herself, whereas the nurturing that Alice wanted was lost in the family battles. Thus, each member's behavior directly influences others' behavior, and shifts in one part of the system reverberate throughout the system.

Circular causality, therefore, draws the therapist's attention away from seeing individuals causing behavior in others to a broader view of the family's repeating and self-perpetuating cycles of interaction. The family's cycles can be functional (adaptive for the family) or dysfunctional (maladaptive for the family by producing symptomatic behavior in one or more family members). Moreover, these repeating and self-perpetuating cycles of interaction weave the family's life tapestry. In terms of family psychotherapy, therefore, the family's dysfunctional patterns become the focus of assessment and intervention.

Finally, circular causality eliminates the "bad guy" assumption. As discussed in a later chapter, families typically present the explanations of their problems in linear terms: If only he or she would quit doing that, we could all live in peace. Defining a problem in this way frequently produces a **family scapegoat** (the family member blamed for the disruptions and tension). Depending on the therapist's linear perspective, for example, Randy might be the cause of the family's problems, or Mr. James could be the culprit.

Circular causality, however, argues that there is no "bad guy"—a family member who is entirely to blame for the problem. Rather, *each* family member is mutually and reciprocally shaping the behavior of others. What emerge from this reciprocal shaping are patterns that are discernible and more or less functional or dysfunctional for the family.

Content Versus Process Dynamics

The shift to a systems model also raises the distinction between content and process in the presenting problem and in the therapy sessions. **Content** refers to the concrete issue being discussed—the "what" that is being said—in the session; **process** refers to how the issue is portrayed in the family's interactions. In other words, process is the systematic series of interactions that underlies the content discussion. For example, the James's arguments could be over any number of content issues: Randy's attitude, his choice of friends, his school performance, curfew, and so forth. Nevertheless, the process of these arguments—the family's underlying repetitive, dysfunctional, problem-solving pattern—was the same regardless of which content issue was center stage at any particular moment in therapy.

To further elaborate, Mr. and Mrs. James presented their problem as their son's behavior. When asked to specify their problem more clearly, the parents expressed a desire to change Randy. Initially, they brought up changes in their son that they wanted to see: improved school performance, obedience to their rules, a better attitude toward his father and mother, and so on. Notwithstanding, the therapist was concerned with the process issues:

- How does Randy's behavior fit into the family patterns?
- Why did Randy's behavior evolve at this time?
- How do the family members solve their problems?
- How does each person shape and reinforce the other family members' behavior?
- What is the function of Randy's behavior for the family system?

Most important, the therapist was concerned with the last question. Papp (1983) points out that a current controversy in the family therapy field is whether the symptom (Randy's behavior) serves a homeostatic function (morphostasis—keeping the family the same) or an evolutionary function (morphogenesis—encouraging the system to evolve new patterns of functioning).

From a morphostatic line of reasoning, Randy might play a part in a covert marital conflict. His acting-out behavior focuses the family's attention on him and thus distracts the parents from their own personal disagreements. It is easier for the parents to argue over Randy than to face their disappointments in each other. Moreover, their marital conflicts do not surface to threaten the family's existence, and the tenuous balance in the family is maintained. From this view, Randy is sacrificing himself to preserve the family unit.

Another morphostatic hypothesis would be that Randy's behavior maintains the child orientation of the family. Adolescence signals a separation from parents and a movement to young adulthood. What is a welcome relief to some parents is a threat to others, particularly in the area of control. If Randy remains a child, the family's balance (on the control dimension) is maintained. Ironically, Randy's acting-out behavior did not further his independence but served to increase adults' control over his life as both school personnel and his parents placed increased limits on him. He protested that he wanted freedom but acted in ways that forced adults to impose greater restrictions on him. Thus, Randy was viewed by the parents not as a young, emerging adult but as a child still in need of control.

In contrast, the evolutionary line of reasoning (morphogenesis) would argue that Randy's behavior is pushing the family to a new level of organization. By rebelling and fighting against what he perceives as his family's restrictiveness— "They want me to be just like them"—Randy is forcing the family to reorganize itself and, therefore, to grow. His behavior is proclaiming loudly that the family's morphostasis, effective when all the children were under the age of 10, is inappropriate for a 16-year-old. Adolescents' symptoms signal a blocked developmental sequence, and a "better fit" between the adolescent and family needs to evolve (Worden, 1991). Thus, from an evolutionary viewpoint, the family in your office might be seen as an organization strained by new demands—internal or external pressures—but responding in old, ineffective patterns and thus increasing their "problems."

As you can see, the shift in attention from content issues (what the family presents as its problem) to process issues (the balance of morphostasis and morphogenesis forces in the family) is a dramatic one for the therapist. The content-oriented therapist would be busy with the James family attempting to resolve or negotiate each of the content issues: curfews, choice of friends, and school performance levels. The process-oriented therapist, however, would be searching for the dysfunctional patterns that underlie the content complaints: What is blocking the family from solving its own problems? How or why are morphostatic forces dominating the James family?

Applicability of Systems Perspective

Individual models of behavior extend poorly to family dynamics. As the early pioneers in family therapy began breaking from their own theoretical pasts and started working with families, they saw a need to conceptualize the wealth of new data available as they added family members to the treatment process. Cybernetics and general systems theory offered the foundation on which to build a new treatment modality that emphasized a systems perspective of behavior, circular causality, and process over content.

Note, however, that a systems paradigm in no way diminishes other established models. Much can be gained from a solid grasp of human developmental theory and individually oriented models, such as psychoanalytic, behavioristic, humanistic, cognitive, and other models. In fact, a well-rounded clinician benefits from a knowledge of all these areas. Nevertheless, a systems perspective offers a unique way of conceptualizing behavior as the clinician moves from an individual level of analysis to the family level. When a string of emotional firecrackers is going off in your office, you can use a systems perspective to order the cacophony and, equally important, to develop intervention strategies that flow from this broader perspective.

Finally, as you will discover with further reading and the courses you will take, the term *systems theory* means different things to different people. Overall, it is a generic term for conceptualizing a group of related elements (family members) that interact as a whole entity (the family). Above all, it is more a way of thinking than a coherent, standardized theory (Nichols & Schwartz, 1991). Its strengths, nevertheless, are its ability to place an individual within the family context, drawing attention to how family members relate and thus opening new avenues to assessment and intervention.

Social Constructionism

Systems theory is a fundamental knowledge base that most family therapists share. As clinical practice evolves, however, theories are revised and refined, new techniques are developed, and established perspectives are questioned. Social constructionism represents a recent epistemological challenge to or, as discussed later, a complement to systems theory.

Like systems theory, **social constructionism** means different things to different people and is also a way of thinking about the world. A common thread running through social constructionist concepts is that meaning or knowledge is constructed through social interaction (Gergen, 1985). What we deem as truth develops through social interaction whereby accepted beliefs are a result of social consensus. For example, at one time, an accepted fact or truth was that the world was flat. Based on new hypotheses (the world is round) and new data (the voyage of Columbus), the once-accepted fact was discarded for a new one. Thus, socially constructed, consensually held beliefs become our definitions of "reality."

To clarify further, most social constructionists would endorse at least one of the following assumptions (Gergen, 1985):

1. The world can be understood in a variety of ways; an absolute reality does not exist. Instead, reality varies from individual to individual, from culture to culture. This assumption reflects the work of cultural anthropologists which demonstrates that different cultures subscribe to many different understandings of the world.

2. People interact and actively construct their understanding of the world. Reality is a social product. What was politically correct 20 years ago might be offensive today.

3. Specific understandings are popular or dominate a given field because they are useful. For example, individual psychotherapy dominated mental health practices until systems theory began to be applied to families. The family then became the focus, expanding treatment options.

4. These socially constructed understandings directly influence the ways individuals perceive and respond to their environments. Consequently, the beliefs I hold about myself and the world around me directly impact my behavior.

[handwritten margin note: Social Constructionist Assumptions]

Although not directly referenced in these assumptions, implied in each is the power of language. Social construction grows out of human dialogue. Through the process of language and discourse, we shape our beliefs. In therapy, therefore, language and the conversational process are of particular importance.

As a newer epistemology, social constructionism is concerned with how people understand the world around them, what meanings they create to explain the world, and how these meanings are constructed. To this end, human beings are seen not as passive recipients of their environment but as active shapers, using their perceptions to "construct" their view of the world.

As a result, at any given time, one model dominates a field only to be supplanted later by a newer social consensus. The field of psychotherapy, for example, has gone through and will continue to go through an evolutionary process. Behavior modification served as a reaction against psychoanalytic thought, and cognitive therapy addresses the areas behavior modification minimizes. Family therapy also has a history in which emerging paradigms or models supplant existing, once-dominant models. When the various systems of family therapy over the past 30 years are reviewed, one model will be seen as dominant in terms of its popularity in books, articles, and conference presentations, only to be supplanted in time by other models and themes.

Currently, the influence of social constructionism can be seen in the popularity of narrative approaches to therapy and a shift from **problem-focused therapy** to **solution-focused therapy**. Although elaborated in later chapters, an introduction can be helpful in orienting the reader to the distinctions between systems, problem-focused family therapy, and narrative, solution-focused psychotherapy.

When we view "reality" as a social construction that is strongly influenced by language, our view of families and psychotherapy undergoes a strong shift. Instead of focusing on changing family interactional patterns, a social constructionist will see therapy as a language- and meaning-generating endeavor in which the client and therapist create meaning with each other (Berg & DeShazer, 1993). We tell our stories in our thoughts and conversations, and these explain who we and others are. Our stories are our constructed realities.

In **narrative therapy**, a client initially presents a dominant story or narrative about his or her problem. Characteristically, the dominant story is so "problem-saturated" that it excludes experiences free of the "problem" and filters problem-free experiences from a person's memories and perceptions (White & Epston, 1990). Adding family members to therapy creates additional stories of the same events (competing stories) or a monolithic, problem-saturated, dominant story. Sometimes, this is a story or narrative devoid of hope.

In the James family, competing stories were demanding the therapist's attention. Mr. James told the story of his attempts to manage and control his "out-of-control" son, Randy. In his story, Mr. James was a caring, responsible father with a son who was rapidly spiraling downward. Mrs. James's story overlapped with her husband's, but it had an added twist. Although her story also featured vignettes of Randy's rebellious behavior, Mrs. James feared a potentially bloody showdown between father and son. Supporting the parents' narrative was the school's story of Randy's "at-risk" behavior. Randy's story, on the other hand, was one of persecution. He was being squeezed on all sides and was reacting accordingly.

Unfortunately, each story was problem-saturated and devoid of hope or possibilities. The family was locked in a struggle for dominance and control. By the time of referral to the therapist, the individual stories were calcified. In the process of therapy, these stories or narratives would compete for dominance by pulling at the therapist.

In narrative therapy, the therapist accepts each story as reality for the respective family member but also believes each narrative has been socially constructed. The therapist engages the family members in conversation and invites them to reauthor the stories to include hope and new, previously unacknowledged alternatives. For example, there are times and ways that Randy is not rebellious but helpful and considerate. Randy could be trying to find his own way in the world, just as his father had done at a similar age. Mr. James does not wish to restrict and punish his son but is striving to guide and protect him. As stories are rewritten, strengths are uncovered and hidden possibilities surface.

Another subtle difference between systems therapy and narrative therapy applied to families is the role of the therapist. Again, this is elaborated in a later chapter (Chapter 3, in which the role of the therapist is discussed). Briefly, most family systems approaches place the therapist in the expert position. In this hierarchical arrangement, the therapist is the expert who will direct the course of therapy and facilitate change.

Narrative family therapy shifts the therapist-family alliance from a hierarchical arrangement to a more egalitarian relationship (Andersen, 1993). The therapist is not an expert doing something to the family but a collaborator with the family. The therapist and family will thus co-construct more healthy narratives to replace the problem-saturated ones.

Again, paying attention to language and meaning, families enter therapy with a set of "problem" behaviors—for example, Randy is out of control. Thus, Randy is the family's problem and he must be changed. (Of course, Randy has a different version of the family story, but his view is overwhelmed by the parents' and school's narratives.) Problem-focused therapy would accept this story as fact and focus on changing Randy—a tack Randy would most surely resist.

A solution-focused approach shifts the figure-ground. Instead of attempting to change Randy (even if the effort is made by changing the family interactional patterns), a solution-focused therapist builds on the family's strengths and wants and not on calcified problems. What does the family do well and what do they want more of? The James family wants more respect and cooperation among its members. Respect and cooperation exist in the family but not in the amount they wish. Consequently, the therapist is there to help them discover or build on solutions that increase the family's satisfaction level. In doing so, the family's strengths are reinforced and maximized.

The Ongoing Debate

Theories emerge to challenge existing views only to be challenged themselves at a later point in time. A debate now occurring within the field of family therapy is how to reconcile the incompatibilities of systems theory and social constructionism. Family systems theory and therapy argue that there are observable patterns that differentiate highly functioning families and dysfunctional families. These patterns are objective in that multiple observers would "see" the same thing. Accordingly, the therapist is an expert at assessing and changing these patterns.

Social constructionist theory and narrative therapy argue that family systems theories are not objective representations of reality but socially constructed models. As such, one model is no more valid than another model. Consequently, what one "sees" is truly in the eye of the beholder. If you are looking for a power hierarchy, you will see it. If you are looking for boundaries, you will find them.

Levine and Fish (1999) refer to systems and social constructionist theory as first- and second-order cybernetics. First-order cybernetic theories (family systems) provide clinicians with various techniques to change the dysfunctional aspects of families. The therapist is an expert who assesses and attempts to change the functional and dysfunctional patterns in families. Second-order cybernetics (social constructionist theories, such as narrative therapy) question the possibility of the therapist's objectivity. The therapist's own view of the family is yet another construction and is not qualitatively better or worse than the family's view of the problem. In therapy, therefore, the family and therapist co-create a new reality or, in narrative terms, a new story line.

Many family therapists are embracing social constructionism because it liberates them from the role of an expert who judges and attempts to change the dysfunctional patterns in families and moves them to a position of co-collaborator with families in creating new and more rewarding stories. In a subtle, but powerful shift, the therapist is no longer focusing on problems and limitations but on building strengths within the family. Objective judgment is replaced by subjective relativism. Ethnic and racial family patterns, for example, are not viewed from a single systems model, such as structural family therapy, but each family is seen within a greater ethnic and racial context.

After a pendulum swings one way, however, it soon swings back in the opposite direction. The subjectivity of narrative therapy replaces the objectivity of systems theory. The question is, are we throwing the baby out with the bath water? Specifically, by embracing the relativism of social constructionism are we denying all objectivity and failing to build an empirical body of knowledge?

If there is no objective reality and, therefore, we do not acknowledge discernible family patterns that may be functional or dysfunctional, then how do we assess a family? How do we make judgments concerning what to change? What do we as therapists do when confronted with spouse or child abuse in a family? Or, when alcoholism is tearing a family apart? Do we objectively judge these patterns as dysfunctional, or do we view them as stories that need to be rewritten? Do we throw out all the research literature on child development and parenting practices and avoid being guided by these findings?

Fundamentally, how do we build a body of knowledge if objectivity is denied? Reviewing the utility of narrative therapy, Etchinson and Kleist (2000) argue that research on its value is sparse because of the constructivist's denial of the possibility of classifying and categorizing family patterns. They conclude: "the breadth of research on utility of narrative therapy approaches is limited. Certainly, no statement can be made about narrative therapy as the approach to use for any particular family problem" (p. 65).

Bertrando (2000) argues that narrative therapy without systems is incomplete and that they complement one another. Narrative approaches to therapy emphasize the subjective meaning people find for themselves as individuals. Systems theory, on the other hand, places individuals within the context of relationships. By applying both, a therapist is continually adjusting his or her viewing lens from the individual to the family system and back again.

To combine both approaches successfully, Pilgrim (2000) adopts a stance of skeptical social realism. Skeptical social realism is the belief that there are facts that are empirically research-based and have explanatory power. We know that certain family patterns, for example, the denial of alcoholism, are detrimental to family functioning. That said, each family constructs its own unique, narrative story of alcoholism. In working with this type of family, a therapist would find himself or herself shifting back and forth between the impact of alcoholism on the family system and the subjective meaning alcoholism has for each family member.

Summary

A systems perspective forms a foundation for an introduction to family therapy. However, as in any field, predominant paradigms will be challenged by emerging paradigms as the field evolves. Family therapy is no exception and has its own share of competing and emerging models of family "reality."

Social constructionism represents an epistemological shift that has opened the field to narrative and solution-focused models of therapy. As the shift contains subtle but significant differences in viewing family therapy, social constructionism can complement systems theory and offer new possibilities for assessment and intervention with families.

From a social constructionist position, systems theory is a utilitarian lens through which family interactions can be perceived. The theory serves as a road map to guide assessment and intervention. As such, it provides coherence to the therapist's thoughts and actions.

Overview of the Book

There are diverse models of family and systems therapy. Among these models are the psychoanalytic, transgenerational, group, symbolic-experiential, behavioral, contextual, Eriksonian, focal, psychoeducational, strategic, and structural (Gurman & Kniskern, 1991). Each of these conceptual models offers its own unique perspective on and assumptions about family functioning, symptom formation, and intervention approaches. This book is not designed to explore any of these in depth or to discuss the assumptions underlying each model. Such a task is much better accomplished in existing texts: Goldenberg and Goldenberg (1985); Gurman and Kniskern (1991); Nichols and Schwartz (1991); Piercy and Sprenkle (1986). Instead, this volume elaborates the themes of systems dynamics, circular causality, and a process orientation, providing a pragmatic overview of the basics of family psychotherapy. In addition, the recent impact of social constructionism, narrative models, and solution-focused models is explored.

The topics and concepts that are sampled cover a broad range of family therapy approaches. They were selected because of their universality and familiarity to most family therapists. Despite an attempt to balance a variety of approaches for the beginning family therapist, the text reflects the author's own bias toward structural and strategic systems models and the more recent narrative, solution-focused approaches. This is most evident in the assessment of family patterns and the preference for making these patterns the focus of treatment, particularly in the "here and now" of the therapy session.

Each chapter is divided into an initial conceptual discussion interspersed with case material and treatment notes. Although not quite a how-to guide, the book should demonstrate the challenge of working with families and increase the reader's comfort in conducting family therapy.

Chapter 2 outlines the steps in the initial phase of treatment: the first interview. Case content is contrasted with process observations that the therapist can make in assessing family patterns and building a therapeutic alliance. The chapter also introduces the Martin family, which will be followed throughout the different phases of treatment. (To protect confidentiality, the case is an amalgamation of families I have worked with in therapy.) By following one case, you should be able to capture the full flavor of working with a family from initial interview through termination.

Chapter 3 examines the therapeutic alliance developed in the initial phase of treatment. This alliance is a mix of family inputs (gender roles, ethnicity, and developmental life cycle) and therapist's inputs (theory and training, gender biases, family of origin, and life cycle). Particular attention is paid to the role of the therapist in engaging the family members, including young children, in the process of therapy. It argues that therapeutic possibilities increase when a strong therapeutic alliance is forged.

For this edition, a new chapter has been added. Chapter 4 discusses the implications of diagnosis and introduces the reader to three empirical approaches to family assessment. Within the field of mental health, the diagnostic handbook is the *Diagnostic and Statistical Manual* (DSM). Built on the medical model, the *DSM* emphasizes an individual family member's pathology and stands in sharp contrast to family therapy's system perspective. Rather than assess individuals, family therapists assess systems. The three empirical approaches discussed in this chapter share a structural systemic approach to families. In addition, each model has developed measuring instruments to guide assessment.

Because family patterns are intricately tied to a systems approach, Chapter 5 offers a practical introduction to assessing patterns of behavior. It gives concrete examples of questions the therapist can ask to further delineate family patterns.

After the therapist has identified family patterns and established a working alliance with the members, the middle phase of treatment is concerned with implementing change. Chapter 6 discusses the delicate balance of change and resistance in the process of therapy. Change is conceptualized in terms of first- and second-order as well as a problem versus solution focus. In particular, the therapist's ability to challenge family norms without overstimulating the family's anxiety level is emphasized. Also, attempts at change are frequently met with resistance; consequently, identifying and responding to treatment impasses are keys to therapeutic success.

Specific interventions and techniques are discussed in Chapter 7. In designing and implementing interventions, the therapist is matching the appropriate technique with the family system at a time in treatment that captures the opportunities for change. To guide you in planning interventions, the change techniques are categorized in sequence, first- to second-order.

Chapter 8 discusses the final phase of treatment: termination. The guidelines include assessing whether goals have been reached, identifying potential problems, and leaving the door open for future contacts.

Glossary

Boundaries Emotional barriers protecting and enhancing the integrity of individuals, subsystems, and families that also include the rules defining patterns of interaction.

Circular causality A sequence of cause and effect in which the explanation for a pattern leads back to the first cause and either confirms or changes that first cause; A causes B causes C, which causes or modifies A.

Circular feedback loops Process in which an individual family member's behavior affects the behavior of other family members; this, in turn, affects the individual.

Content Concrete issues being discussed in the therapy session.

Epistemology By strict definition, the branch of philosophy concerned with the development of knowledge. Within the field of family therapy, the term is used as a synonym for a person's belief system, perspective, or worldview.

Family scapegoat One family member whom the other members blame for the family's difficulties and emotional upheaval.

Family system A particular family's structure or organization and the members' interactive patterns.

Feedback A circular message within a system.

Homeostasis A system's tendency toward stability or a steady state.

Linear causality A cause-and-effect relationship in which the sequence does not come back to the starting point: A causes B causes C causes D and so on.

Morphogenesis The formation and development of structures in a system; delineates the system-enhancing behavior that allows for growth, creativity, innovation, and other change.

Morphostasis Similar to homeostasis, it is the ability of a system to maintain its structure in a changing environment.

Narrative therapy An approach to therapy in which the belief system of an individual or a family is the focus of change.

Problem-focused therapy An approach to therapy in which behavior patterns are seen as problems that need to change.

Process Interpersonal dynamics and patterns of interactions underlying the content issues.

Roles Individually prescribed patterns of behavior reinforced by the expectations and norms of the family.

Rules Overt or covert agreements within a family that organize the members' interactions into a reasonably stable system.

Social constructionism An epistemological perspective that views beliefs as consensually held and reinforced—products of social interaction.

Solution-focused therapy An approach to therapy that mobilizes the family's strengths to increase desired behavior.

Subsystem boundaries Boundaries defining smaller units embedded within a larger system such as individuals, siblings, parents, and extended family.

2

The First Interview: Initiating Assessment and Engagement

Developing the Capacity to Observe

Basic Interactive Concepts: Preliminary Observations

The First Interview

Summary

Glossary

The first interview initiates two crucial processes for therapeutic success: engagement and assessment. Engagement involves the forming of a therapeutic, trusting alliance between the therapist and the family that permits them to explore together the inner workings of the family relationships. (The engagement process is introduced in this chapter, and a more detailed discussion follows in the next chapter.) Assessment is the process of identifying the family's interactional patterns and then focusing on the ones directly related to the problem behavior. After the first interview, ideally the therapist begins to formulate working hypotheses about the family's patterns that are producing and maintaining the symptomatic behavior.

In traditional psychiatric models, diagnosis is a two-step process. First, the therapist makes an assessment of an individual's internal experience through the person's self-report and the therapist's observations of the person's behavior. Second, these data are placed into categories and given a label, which serves as a shorthand means of summarizing the individual's symptoms. The movement to a family systems perspective, however, radically changes the concept of assessment and diagnosis.

An important shift is that one family member is not singled out as possessing a disorder. Rather, the family becomes the unit of analysis. The data the therapist gathers consist of intrapersonal experiences—how each family member thinks and feels about the problem, particularly, his or her view of others' behavior and motivations—and observable interactional patterns that occur in the sessions. Obviously, as more family members are added to this assessment, the wealth of clinical material at the therapist's disposal will increase dramatically. The question, therefore, is how to organize this material in a meaningful way to guide the therapy process.

As a guide for the therapist, specific diagnosis/assessment schemata grow directly out of the various theories of family therapy (Liddle, 1983). For example, a symbolic-experiential family therapist would assess, among other dimensions, the family members' ability to tolerate interpersonal stress and to play with one another, whereas a strategic therapist would view the symptoms as metaphors for adaptation in the family.

Based on a comparison of six schools (Bowen, symbolic-experiential, structural, strategic, brief therapy, and systemic), Liddle (1983) concluded that although many differences exist, all the models share an appreciation for the need to understand family rules (cyclical behavioral patterns). Also, all the models link the rigidity of roles and patterns of interaction to dysfunction (Liddle, 1983).

Thus, all family therapists, to one degree or another, concern themselves with rigid patterns or cycles that accompany any problem (Hoffman, 1981; Minuchin & Fishman, 1981). Consequently, one of the most challenging aspects of the movement to systems thinking, and one of the most difficult for beginning therapists, is developing the capacity to discern family interactional patterns as they evolve in the treatment sessions.   *Most Difficult aspect of systems*

Developing the Capacity to Observe

Skill in identifying family patterns depends largely on the therapist's capacity to observe. Frequently, clinicians trained in individual therapy are reluctant to meet with families because of the wealth—and sometimes overload—of data generated from family interviews. Meeting with individuals and focusing on their intrapersonal dynamics is more clear-cut. More to the point, the dyadic nature of individual therapy allows the therapist to control the pace. There are no tempers flaring, people interrupting one another, or angry stares flashing across the room that sometimes mark a family session. Moreover, attempting to understand the individual dynamics of four, five, six, or more people at the same time is simply overwhelming. Subsequently, discerning patterns becomes the first step in making sense of a family session.

A key to discerning patterns is observing the verbal and nonverbal communication between family members. For example,

Observe Verbal & Nonverbal communication

- Where do people sit in relationship to one another?
- Who speaks for the family as well as for other family members?
- How does the spokesperson introduce the family's problems?
- How do other family members react to the spokesperson's presentation? Does anyone object or agree?
- Who supports whom most frequently during the discussion?
- Which relationships are the most conflicted?

- What patterns are common to the family's disagreements?
- Who gets involved in these arguments? Who stays out of them?
- At which points is the therapist invited into the disagreements?
- Who consistently elicits the therapist's support?

With these and similar questions in mind, the therapist is simultaneously listening to the family's concerns and observing the consistent patterns in the family. Basic patterns frequently emerge as soon as the therapist asks what the problem is; they will reemerge several times in the first interview. The content of the conflict might vary but the patterns consistently reappear. A mother complains about her daughter, for example; the daughter counters her mother; anger escalates; the mother invites the father into battle but he declines; the father abdicates and looks to the therapist to solve the problem; the mother feels increasingly frustrated and unsupported, which only furthers the argument with her daughter.

The next section introduces several basic concepts as a means of identifying patterns. In keeping with the tenor of the book, the list borrows from various family therapy theories that are familiar to most family therapists.

Basic Interactive Concepts: Preliminary Observations

Triangulation and Scapegoating

Bowen (1978) maintains that a dyad (mother-father) is an unstable relationship system that forms a triangle (mother-father-child) under stress. Hoffman (1981) adds that triadic relationships are at the heart of family systems therapy.

"Triangling" a third party into a dyadic conflict is a common pattern for all of us. In a conflict between two friends, each will turn to a third friend to get his or her point of view. In a disagreement between a parent and child, the parent turns to the other parent for support, and the child turns to a friend or sibling for support: "Let me tell you what she did then!"

Triangulation is a recurring pattern in human relationships, but when does it become dysfunctional? Hoffman (1981) speaks of the pressure on a child when each parent attempts to enlist the child's support against the other. In this scenario, the child is inappropriately elevated into the marital conflict and, under this stress, develops symptoms.

Covert marital conflict might be managed by triangling in a child. In these cases, the child's symptoms dominate the family as the parents argue over which of them is to blame for the child's behavior. This redirection allows the repressed marital anger to be displaced into the parent-parent-child triangle. Ironically, this pattern protects the family's existence because the marital conflict that could lead toward separation or divorce remains hidden or unaddressed. The parents can then express their anger at each other as parents, not as spouses, or toward the child. The overt conflicts concerning the child serve as a steam valve for the boiling family tensions.

Marital conflict chronically managed by triangling in a child is dysfunctional on several levels. First, the marital conflict, never fully addressed, continues to leave a "lump underneath the carpet." Second, the child is inundated with stress messages that he or she can do little about. Third, the child is, at best, torn by loyalty to each parent and, at worst, subtly asked to choose one side against the other. Finally, the family avoids developing effective problem-solving skills.

A variation on the theme occurs when a scapegoat is selected by the family. In these cases, the pain caused by the dysfunctional triangles is projected onto one of the family members (frequently one of the children): "We would be happy if it were not for you." Consequently, all stress, frustration, and anger is directed toward this family member. Tragically, with time, this particular family member will absorb these accusations and fulfill the family's prophecy: "They don't think I can do anything right anyway, so I don't care either!"

Interviewing these families will leave the therapist with a headache. Clearly, there is a tremendous amount of anger in the room, but all of it is being directed at one family member. Any attempts to move the discussion to other problems in the family or between other family members are met with denial. One piece of evidence after another is exhibited to prove the parents' point: "He did this. He did that. He doesn't listen. He won't obey. He is out of control." In addition, the family has come in only to drop off the scapegoat to be fixed: "Why do we all have to come? He is the problem! Shouldn't you be seeing him alone?"

A more seductive form of scapegoating occurs when parents present themselves as victims. In these cases, the scapegoating has been going on for so long that the child, often now an adolescent, is a terror. The parents sit pleadingly, looking at the therapist, while their adolescent son, with a disdainful look, is flicking matches in the corner. These scenes call out for the therapist to do something with this teenager and, in the process, join (triangle) with the parents.

Boundaries

The structural theory of Salvador Minuchin (1974) places a heavy emphasis on boundaries delineating the family's structure. As we saw in Chapter 1, boundaries are unwritten rules that define family interactions: Who participates and how? For example, is a child permitted to express anger at a parent? Can a parent form a coalition with a child against the other parent? Can a grandfather correct a grandchild while the father is in the room? Does the husband always put his mother's needs above his wife's needs?

Boundaries serve to protect the differentiation of the family system (Minuchin, 1974). In a clearly defined family structure, grandparents serve as an extended support subsystem for the nuclear (parents-children) family. The parental subsystem makes the executive decisions for the family and permits the parents to mutually support one another while the children are free to interact with one another, learning the values of competition and cooperation.

Although not elaborated by Minuchin, the interpersonal boundaries around each individual family member can be conceptualized. These boundaries delineate the "space" needed for personal growth. With clear individual boundaries, one's thoughts and feelings are respected; a person is not confined to a limited, acceptable range of behavior rigidly reinforced by family rules. Instead, differences are accepted in a family as a natural consequence of the family members' unique personalities. This is particularly important in families with adolescents because appropriate and clear interpersonal boundaries permit the adolescent to individuate while at the same time remaining connected to the family (Worden, 1991).

To return to the structural framework, boundaries (or transactional patterns) range on a continuum from enmeshed to disengaged. Enmeshed patterns blur boundaries. Families with these patterns lack any clear demarcations of generational hierarchy (grandparents-parents-children). In turn, any member's sense of autonomy is sacrificed to the cost of belonging. Responding to family needs comes first, before individual desires or wants. A narrow range of acceptable behavior (thoughts, feelings, and actions) is permitted—the cost of belonging—and reinforced through guilt. Telling people what they should think and feel is permissible. Deviance threatens the system's unity and, consequently, will be labeled "mad" or "bad" behavior. Thus, individual growth is greatly restricted.

In therapy, **enmeshed boundaries** exhibit these characteristics:

1. family members speaking for one another
2. a parent telling children what they really think and feel or telling them what they *should* think and feel
3. guilt used as a means of controlling others
4. hints that neither parent has psychologically separated from his or her own parents

[handwritten margin note: Enmeshed boundary Characteristics]

For example, in the course of ongoing treatment, a boy 9 years of age whose depressive symptoms led the family to seek therapy said, "I am lonely." Quickly, the family was energized. The mother said, "You are not lonely! You have your grandparents, your parents, and your brother and sister." The father concurred and observed, "That's the silliest thing I ever heard. What's wrong with you to say such a thing?" In these interactions, the boy was being taught that his thoughts and feelings were not valid unless they concurred with the family norms. Furthermore, the boy was being clearly told that loneliness was not permitted in the family or, at the very least, he had better not verbalize those feelings.

In contrast to engaged boundaries, **disengaged boundaries** sacrifice belonging for autonomy. Overly rigid or impermeable boundaries between people inhibit communication and rob the family of much needed mutual support. Privacy is taken to the extreme. Little sharing of thoughts and feelings occurs, and family members typically seek support outside the family in friends, activities, alcohol, or drugs.

Families with disengaged boundaries are extremely reluctant to be in family therapy. It is far too threatening. The members have operated by staying away from one another, and now this therapist wants to bring them together. As a result, the engagement phase of treatment is marked by continuing efforts of the family to persuade the therapist to meet individually with the scapegoat.

Sometimes, labeling a family as purely enmeshed or purely disengaged is erroneous and misleading. More often than not, close examination of interpersonal boundaries between individual family members reveals a potpourri: son is enmeshed with mother but disengaged from father; father is disengaged from his own father but enmeshed with his daughter; parents are disengaged from one another, but each is enmeshed with one of the children.

From the structural position, enmeshed and disengaged boundaries inhibit effective problem solving in families and hamper individual members' growth. At either extreme, the patterns are dysfunctional because the members are unable to balance their strivings for autonomy and their need to belong.

Although the earlier discussion presents the classic view of boundaries, the concept is currently undergoing revision. Green and Werner (1996) argue that the concept of boundaries needs refinement and further differentiation. Specifically, boundaries are not unidimensional, from enmeshed to disengaged; rather, they are made up of two separate dimensions: closeness-caregiving and intrusiveness.

The closeness-caregiving dimension is characterized by expressions of warmth, caring, and physical affection. Family members seek and enjoy time together. Also, they support one another emotionally and are consistent in these responses.

On the other hand, the intrusiveness dimension is characterized by possessiveness and jealousy. Individual, alone time is threatening to the family system. Emotions are highly negatively charged and frequently expressed in aggressive comments. Decisions are based on who is dominant. Finally, individuality is not valued. Personal opinions or beliefs that differ from the family norms are discounted or minimized.

Differentiating two separated dimensions (high-low) of the concept of boundaries further refines a clinician's observations and assessment. Thus, rather than viewing a boundary as either enmeshed or disengaged, the closeness-caregiving and intrusive dimensions suggest four extreme combinations:

High closeness-caregiving and low intrusiveness. This boundary would be optimal in terms of family members' psychological well-being (Green & Werner, 1996). Family members are responsive and actively nurture one another, while respecting individuality. Disagreements occur in the family, but the basic sense of love and commitment is never in question.

Low closeness-caregiving and low intrusiveness. In these relationships, individuality is fostered but without emotional support. Benign neglect characterizes these relationships. Family members seek closeness and caregiving outside the family.

High closeness-caregiving and high intrusiveness. Double binds highlight these boundaries. Family members are actively nurtured but also highly controlled. Consequently, attempts at separation might result in efforts by the family system to pull the person back into the family. Separation is defined as disloyalty. In these relationships, guilt serves as a powerful means of control. At the very least, if the family does not perpetuate the guilt, the separating individual experiences self-inflicted guilt for violating the family norms.

Low closeness-caregiving and high intrusiveness. Clinically, this boundary appears in families with rebellious adolescents. Here, without the mitigating effect of emotional support, the teenager fights against the parents' attempts at control. A teenager will tolerate or even accept parents' limits if they are combined with the belief that he or she is loved and respected. Likewise, in a couple relationship, such boundaries are seen as struggles for control. The love in the relationship has been replaced with the question "who will control whom?"

Rather than categorizing an entire family system as falling at one end or another on this continuum, families should be seen as a complex system of dyadic relationships. A husband, for example, is emotionally distant from but controlling toward his wife, but as a father, he is close to but also controlling of his daughter. Likewise, a wife is close to and supportive of her husband but close to and intrusive toward her teenage daughter. From this perspective, the boundaries of the various dyadic relationships create a rich tapestry of family interactions.

Power

Akin to the concept of a generational hierarchy (clear boundaries among grandparents-parents-children) is the definition of power in a family: which members have the power in the family, how they got it, how they maintain it, and at what costs to other members. For the purpose of the following discussion, and defined simply, **power** is the ability to influence others.

Each family member has individual wants and needs. Sometimes, through individual action, members can satisfy their needs, but more often than not, family membership implies the cooperation and consideration of others if the majority of needs are to be met. Likewise, diverse individual needs can conflict, leading to frustration, hurt, and disappointment. A teenager cries for more freedom, whereas the parents enforce restraint. A husband attempts to influence his wife, whereas she attempts to influence him. Understanding these patterns, however, is frequently a difficult task because there is typically more there than meets the eye.

For example, a dominant, authoritarian father may initially appear to possess the power in the family. His wife and children behave in ways to avoid his anger. On closer examination, however, the power is like shifting sands. The teenage son has the power to rebel and not follow orders. The father is powerless to change his son's rebellious behavior, no matter how much he threatens. The mother has the power to further her son's rebellion against his father by silently encouraging her son.

What one sees when looking closely at family patterns is the way attempts to gain or hold onto power are frequently countered by others, almost in an effort to balance the power in the family. To continue with the above example, the mother has the power, by gathering the children around her, to exclude the father from the family's nurturing emotional life. The father, sensing his emotional exclusion but putting it in control words, accuses the mother of undercutting him: "You baby and protect that boy too much." For his part, the son allies with his mother because she gives him the freedom he wants when the father is not around. Thus, although a therapist may be quickly drawn into viewing the authoritarian father as the only one possessing power in the family, closer examination reveals power (again, the ability to influence) being expressed by each family member.

Power, therefore, has both overt and covert qualities. What initially appears to be the power hierarchy in the family shifts as the family patterns emerge. To avoid being bogged down in the overt and obvious power patterns in the family, the therapist asks a few simple questions:

1. In what way is each family member attempting to influence others?
2. How is the overt power in the family counterbalanced by covert power?
3. How is each family member attempting to influence me (the therapist), particularly if someone is presenting himself or herself as the victim?

Intimacy

Believing that there is one absolute way in which family members should express their closeness with one another is erroneous. Members of some families are constantly touching one another both physically (a touch on the shoulder) and verbally ("I really do care about you"). Others sit stiffly, arms tightly at their sides while

Question to ask to determine covert power.

another member cries. To judge as "good" or "bad" either of these styles or patterns misses the point: Each family has evolved its unique ways of expressing affection and thus sharing closeness.

Appreciating the family's style of **intimacy** (the ability to form caring, expressive bonds while respecting individual boundaries) serves to guide the therapist during the engagement and intervention phases of therapy. For example, forcing people to spend time together or to share intimate thoughts might be ill-timed and could cause unnecessary anxiety and resistance. Likewise, attempting to create distance in an enmeshed relationship might also stir anxiety and create unnecessary resistance.

Again, a few simple questions will guide the clinician:

1. How is intimacy expressed in this family (that is, are family members comfortable with touching one another, sharing compliments, saying, "I love you")?

2. Is there too little or too much intimacy for the members' needs?

3. How does the family's expression of intimacy differ from my own? Will this be a problem in my working with them?

[handwritten margin note: Questions to ask to determine intimacy style.]

Communication Patterns

Although certainly an overused word, communication is at the heart of family patterns. Rather than attempting to elaborate on the variety of communication patterns and to avoid a redundancy of the previous discussion, I offer the following guidelines to improve one's observational skills.

Verbal behavior:

- Who speaks to whom?

- Do family members speak for one another?

- How often do sentences begin with *you* instead of *I*?

- Who tends to dominate the discussion?

- Does anyone try to interrupt that person?

- What types of words frequently occur in the discussion—judgmental and evaluative words (*stupid, bad, good, foolish*), or supportive words (*love, care, understanding*)?

- What tones dominate the discussion—for example, hostility, pleading, anger, hurt, confusion?

- Do family members listen, or do they constantly interrupt?

Nonverbal behavior (frequently more revealing than verbal behavior):

- Do family members acknowledge each other when talking—a nod of the head, eye contact?

- Who acknowledges whom and who nonverbally avoids whom?

- Where do members consistently sit in relation to one another?

- Who leads the family into the office?

- When members speak, do they continually look at the therapist and not at the person to whom they are speaking?

- Is physical contact made between family members?
- What is the quality of that contact—comforting, forced and stiff?

Although more guidelines could be added, the point is that the verbal and non-verbal interactions between family members are grist for the family therapist's mill. Developing the ability to listen to the speaker while observing other family members is a key therapeutic skill. Furthermore, by following action and reaction communication patterns, your skill is enhanced: How does a family member react when he or she is accused? How does his or her response fuel further exchanges and potentially triangle in other family members or the therapist?

The First Interview

In the initial session, many therapeutic agendas are set in motion: The family and therapist begin to evaluate one another and begin to form a therapeutic alliance; the family is introduced to the therapy process; the family's complaints and patterns are explored; and goals are set for treatment. This section of the chapter introduces the Martin family, a recently blended family, which will be followed through each phase of the treatment process. By following one case from the first interview through termination, you will be able to gain a coherent picture of family psychotherapy. A blended family was selected because it is estimated that one child in five under the age of 18 is a stepchild and that this type of family will actually outnumber all other kinds of families by the year 2000 (Glick & Lin, 1986).

Because of the variety of therapeutic agendas that need to be accomplished—and in the interest of clarity—the first interview is divided into the following stages, interwoven with the therapist's treatment notes.

1. Initial phone call
2. Greeting
3. Defining the interview
4. Defining the problem
5. Moving to a systems definition
6. Establishing goals and clarifying an intervention plan

Initial Phone Call

The Martin family was self-referred. Mrs. Martin made the initial phone call concerning her stepdaughter of one year, Cindy. "Cindy," Mrs. Martin said, "has caused increasing problems in our home. We are fighting all the time, and my husband and I are at wit's ends. We don't know what to do anymore. We need help!" With this as an introduction, the therapist scheduled an appointment and awaited the first interview.

Greeting

The Martin family (Mr. and Mrs. Martin who had been married one year, Mrs. Martin's two children from her first marriage [Robert, 17 years of age, and Karen, 7 years of age] and Mr. Martin's daughter from his first marriage [14-year-old Cindy]) arrived on time and were sitting quietly in the waiting room. As the therapist introduced himself, Mrs. Martin was the first to rise to shake his hand. She turned and quickly introduced her husband, who extended his hand, and then introduced the children, Robert, Karen, and Cindy, who each nodded to one degree or another. More noticeably, as the children walked past the therapist to his office, Robert looked the therapist in the eye and extended his hand, Karen giggled, and Cindy followed with stooped shoulders, staring at the floor.

The therapist had arranged individual chairs in a circle, and he asked the family members to sit wherever they wished. Mrs. Martin pointed to the chairs for Robert and Karen to sit in as Mr. Martin waited hesitantly for Cindy to choose her seat. Lingering in the doorway, Cindy moved to the chair closest to the door and pushed it farther into the corner. Mr. Martin then took the remaining seat.

After everyone was seated, the therapist began by asking global family questions.

> **Therapist**: Did you have any trouble finding the office? Were my directions clear?

Then the therapist began to contact each of the children individually, going from youngest to oldest:

> **Therapist**: Let me get all the names right. You are Karen, aren't you? How old are you? Where do you go to school?

Completing this process, the therapist next addressed Mrs. Martin and then Mr. Martin.

Treatment Notes

During the initial phone call, an observant therapist is already gathering data. Which parent called? Is this the spokesperson for the family? Is this the most motivated parent?

Likewise, in the initial contact in the waiting room, the family members have begun to present themselves to the therapist. Mrs. Martin continues her leadership role in the family. Mr. Martin follows his wife's lead. Robert mirrors his mother's behavior. Karen appropriately reveals her anxiety with her giggle. Cindy's nonverbal behavior clearly pronounces that she does not want to be there and expects the worst in the next hour.

The family members' choice of seating continues their presentation. Mrs. Martin strategically places her children to her left. Mr. Martin appears torn between his wife and daughter. Cindy, partly out of protest and partly out of fear, avoids entering the room until the last moment and then proceeds to extricate herself physically from the family circle.

For the therapist's part, he attempts to welcome the family and allow them to catch their breaths by asking global conversational questions. Although the conversation seems like chitchat, it serves the valuable function of reducing the family's initial anxiety.

Next, each family member is contacted individually. Notice that the therapist moves from youngest child up to the parents. This serves several purposes. First, individual members are acknowledged. Second, the concept of family systems is introduced by avoiding moving directly to Cindy, the identified problem; Cindy is addressed as the second youngest family member and not as the focal point for the meeting. Third, by talking first with Karen, the youngest, the therapist is giving the older family members the opportunity to observe him: Does he seem friendly? Will I be comfortable talking to him? Will he ask probing questions? Do I need to be defensive with him? Finally, Mrs. Martin is the first parent addressed because she had originally contacted the therapist: "Mrs. Martin, I guess it's your turn since we have already talked on the phone."

Overall, the purpose of the greeting stage is to acknowledge the family members and make them somewhat comfortable in the office before moving on to the task at hand. Spending too much time in the greeting is a mistake. The family has come for a purpose and is confused if this is not soon addressed. More specifically, research has shown that the lack of structuring in the early treatment sessions is one factor associated with deterioration in clients' conditions during family therapy (Gurman, Kniskern, & Pinsof, 1986). Thus, a brief greeting stage followed by a structuring of the interview communicates to the family that the therapist is moving purposefully.

Defining the Interview

The Martin family brought a great deal of anxiety to the first interview. Not only were the family members in pain, but to expose their pain to an outsider in a setting they did not understand was even more unsettling. Consequently, by providing a format, the therapist structured the meeting and reduced to some degree the family's anxiety about the unknown:

> **Therapist**: The chief purpose of this meeting is to give all of you the opportunity to meet me and to let me meet you. I understand that a lot has been occurring in your family that has been upsetting for all of you. What I would like to do in this first meeting is to hear everyone's point of view about what's been going on. Finally, at the end of our meeting, I would like to share with you my perceptions, give you my recommendations, and allow time for you to ask me questions.

Treatment Notes

On a content level, the therapist is laying out the progression of the interview. On a process level, he is again underlining the family theme and a respect for individual perspectives. He is emphasizing that there are many sides to a story (circular causality), and each member is encouraged to share his or hers. Finally, on a process level, he is trying to form a reciprocal, therapeutic alliance by welcoming the family's questions. In doing so, he is inviting the family members to participate actively in the treatment process and is communicating that therapy is not something that will be done to the family; rather, the family members will be co-contributors in shaping the process.

Defining the Problem

At this point, the therapist directed the meeting to the task at hand. He was interested in each family member's perspective on the problem: "Why has each of you come to this meeting?" As well as telling their sides of the story, in this initial step, the family members were presenting their viewpoints: Who is to blame? What rules or values has that person violated? How has the family tried to rectify the problem?

> **Therapist:** I'd like to find out what you each thought about coming here today and why you think you are here. Who would like to start?

> **Mrs. Martin:** We need to come because we have to get Cindy straightened out. As I told you on the phone, Cindy has been increasingly angry around the house. We have to ask her 20 times to do something, and even then we end up arguing. On top of that, her schoolwork is the pits.

> **Mr. Martin:** Well, I guess coming is a good idea because anything would be an improvement. There is continual fighting around our house. My wife and Cindy are always at it.

> **Robert:** I came because Mom made the appointment. We are here because of Cindy.

> **Karen** (giggling and quickly looking at her mother): I don't know. I guess because of the fights.

> **Cindy:** I don't know. Ask her (pointing to her stepmother).

After the initial opening by the therapist and the family members' responses, each participant was asked to expand his or her view of the problem. Mrs. Martin began by delineating what she saw as Cindy's disruptive behavior. From her perspective, Mrs. Martin had tried over the previous year to be a combination friend and mother to Cindy. She had tried to talk with Cindy to find out what was bothering her, but Cindy rebuffed her attempts. She saw Cindy as having a "bad attitude" at home that was increasingly mirrored in poor school performance. Mrs. Martin, who felt she had tried her best to help Cindy, wanted Cindy changed.

Mr. Martin explained that Cindy had lived with her mother for several years after the divorce (Cindy's parents had been divorced four years before), but that increasing arguments between Cindy and her mother had led Cindy to choose to live with her father. Mr. Martin had high hopes that he and his new wife could give Cindy the stable home she had lost when the divorce occurred. Mr. Martin could identify the guilt he felt—"Perhaps the divorce is still affecting Cindy"—and his divided loyalties—"I wish my wife and Cindy could get along with one another so that I would not feel so much in the middle." Mr. Martin wanted the fighting to end.

From all accounts, Robert had moved smoothly through adolescence (his father had died years earlier, but Robert evidenced little signs of unresolved grief). He was doing well in school, participated in sports, and was active socially. He was a stable support for his mother and was happy she had remarried. Because he was out of the house more than he was in it, Robert was the most peripheral to the conflicts. He did not feel he had to support or defend his mother in the arguments, but wished they were not occurring. Robert wanted to remain on the periphery of the battleground— he had agreed to come to the session only at his mother's insistence—but thought Cindy needed to "get her act together."

Karen also was doing well in school, but Mrs. Martin thought she was beginning to see a change in her attitude (her secret fear was that Cindy would influence Karen). Karen played with her doll and occasionally sat on her mother's lap. Mrs. Martin would stroke Karen's hair as Karen brushed her doll's head. Although seemingly concentrating on her doll, Karen would quickly look around the room as the tension built.

Initially, Cindy sat silently smoldering. When asked her view of the problem, she grudgingly responded, "I don't know." However, as the therapist prodded her to speak, Cindy opened up. "My stepmother is way too strict. She expects people to jump whenever she says so. She is always on my back. She never picks on the other two, only me." Cindy wanted to be left alone.

At this point, the therapist opened up the meeting: "Would anyone like to add to or correct what someone else said?" After a brief silence, Mrs. Martin pursued Cindy. "What do you mean, I pick on you? You never do anything around the house." With this, the fuse was lit and the conflict soon erupted in the office. Mrs. Martin and Cindy went head to head while each watched Mr. Martin out of the corner of her eye, Robert tightened his jaw, and Karen left her chair to sit on her mother's lap.

Treatment Notes

Seemingly a straightforward question-and-answer procedure, defining the problem further explores the family's motivation, begins to build a feedback loop between the therapist and family, allows each family member to tell his or her personal story, invites the family to test the therapeutic limits, challenges the therapist's capacity to listen to and "hear" what is being said.

First, by asking the family members why they came to the meeting, the level of motivation is tested. Who wanted the meeting? Who was the driving force to have the session? Who did not want to come? Who couldn't care less, one way or another? Who came willingly? Who was pressured into coming? What type of pressure was employed (threat of punishment, guilt, pleading)?

Also, asking all the members why they think they are in the counseling session reveals more about the family's communication style. What was each member told about the purpose of the meeting? Was the communication direct and honest—"We are going because of the problems in this family"—or indirect, confused, or vague— "It does not matter why we are going; the man wants us all to be there"?

Finally, by throwing the question out to the family as a whole, a spokesperson is invited to step forward. This family member is typically the one who possesses the clearest definition of the problem, at least in his or her own mind. The spokesperson is probably the one who initiated the contact to begin with and is the most motivated for change. The question, though, is what to change. Rarely does the spokesperson speak of changing the family; rather, someone needs changing and you can be assured it is not the speaker. Regardless, the spokesperson is the one who brought the family in and, in all probability, will be the one to bring the family back for another session. Consequently, family engagement possibilities increase as the spokesperson becomes engaged with the therapist.

As mentioned in the first chapter, feedback loops are cycles of communication. Feedback modifies feedback modifies feedback. The family has long-standing and well-established feedback patterns: Who talks to whom about what with what effect?

In engaging the system, the therapist enters the family's feedback loop and begins to modify it with his or her own feedback (communication) to the family. As the alliance is coalescing, the therapeutic system (family + therapist) begins to establish its own feedback loops (the collaborative effort).

By asking each member his or her point of view, for example, the therapist is communicating the importance of everyone's experience. In addition, a communication norm is being established in which everyone's opinion will be heard and valued. This pattern might not hold outside the therapy setting—and probably won't for many families experiencing difficulties—but at least in the therapist's office, this norm will be firmly imposed.

Individually engaging the family members is also an attempt on the therapist's part to develop a basic empathy for the separate perceptions: What is it like to be in your shoes? Even though the therapist is viewing the family from a systems perspective, the family is still a group of individuals, each of whom will decide for himself or herself, "Can I trust this person (therapist)? Will he listen to me? Will he try to understand my perspective? Do I want to share anything with him?" Thus, engagement occurs on a person-to-person level first.

As each family member is invited to tell his or her story, a key to establishing the person-to-person engagement is to make sure that all words and phrases used by clients are given an explicit meaning. For instance, at one point Mrs. Martin refers to Cindy as having a "bad attitude." If the therapist leaves the term unchallenged or unclarified, there will be the possibility of six different interpretations. Instead, he asks Mrs. Martin to define the term:

> **Therapist:** I am not sure what you mean by Cindy's "bad attitude." Would you give me some examples?

> **Mrs. Martin:** Well, she always challenges what I say and never just quietly obeys.

Notice that with this question, the problem has begun to be redefined as between people and not within a person. Also, defining the problem becomes an interactive process between the therapist and family members. And finally, the therapist, in the process of asking clarifying questions, is establishing feedback loops:

> **Therapist** (in response to Mrs. Martin's definition of a bad attitude): Let me get this straight and tell me if I am wrong, but you believe Cindy is being deliberately disrespectful when she questions your decisions.

In phrasing the question in such a manner, the therapist is in a win-win position. If he is accurate in his impression, Mrs. Martin agrees and feels understood. If she disagrees, the therapist responds, "I am sorry. I guess I missed hearing you. Let's try again because it is important for me to understand your dilemma." Here, the therapist's inaccurate empathy is used to foster further feedback loops with Mrs. Martin and, probably, to facilitate the engagement process.

Moving to a Systems Definition

After exploring each family member's definition of the problem, the therapist is in a position to underline the differences and move on to a systems definition. Such a def-

Explore definition ➤ underline differences ➤ system

inition highlights the interpersonal aspects of the problem and hints at circular causality. To begin accomplishing this, the therapist asks the family members to comment on the differences between their perceptions:

Therapist: Mr. Martin, your wife says she believes that both of you should hold the line and avoid Cindy's manipulation, but you at times seem to hold a different opinion. I wonder if you could explain this difference of views between the two of you and how both of you deal with it.

With this question, the therapist moves away from the focal conflict to the marital subsystem.

Therapist: Mrs. Martin, you and Cindy certainly see things in different ways. Has this always been the case and, if not, when did it begin?

A therapeutic assumption is made that if this conflict had existed from day 1, Mrs. Martin would have been reluctant to marry Cindy's father. In all probability, the relationship between Cindy and her was at least cordial in the beginning, only to sour at some later point. With this question, the therapist is seeking to identify a time when a positive relationship existed between the two and is further trying to learn whether a specific event or theme led to the disruption.   *time clarification*

Therapist: Cindy, the differences with your stepmother are clear, but I was wondering if you have differences of opinion with other family members?

Again, rather than rehash a litany of complaints between Cindy and her stepmother, the therapist redirects Cindy's attention to other family members. First, this defuses the focal conflict; second, it shows that Cindy's opinions of what others have said are equally important; finally, she is invited to participate as an equal of other family members and not as the scapegoat.

Therapist: Robert, you seem to me to be very observant. It looks like you pick up a great deal more than you comment on. I wonder if you could tell me what you observed in the last few minutes.

This is a nonthreatening invitation for Robert to participate in therapy.

Therapist: Karen, that's a pretty doll you have there. What is her name?

Karen: Pocahontas.

Therapist: How long has Pocahontas been a member of your family?

Karen: Two years.

Therapist: Does Pocahontas ever worry about things?

In joining with young children, a therapist searches for common ground. Karen's doll, Pocahontas, serves as a means of exploring Karen's view of the world.

All the above questions are analogous to fishing: You never know when you will get a bite. For instance, some of the questions might result in a blank stare, a shrug of shoulders, and an "I don't know." You hope that one or two open the door to exploring the differences between people and their views of one another. Furthermore, by exploring or at least questioning the differences between family members, the therapist shifted the interview from the static blame game to a more fluid focus on interactions: How do you differ? How do you explain the differences? When did the differences appear? How do you manage them? How destructive do they get?

As the interpersonal dynamics became the focus of the interview, it was possible to ascribe a systems definition to the family problems:

Therapist: From what all of you have told me, the fights between Mrs. Martin and Cindy have not always been there. In fact, at one time, the two of you got along fine. Something has obviously changed that. I think part of our job is to figure out what happened and how to make it different.

Therapist: From what I have heard, one difficulty that exists is the difference of opinion between the parents on when to pull back on the reins and when to trust Cindy's judgment. I believe it must be difficult to draw this line, and sometimes you are bound to disagree. A problem, however, is that Cindy receives mixed messages. Sometimes she gets a green light and other times it is red. Sometimes her stepmother disagrees with her behavior while at the same time her father approves of it. It seems to me that it would be helpful if a consistent agreement could be reached; this would make life easier for both of you and certainly for Cindy.

Therapist: I am not sure if all of you have noticed it, and tell me if I am wrong, but a pattern seems to appear consistently. A disagreement occurs between Cindy and Mrs. Martin; it escalates without resolution; Mr. Martin enters to try to resolve the matter and prevent further arguing while Robert and Karen are emotionally involved spectators.

Therapist: It is evident that this past year has been a very painful time for all of you, and from what you have told me, it has affected each of you differently. Each of you also seems to have a unique perspective on the problems. Because of this, I will need input from all of you if we are to reduce the tension in your family.

As you can see, underlying all these systems definitions is the movement from individual blame to interpersonal dynamics. At this stage of the first interview, what the therapist believed was sometimes irrelevant to what the family believed. Remember that in the engagement process, the therapist and family are forming a therapeutic system. Consequently, some type of consensus needs to be reached among all the participants on the nature of the problem, or at least on how to approach it. The therapist was able to "sell" his point of view only to the extent that the family was willing to "buy into" it. On the other hand, if the therapist is busy trying to teach or fit the family into a specific theoretical model—"Your family is poorly differentiated," "Your family possesses poor interpersonal boundaries," "We need to improve the executive subsystem in the family," "You are projecting your family-of-origin issues onto your daughter"—the family members might feel confused, misunderstood, talked down to, or even irritated, and this would lead to the inevitable question, "What does this have to do with Cindy's bad attitude?"

In moving the Martin family to a systems definition of its problems, the therapist was applying one of the key "arts" of family therapy: the ability to translate his theoretical model into concrete realities that fit the family's worldview. For example, one of the first clinical impressions that struck the therapist was the dysfunctional triangle involving the parents and Cindy. Cindy was clearly a focal point of the parents' inability to co-parent effectively. This situation raised questions about the extent to which Mr. and Mrs. Martin had formed a parental unit and hinted at possible marital conflicts (Mrs. Martin, for instance, might have been furious at the lack of support she was receiving from her husband).

It would serve little purpose, however, for the therapist to expound on his wonderful conceptual understanding of the family's dynamics. Rather, this hypothesis needed to be translated into concrete terms. Of the four examples given above, the second systems definition struck a responsive chord. Mrs. Martin welcomed the opportunity to discuss the co-parenting dynamics in hopes of gaining more support from her husband. By including all the family members in the definition of the problem and potential solution, the therapist was offering hope to the parents that their differences could be resolved and, at the same time, was freeing Cindy from a scapegoat position. At this point, with a consensus reached on the definition of the problem, the family was willing to pursue further this "therapy business."

Treatment Notes

Up until this stage of the engagement process, the interview has progressed smoothly. The family members have been willing to tell their sides of the story and have welcomed the therapist's attentive ear. In moving to a systems definition, however, the family's resistance to change might first be encountered with their attempts to seduce the therapist into playing a supportive role in the drama. Although the concept of resistance will be elaborated in a later chapter, its appearance in the initial phase of treatment highlights several clinical concerns.

Long-standing family patterns are an outgrowth of the family's worldview or paradigm. Even if these patterns are unsatisfying, they provide family members with a sense of security and predictability as well as the feeling that the members are acting "right" (Anderson & Stewart, 1983). Consequently, family members enter therapy with their unique views or stories of the problem, and sometimes the members' opinions coalesce around a central theme: Cindy's behavior needs to change.

From a systems perspective, the family's view of the problem becomes more important than the problem itself. As long as Cindy stays within her scapegoat role—a collusion between her and the rest of the family—other aspects of the family's functioning (for example, Mr. and Mrs. Martin's co-parenting capacity) go unnoticed. The more rigidly this view of the problem is held, the more rigid everyone's roles and the family's patterns become. Cindy feels blamed and victimized and in her anger acts out more. Mrs. Martin is overwhelmed in her efforts to parent Cindy and fears her stepdaughter's influence on her own daughter. Mr. Martin is torn between his daughter and his new wife. Robert and Karen blame Cindy and just want to be left alone. With these beliefs in place, the Martins continue to ride the merry-go-round.

For the family, the merry-go-round is an up-and-down ride going nowhere, but at least it is a known and familiar ride. When the therapist enters the picture, he initially, and briefly, rides the ride until he is familiar with its unique rhythms. He then steps off and attempts to point out other rides the Martins could take. The Martins, however, had ridden the merry-go-round so long that they did not want to get off; besides, the therapist appeared to be looking at the terrifying, triple-loop roller coaster (potential parenting or marital problems).

Concretely, in the engagement process, a family might resist the therapist's systems definition: "What do these questions about our parenting and marriage have to do with Cindy's bad attitude?" At this point, the therapist needs to rethink the definition:

- Does the family not understand my definition?
- Have I missed something, and am I off track?
- Is the definition resisted because it does not fit the family's experience?
- Is this too threatening a definition for the family to adopt at this time?
- What makes this definition too threatening to the family?
- Is there another way to phrase the definition?

With these questions, the therapist is looking inward—"Have I missed a key experience of the family or poorly phrased my definition?"—and outward—"What is so threatening to the family?"

Because a systems definition is a cooperative effort, a therapist errs by insisting on only his or her definition. Therapists who push their viewpoints believe and take pride in the fact that they are "telling it like it is"; they are often surprised when families cancel or fail to make follow-up appointments. More to the point, successful engagement is dependent on the family's willingness to cooperate. The members need to feel listened to and to share in the therapist's definition of the problem. From this solid foundation, the chances of treatment success increase.

Establishing Goals and Clarifying an Intervention Plan

As mentioned earlier, failure to structure early treatment sessions has been reliably associated with a deterioration in treatment effectiveness (Gurman, Kniskern, & Pinsof, 1986). Other crucial factors influencing a successful therapeutic outcome are the therapist's encouragement of clients' initiative and clients' assumption of an active role in resolving their problems (Orlinsky & Howard, 1986). With this in mind, the systems definition constructed between the therapist and family lays the foundation for establishing the goals of therapy.

Goals of therapy for the Martin family could range from straightforward symptom relief (less fighting in the home) to more global objectives (improved communication, improved self-esteem, a better attitude) and should be established in a collaborative manner. Still, the broader the goals the therapist and family set, the easier it is to lose sight of them in the give-and-take of therapy sessions. Without a clear focus, frustration can develop and family members can legitimately ask, "Where are we going? Are we getting anywhere?" The therapist proceeded this way:

> **Therapist:** If our sessions are going to be worthwhile, it is important for us to reach agreed-on goals. I'd like each of you to tell me what you would like to get out of our meetings, and I will also tell you my opinions.

The therapist has begun the collaborative effort of reaching consensus on therapeutic goals.

Each family member expressed in one form or another his or her own personal goals. Mr. Martin wanted a decrease in the arguments. Mrs. Martin wanted fewer arguments and felt Cindy's bad attitude needed to change for that to happen. Cindy wanted her parents to quit picking on her and leave her alone. Robert wanted the fights to end. Karen said she did not know.

> **Therapist:** Well, there is clearly a variety of goals, but despite these differences, a common theme appears to be a desire to decrease tension in the home by reducing the arguments. I think this is a workable goal, but I think it would be helpful to know when we have reached this goal. How would we know that?

Rather than leaving the goals as abstractions, an attempt was made to define them in more specific and concrete terms.

> **Therapist:** While we are discussing goals, I would also like to hear the positive things that are going on in the family and your ideas on increasing them.

More often than not, goals are stated in terms of reducing negatives. The opposite side of the same coin, however, is an identification of what is positive in the family and how to increase those behaviors. Thus, the treatment goals are redirected from focusing on a problem—how to change Cindy—to increasing the positive actions already in the family's repertoire—"What is going on when all of you are getting along?"

From a systems perspective, the goals are interpersonal in nature. Nevertheless, a family member might state an intrapersonal goal:

> **Mr. Martin:** I want to feel at peace in my own home.

Although certainly legitimate goals in and of themselves, intrapersonal goals are easily translated into systems goals.

> **Therapist:** Mr. Martin, I can understand your desire for peace in your home. What do you believe you need to do to make this happen?

Again, the therapist refocuses on the family and the responsibility of each family member to change it.

Ideally, therapeutic goals flow directly from the systems definition of the problem. Defining the goals in soluble terms that involve the family members is important. A key to doing this is to change nouns into verbs. For example, Cindy's "bad attitude" (a static, intrapersonal term) was translated into improving the relationship between

Cindy and her parents (a fluid, interpersonal goal) on which all the family members could agree.

Accepting "changing Cindy's attitude" as the goal would probably have doomed therapy from the start. A person either does or does not have a bad attitude. Consequently, therapy would have involved attempts to discern Cindy's attitude: Is it bad or not? Has it changed or not? Obviously, this would only have further maintained the family's basic scapegoating patterns.

Instead, by defining a goal as improving relationships, the therapist and family members involved everyone in the solution. Cindy alone did not have to change—an idea she found revolting and would have fought against with all her might; instead, the family relationships became the focus of treatment. As a family, the Martins agreed to begin family therapy with the stated goal of decreasing the tension in the home by reducing the number of arguments.

Treatment Notes

Clarifying the intervention plan is the final issue addressed in the first interview. Specifically, the intervention plan is the rough skeleton of the treatment process: How long will the sessions last? How frequently will we meet? How many sessions will we have?

Because of the legacy of individual psychotherapy's "50-minute hour," weekly, one-hour sessions have evolved as an acceptable pattern for family therapy. Nevertheless, no set standard exists. Rather, intervention plans are the result of many factors: time and financial limitations of both the therapist and family, the goals of therapy, and the therapist's theoretical position.

For example, some therapists operate within settings—clinics, HMOs—that emphasize short-term, brief treatment. Five to 10 sessions represent the acceptable standard. In other situations, the family's financial and insurance coverage limits the number or frequency of the sessions. The goals of therapy can be short- or long-term and might reflect the therapist's theoretical position or the family's needs. Thus, the exact nature of the intervention plan is unique for each case. The therapist meets weekly or biweekly for an hour with some families; with others, the intervention plan might involve monthly two-hour sessions.

The luxury of experimenting with time and frequency enhances one's therapeutic options. You may find that the first interview consistently takes one-and-a-half hours or that longer family sessions spaced farther apart make more sense. Experimentation teaches what works best. As a beginning family therapist, you should experiment with different time schedules. Some therapists find an hour too short a time period for a family session. Others find that working with families intensely for two or three hours spaced over longer periods of time suits them better.

In keeping with the tone of the book, the design of the treatment plan is a collaborative, conjoint effort between the therapist and the family members. With the Martin family, weekly, hour-long sessions were agreed to for several reasons. First, the family was in a moderate crisis state. The arguments were becoming more frequent and intense and relief was needed. Second, weekly sessions would allow for a continuity of treatment to develop. The arguments were based on the struggle to form a new stepfamily, and building a solid foundation for a stepfamily would take time and consistency. Third, the family's work and financial restraints would allow only weekly sessions. Finally, because the goal of reducing the arguments was clearly stated and thus served as an end point, the number of sessions was left open-ended.

Summary

If managed well, the first interview has resulted in a tentative therapeutic alliance between the therapist and family, and the family patterns have begun to be discerned. From the therapist's perspective, he or she gains an appreciation of each of the family members, forms early working hypotheses concerning the system's dynamics, reaches consensus with the family on a definition of the problem, and proposes an intervention plan. The family members, ideally, feel they have been listened to and understood, have an initial sense of trust in the therapist, and view the intervention plan as a reasonable one. Table 2.1 presents a series of questions that can be used as a guide.

Glossary

Disengaged boundaries Overly strong boundaries that rigidly divide the system's subsystems.

Enmeshed boundaries Overly weak or diffuse boundaries that poorly delineate the system's subsystems.

Intimacy Caring, expressive, affective bonds formed with another while respecting individual boundaries.

Power The ability to influence others.

Triangulation A way to diffuse dyadic conflict by expanding the relationship to include a third person (child, therapist, etc.).

Table 2.1   Questions Guiding the First Interview

Reasons for Referral

1. Why is the family seeking treatment at this time?
2. Are the family members in agreement on their problems?
3. What is the level of motivation in the family to pursue therapy?
4. Are outside referral sources involved? What is the relationship between the family and the referral source?

Family's Agenda for the Therapist

1. What role or roles do family members expect the therapist to play? Judge? Referee? Ally? Savior?
2. Do individual family members seek alliance with the therapist? What are his or her agendas?

Greeting Process

1. Who is the spokesperson for the family?
2. Who appears to have the power in the family? To whom do family members look when they are speaking?
3. Who brought the family into therapy? What is that person's agenda? Will this person decide whether the family will continue in treatment?
4. Who are the motivated family members? Are they seeking help for themselves or change in another family member?

Defining the Problem

1. How does the family define its problem?
2. Is one person blamed for the family's difficulties? How long has the blaming been going on? How rigid is this paradigm? Is there family consensus on this point?
3. How willing are the family members to examine other possible explanations?
4. Does the family's definition of the problem suppress potential, threatening anxiety?

Developing a Systems Definition

1. What differences are identifiable in the family members' presentations?
2. What differences do the family members recognize? How are these differences managed?
3. What differences and potential conflicts are denied or rejected?
4. What resistance is evoked with the attempted shift to a systems definition? What is the basis of the resistance? What fears are being evoked?
5. What systems definition will permit the establishment of feasible goals and be acceptable to both the therapist and the family members?

Planning Interventions

1. What interventions will the family accept?
2. What interventions will push the family's anxiety past manageable limits?
3. On what family strengths may the intervention plan be built?

Table 2.1	**Questions Guiding the First Interview (*continued*)**

Treatment Notes

Triangles and Scapegoating

1. What triangles are central to the family's problems?
2. In what ways are the triangles created?
3. Does scapegoating exist in the family?
4. What purpose does the scapegoat serve?

Boundaries and Coalitions

1. How clearly defined and maintained are the family's boundaries?
2. What boundaries are enmeshed and/or disengaged? More specifically, what boundaries reflect (a) high closeness-caregiving and low intrusiveness, (b) low closeness and low intrusiveness, (c) high closeness and high intrusiveness, and (d) low closeness and high intrusiveness?
3. Do cross-generational coalitions exist in the family?

Power and Control

1. Who controls the family? How? Guilt? Forcefulness? Coercion? Threats?
2. Are alliances with the therapist sought to oppose other family members?
3. Are these roles reflected in the family's interaction patterns concerning intimacy, communication, conflict resolution, and power differentials?
4. What are the therapist's gender biases?
5. Are there gender patterns within the family that could bias the therapist and make this family difficult to work with?

Intimacy

1. How is intimacy expressed in the family?
2. What interpersonal distance exists between family members?
3. Are certain family members expressing a greater desire for intimacy than others?
4. How are requests for intimacy managed?

Communication

1. Do family members speak to one another directly? Who speaks to whom? Are the messages clearly sent?
2. Do family members interrupt one another? Who interrupts whom?
3. Do family members listen when someone else is talking? Who is listened to and who is not?

3

Engagement: Establishing Therapeutic Boundaries

Therapeutic Alliance: Conceptual Notes

Case Presentation

Treatment Notes

Summary

Glossary

Although initiated in the first interview, the **therapeutic alliance** between the therapist and family becomes more firmly established in the initial several sessions. In this alliance, the family and therapist evolve a basic level of trust, a working relationship, and a shared agenda—that is, an agreed-on definition of the problem and treatment plan. Bordin (1982) refers to the relationship between the therapist and client(s) as a "working alliance" made up of three parts: (1) a consensus between therapist and client on the goals of therapy; (2) an agreement and collaboration on the relevance and implementation of various therapy tasks; and (3) a strong, positive affective bond between therapist and client.

In the family therapy literature, the process of forming a therapeutic alliance has been referred to by a number of terms, including *establishing rapport* and *joining*, but a description of the "how-to" of this process varies, depending on one's theoretical model.

For example, **joining** emphasizes the therapist's actions in response to the family system; specifically, the therapist accommodates (flexibly adapts) to the family's patterns and styles of relating:

> To join a family system, the therapist must accept the family's organization and style and blend with them. He must experience the family's transactional patterns and the strength of those patterns. That is, he should feel a

41

family member's pain at being excluded, or scapegoated, and his pleasure at being loved, depended on, or otherwise confirmed within the family. (Minuchin, 1974, p. 123)

As a therapeutic technique, joining combines three accommodating operations:

1. **Maintenance**—The therapist confirms or supports a family member's position: "Mrs. Martin, you must find it very difficult being the mother in this blended family."

2. **Tracking**—The therapist, through a series of clarifying questions, tracks or follows a sequence of events: "Mrs. Martin, when Cindy has not picked up her room, what do you do or say? Cindy, how do you react? Mrs. Martin, how do you respond? Mr. Martin, when do you enter the picture?"

3. **Mimesis**—The therapist adopts the family's style and tempo of communication. For example, the Martin family was deliberate and controlled in the initial interview. A deadly seriousness pervaded the room. As a result, the therapist also adopted a serious demeanor. At least in the initial sessions, a therapist would err by being jovial or expansive if the family was serious; not only would the family members believe they were not being taken seriously, but also they would not feel understood.

At the other end of the spectrum, Whitaker and Keith (1981) argue that the therapist does not have a choice in joining the family. Rather, the family's willingness to continue the treatment sessions indicates that the therapist has already been assigned a role in the family drama (judge, savior, ally). Nevertheless, Whitaker and Keith do add that to complete the joining process, the family therapist must develop a basic empathy with the family.

The first section of this chapter discusses the engagement process from a conceptual point of view and is divided into three interrelated parts: (1) family inputs, including background and values; (2) the therapist's input, including life patterns and training; and (3) the role of the therapist. In the following section, case material is presented, and then the pragmatic issues of establishing therapeutic boundaries are addressed.

Therapeutic Alliance: Conceptual Notes

Family Inputs

As a social group, a family brings to therapy a host of factors: generational ties from two extended families, historical references (a sense of past, present, and future), and an established repertoire of values, norms, roles, and interactive patterns. Three primary issues in the family therapy literature are gender, ethnicity, and the family's stage in the life cycle.

Gender

The "differences" between men and women, or the "battle of the sexes," is an endless topic for talk shows and popular literature. Men and women are divided into hunters and gatherers, nurturers and warriors, little girls and little boys, and even aliens from different planets. These "differences" appear to be an innate given.

From a social constructionist position, however, the differences are socially constructed and are reflected in societal roles each sex fulfills (Beall, 1993). To support this position, social constructionists point to cross-cultural differences: "Some cultures perceive more than one gender and cultures vary in their belief about the nature of males and females" (Beall, 1993, p. 134). Thus, innate sex differences disappear when viewed from a multicultural perspective.

The argument for innate sex differences is also weakened by meta-analytic studies of gender differences in cognitive abilities (Hyde, 1981), personality traits (Cohn, 1991), and social behavior (Aries, 1996). In these studies, male-female differences accounted for generally less than 10% of the variance and typically less than 5%. In other words, men differed more from other men and women differed more from other women than men and women differed from each other.

The social construction of gender is reflected in culturally defined male and female roles, which begin when we are first wrapped in a pink or blue blanket at birth. These socially ascribed roles influence our identity and how we interact with the world around us. By the age of 2 or 3, children identify themselves as male or female and can classify toys, behavior, and people according to gender (Cross & Markus, 1993).

Cultural gender roles are also incorporated into our self-concept (Cross & Markus, 1993; Geis, 1993). The traditional feminine role is characterized by affiliative responses to others in terms of caring, nurturing, passivity, and deference, whereas strength, dominance, autonomy, aggression, and achievement are more characteristic of the masculine role (Best & Williams, 1993). Thus, the quality of a woman's interpersonal relationships would be a key element in her self-concept. The male role, emphasizing independence, assertiveness, and achievement, focuses men on competitive relationships and their hierarchical status within their reference groups.

Roles not only prescribe specific behaviors but they also vary in the status they possess. In traditional, Western European roles, women are assigned the role of reproduction (child care, home maintenance); men are given production activities (the family's economic survival) (Cancian, 1989). Specifically, men's domain is the public work world where independence, assertiveness, and control of emotions are valued. In part, because of their ability to bear children, women have been given private, reproductive roles in which relationships are valued and fostered.

Cancian (1989) argues that this split between reproductive and production roles placed men in the economically superior role, whereas women's work at home rearing children and doing household chores became defined as love. Because a family's survival was dependent upon production—that is, bringing in the crops, making money—the production/male role became more important and powerful. A woman was to support her husband's "making-a-living."

From a social constructionist viewpoint, this division of roles leads to separate socialization paths. Tenderness and the expression of emotion become the jurisdiction of women. The male role, on the other hand, demands independence, competitiveness, and an absence of feeling. Because the sexes are raised to assume different roles within a society, men and women are likely to experience the same event in different ways. The following highlights these differences in areas directly related to family therapy: intimacy, communication, response to conflict, and power.

Social constructs and the role they play in families.

Intimacy

The expression of intimacy needs is learned early in childhood and family experiences. Chodorow (1978) argues that mothers teach their daughters to be empathic and responsive to the needs of others, whereas sons are encouraged to loosen their attachments. Stiver (1991) adds that, very early, mothers and their daughters develop the capacity to flow back and forth as both the giver and receiver of emotional supplies.

A woman's role, therefore, values relationships and connections with others. The male role, on the other hand, fosters independence, separateness, and achievement in the public world. Consequently, within relationships, women fear the loss of connection, whereas men fear the loss of autonomy—a basic conflict in male-female relationships (Low, 1990).

Tavris (1992) labels men's and women's different ways of expressing intimacy as a "doing-versus-talking" dimension. For men, if you care for people, you do things for them. In providing for his family, a man might work two jobs and never be home, watch the kids on the weekend, or help a friend work on his car. For women, love is talking about, maintaining and improving the quality of the relationship, and acknowledging the other person's feelings. Tavris (1992) attributes these differences to emotional systems fostered in childhood, when boys develop "side-by-side" relationships in which intimacy means sharing the same activity and girls develop "face-to-face" relationships in which ideas and feelings are shared.

Communication

A bestseller for a number of years has been Tannen's (1990) *You Just Don't Understand: Women and Men in Conversation*. With this book, couples can now explain their misunderstandings and arguments: They do not speak the same language!

For Tannen (1990), the differences in communication styles are based in gender roles. Socialized to succeed in the public world, men are instructed in public or "report talk." Report talk emphasizes competency and skill designed to further one's influence and status in the group. Being able to influence others, and, in its negative forms, dominate and control, is more important than having listening skills. Moreover, better problem-solving skills will increase a man's status in the workplace.

In contrast, women's private communication or "rapport talk" emphasizes sharing similarities and listening. Sharing emotional experiences serves to maintain and build relationships. In rapport communication, if you take the time to listen to me, I believe you care for me.

Equally important, sex role status strongly influences communication. In a study of group discussions, Carli (1990) found that men agreed more with women who spoke tentatively than with women who spoke assertively. Whether a man spoke assertively or tentatively, however, had no bearing on his being heard by other group members. From a social role perspective, women who spoke assertively violated the social norms and were cut off from being heard by the group. In the study, women were more likely to be heard if they first qualified their statements—for example, if they began their statements with, "I don't know," or "I could be wrong, but . . ."

Given the differences in socialization and the effects of status on communication, it is no wonder that Tannen's (1990) book struck such a responsive chord. Practiced in the art of public talk, men focus on problem solving, seeking and maintaining one's place in the status hierarchy, and minimizing feelings. Women, on the other hand, are experts in emotional and expressive communication; they focus on developing and maintaining relationships. Given the power of gender roles, the ubiquitous "communication" problem is frequently a complaint within families.

Conflict

The meaning of conflict and the ways it is managed are also shaped by socially constructed roles. For example, conflict is a threat to connection for women but a means of negotiating status for men (Tannen, 1990). Ascribed the role of maintaining relationships, a woman may placate rather than risk her mate's anger, or she may seek to break through his emotional aloofness. For men, however, conflict signals a difference of opinion; someone is right and someone is wrong. Consequently, for a man, to maintain status, all is fair—from controlling the discussion with logic to threatening to cut off contact with anger.

Besides the different meanings of conflict, the effects of socialization are seen in physiological and behavioral responses. In marital conflict, as measured by heart rate and blood pressure, men reach a state of emotional, physiological overload faster and stay at that level longer than their wives (Gottman, 1994). This leads to a familiar clinical pattern in which the woman is emotionally pursuing an aloof and emotionally distancing man.

For example, during the course of a negative exchange, the man becomes rapidly, physiologically distressed and responds by withdrawing and shutting down emotionally. From a physiological perspective, the emotional withdrawal is an attempt to reduce his distressed physiological arousal. The woman, however, experiences his withdrawal as rejection and a threat to the relationship. To reduce her distressed physiological state, she pursues him to stay in contact and secure the relationship.

Gottman (1994) attributes these styles to biological differences and the effects of socialization. His hypothesis is that without being taught how to manage emotions, men experience more intense physiological reactions to emotional stimuli than women. Hence, a man's lament, "I can't stand it when she cries because I don't know what to do." Women, on the other hand, responsible for the maintenance of relationships, are distressed when the relationship is threatened. Women experiencing chronic emotional isolation from their partners reported greater health problems in a four-year follow-up study (Gottman & Levenson, 1992).

Thus, men can regard conflicts as potentially explosive situations that need to be controlled. Control is managed through threats of and actually creating distance and disengagement. For women, conflicts with loved ones risk dissolution of the relationship and raise the fears of isolation and vulnerability (White, 1989). Unfortunately, within traditional gender roles, each sex's approach to conflict directly threatens the other.

Power

Power is the capacity to influence our environment. However, within traditional gender roles, a power differential exists between men and women. "Historically, the distribution of power between men and women has been unequal in economic, political, and religious institutions, as well as in family life" (Low, 1990, p. 250).

This power differential to a large degree is based in economics. When production and reproduction roles were relegated to the respective sexes, production was defined as work and reproduction an expression of love. The man worked all day in the factory to support his family while the woman worked all day taking care of the house and children because she "loved" her home and family.

Within these parameters, the man's job was the priority for the family; because he controlled the economic resources, his wishes and needs took precedence—he was entitled! As evidence of the power of resources, studies demonstrate that when women contribute financially to the family's standard of living, their power rises (Blumstein & Schwartz, 1991). Nevertheless, traditional roles and expectations change slowly, if at all. Even when the couple has a two-paycheck marriage, the woman assumes the burden of the domestic responsibilities (Blumstein & Schwartz, 1983).

Thus, despite changes in economic facts of life, when two or more paychecks are needed to sustain a family's standard of living, traditional gender roles still exercise considerable influence. Even in cultures in which law and ideology favor equal rights for men and women, men still have more power than women in the family and society (Best & Williams, 1993; Williams & Best, 1990a, 1990b). This distribution translates into family relationships in which men are more likely to be listened to and to have the decision-making power.

The power differential inherent in traditional gender roles also influences communication patterns. In the subordinate position, women are more likely to influence men through pouting, crying, manipulation, or "soft" strategies, such as acting nice or flattering the man. Men, however, are more likely to use persuasion through reason and force if necessary to influence the other (Falbo & Peplau, 1980; Hatfield & Rapson, 1993).

In the previous chapter, several basic interactive concepts were introduced: triangulation, boundaries, power, intimacy, and communication patterns. Each of these can be strongly influenced by gender roles. Consequently, gender will figure prominently in the family's presentation in therapy as well as in the therapist's assessment of family dynamics. For example, is the father emotionally aloof and detached or fulfilling his prescribed gender role? Is the mother intrusive in her daughter's life or fulfilling her role as well as she can? Are the family norms for male or female behavior being violated by the family scapegoat? Does the family power hierarchy reflect gender and cultural values? Are the family members struggling with their own definitions of male and female norms?

Ethnicity and Multiculturalism

Viewed from a systems perspective, a family is not a self-contained unit operating autonomously but a subsystem of broader community and culture systems. Just as the strength of family therapy is the ability to place an individual's symptoms within a family context, family patterns can also be placed within a broader cultural context. This broader cultural context is the family's **ethnicity** or ethnic heritage, a heritage steeped in norms and values transmitted over generations, norms and values that provide an identity for the family members and also guidelines for their behavior.

It is through culture that we organize and understand our experiences in the world (Saleebey, 1994). Ethnicity, in particular, provides a common ancestry of shared customs, norms, and values. This sharing provides a sense of belonging and historical continuity (McGoldrick, Pearce, & Giordano, 1996; McGoldrick, Preto, Hines, & Lee, 1991).

Because ethnicity provides a sense of belonging and historical continuity, McGoldrick, Pearce, and Giordano (1996) argue that it is a powerful influence on the individuals in a family. Specifically addressing treatment, they point out that family stresses are compounded when ethnic stresses or transitions interact with life cycle transitions. For example, parents with strong ethnic values that foster mutual dependency among family members clash strongly with an emerging adolescent who adopts peer-related values of autonomy. Likewise, for some people, the influence of extended ethnic family members is a powerful force in the nuclear family's life. What extended family members might think and how they could react is frequently an important influence on a nuclear family's problem-solving ability.

To use a more concrete example, Nancy Boyd-Franklin (1987, 1989) has written extensively on black families in therapy. She observes that for black families the traditional sources of help have been extended family members, very close friends, and church leaders; because of the legacy of racism, black families tend to be extremely reluctant to enter treatment, which can be seen as intrusive and yet another labeling process of the establishment: "We will be told we are crazy." Consequently, empowering the black family and mobilizing them to interact successfully with external systems are key therapeutic goals.

Regardless of the specifics, ethnicity can powerfully shape and control family members' behavior. Reiss (1981), for instance, speaks of the family's capacity to construct its own view of reality: a **family paradigm** that guides the behavior of the family members and serves as a guideline for making sense of the world.

Reiss's (1981) family paradigm is similar to social constructionists' views of family narratives or stories. For example, families may be seen as interpretive communities or "storying" cultures (Pare, 1995). Cultures, therefore, are communities of individuals who see their world in a particular manner. These shared interpretations of reality provide meaning for their lives and guide their actions. Regardless of the labels we apply, the threads of ethnicity reinforce the paradigm or family story.

For example, the simple statement, "We are a close family," can have extremely divergent meanings when the word *close* is further defined. For a strong ethnic family, closeness is a primary motivational force. Extended family members live in close proximity; Sunday dinner at the grandmother's house is mandatory; and in-laws consistently feel they are outside the large, blood-related extended family. For another family, the definition of closeness is, "Well, we see them about three times a year and call about once a month, but you always know that they are there for you."

With such diverse definitions, a clinician errs in ascribing any meanings without first understanding the family's ethnic paradigm or narrative. Words such as *love, close, distant, hurt,* and *anger* have specific meanings for each family. Consequently, it behooves the therapist to discover what these words mean for a particular family. By doing so, the therapist is gaining valuable knowledge of the family's functioning, and the process of engagement is being enhanced because the family members sense that the therapist is attempting to understand them.

In the Martin family, Mrs. Martin grew up in a traditional Italian family. Being from the second generation of the family in the United States (both her parents immigrated from Italy), Mrs. Martin combined traditional Italian values with middle-class American ones. From her framework, children were closely guided and protected, and above all else, they respected their parents. Cindy's behavior was a clear affront to her stepmother's values. To compound the matter, Mr. Martin was third-generation Irish and had given his daughter much more freedom than would ever be allowed in an Italian family. Thus, a clash in values was one of the cracks in the stepfamily's foundation.

Besides clashes within the family, potential differences exist between the therapist's and family's ethnic paradigms. Spiegel (1982) points out that no matter what their ethnic origins, middle-class therapists have been socialized in terms of mainstream values: The therapist expects clients to keep appointments, be motivated toward change, and work at therapeutic tasks. More specifically, personal autonomy is emphasized over emotional dependency. Therapy suffers when the family's values are at odds with the therapist's. For example, members of a strong, traditional ethnic family who value emotional dependency on one another will quickly and unilaterally terminate treatment with a therapist who is pushing autonomy.

When the therapist and the family do not share a common cultural background, the therapist walks a fine line between classifying certain family patterns as dysfunctional just because they deviate from the therapist's values and attributing actual dysfunctional patterns to culture (Celano & Kaslow, 2000). It is helpful when the therapist is aware of his or her cultural biases while being able to fully appreciate the family's paradigm or narrative. Finally, engaging or joining is enhanced when the therapist uses culturally compatible interventions that benefit the family early in the treatment (Celano & Kaslow, 2000).

Family Life Cycle

Family stresses can be compounded by life cycle transitions (Carter & McGoldrick, 1988). If we view the family as a system moving through time, transition and change are inevitable. This developmental perspective assumes that there are family tasks at each stage that need to be accomplished and that the transition from one state to another is always accompanied by a normal degree of crisis (Gerson, 1995; Preto & Travis, 1985). Furthermore, symptoms can appear in any stage of development, signaling that a family is experiencing difficulty negotiating that particular stage.

Carter and McGoldrick (1988) outline six stages of the **family life cycle**:

1. Leaving home: single young adults
2. The joining of families through marriage: the new couple
3. Families with young children
4. Families with adolescents
5. Launching children and moving on
6. Families in later life

Carter and McGoldrick (1988) also identify accompanying emotional processes at each transition and the changes in family functioning required to proceed developmentally. For instance, the emergence of adolescence in one or more children (as in the Martin family) requires increased flexibility of the family's boundaries to allow

Stages of Family Life Cycle

the adolescent's quest for autonomy. A shift in parent-child relationships is also needed to permit the adolescent to move in and out of the family system.

Through the process of adolescence, the relationship is transformed from parent-child to parent-adolescent to parent-young adult. This developmental change reflects a new balance between individuality and connectedness within the family (Worden, 1991). The adolescent developmentally seeks autonomy and a sense of identity separate from the family; at the same time, he or she does not wish to be cut off completely. Employing the family as a home base (stability), the adolescent is then free to explore the world but also to return as needed. Combrinck-Graham (1985) captures this fluidity by describing family development as a process of oscillations between centripetal (turning inward) and centrifugal (turning outward) movements. At times, family members pull together—for example, at childbirth or illness; at other times, individuality and separateness are emphasized—for example, when one member is starting a new job or heading off to college. Gerson (1995) refers to the same process as a rhythm of expansion and contraction.

Family stress is often greatest at transition points from one stage to another, and symptoms are most likely to appear when there is an interruption of the unfolding life cycle (Carter & McGoldrick, 1988). In particular, divorce and remarriage are two major disruptions of the life cycle that place tremendous strains on the family. In the case of the Martin family, death of a spouse (Mrs. Martin's first husband), divorce (Mr. Martin's), and remarriage had laid the groundwork for many of the family's problems. As a final note, Simon (1989) argues that the therapist's own stage in the life cycle has an impact on therapy. How the two life cycles combine is an important part of the fit between therapist and family. A therapist who has already moved through the family's current stage of development and its accompanying dilemmas might have personal knowledge of what the family is going through and can easily empathize with them. However, if the therapist moved easily through the stage, he or she might minimize the family's problems. Worse yet, a therapist in the same stage as the family could be just as stuck as they are.

In conclusion, a basic understanding and appreciation of the family life cycle greatly enhances the building of the therapeutic alliance. A life cycle approach sensitizes the therapist to developmental issues with which the family could be struggling and suggests initial hypotheses to guide assessment and intervention.

Therapist's Inputs

Just as the family operates from its own paradigm, the therapist's paradigm is equally strong. Therapists bring to therapy their academic/training experiences, the cultural impact of gender on their theories and personal experience, and their own issues involving their family of origin and life cycle. All these factors shape their own worldviews and their capacity to form therapeutic alliances with their client families.

Theory and Training

Each model of family therapy addresses, to one degree or another, functional and dysfunctional patterns in families, important assessment issues, goal setting and the structure of the therapy process, the role of the therapist, techniques unique to the model, and the curative factors in the change process. Nichols and Schwartz (1991) point out that many of the concepts and methods of a family model will be determined by the model's assumptions about people. For example, if power is seen as a key dimension in family life, learning how to defuse and redirect power in the family becomes paramount. If love and intimacy are seen as most strongly influencing family relationships, therapy would focus on the sharing of the members' feelings.

Simply put, each model presents its own worldview (paradigm) of family life. Thus, the adoption of any theoretical position reflects a "goodness-of-fit" among the model, the therapist, and the family, particularly in terms of utilitarian value: Do the family's data fit the theory? Does the model facilitate the therapist's understanding of the family and guide his or her interventions?

By this stage of training, you have probably been exposed to several of the family therapy models. Some have been exciting and stimulating, while others have appeared vague and confusing. Some have made intuitive sense, whereas others have not matched your experience or personal style.

Despite the potential for confusion and uncertainty, the best advice, particularly for the beginning family therapist, is to learn one model well. First, knowing one model well provides a reference point for comparing other models: What are the differences in the models' descriptions of functional and dysfunctional family patterns? What is the difference in the therapist's role in the change process compared with another model?

Second, by learning one model well, therapists become consistent when working with families. Each model possesses an internal logic to guide the therapist's actions. This logic serves as a beacon through the strong winds and seas of therapy sessions. Along the same line, consistency on the therapist's part projects to the family a confidence of belief, a sense of "knowing what I am doing." The therapist acts with a confidence that is crucial to engaging the family.

Still, a note of caution needs to be added. As Papp (1983) points out, no single approach is right for all families and situations. This point is further underlined by a review of the research that found no support for the universal applicability and efficacy of any one family therapy approach (Gurman et al., 1986). Thus, for a beginning family therapist, the best path is to learn one model well while staying open to other viewpoints.

The Effects of Gender

Two basic premises of systems theory is that all parts of the system affect one another and that the family's patterns serve a functional purpose. The concept of co-dependency, for example, implies that both parties equally collude in the abuse of alcohol; that is, the nonabusing partner, through either conscious or unconscious motivations, facilitates or encourages his or her partner's substance abuse. The abusive behavior, furthermore, could serve as a defense against the couple's fear of intimacy, or bind the free-floating anxiety in one or both partners, or serve any number of other functions.

The heart of the feminist critique of systems theory is this assumption of equality. From a systems perspective, males and females equally influence one another; however, this position does not take into account the differential in power and status between men and women in the larger social systems in which families are embedded (Luepnitz, 1988; Walsh & Scheinkman, 1989; Walters, Carter, Papp, & Silverstein, 1988). Thus, a woman labeled co-dependent might remain in a dysfunctional relationship because she is economically dependent. Also, systems theory does not address the nuances of separate gender role socialization. Again, from the earlier example, the woman labeled co-dependent could be seen as fulfilling her caregiving, nurturing role.

The confusion between personality traits and role behavior is referred to as the **fundamental attribution error**. This error occurs when one attributes an individual's behavior to personality traits while ignoring or underestimating situational or role constraints (Geis, 1993). In other words, male and female behavior could reflect gender roles more than internal, individual personality traits (Aries, 1996). Consequently, in the assessment of family patterns, the influence of cultural, gender roles supersedes an automatic assumption of equality or innate personality traits.

As therapists, however, we are not immune to what we treat. We possess our own **gender biases**. Hare-Mustin (1989), for example, has found that many family therapists value as treatment goals differentiation—separating emotions from feelings and establishing clear interpersonal boundaries—and the negotiation of differences (male-oriented behaviors); lower-rated goals are an increase in caretaking and nurturing (female-oriented behaviors). Systems models frequently endorsed by the therapists reduce the family to an abstract and mechanistic structure while minimizing the value of intuition and feelings. Therapy, consequently, focuses on changing family structure and minimizes feelings.

Newberry, Alexander, and Turner (1991) believe, however, that the family therapist's role requires behaviors that are both instrumental (goal-directed, assertive, structuring behavior) and expressive (emphasis on creating interpersonal closeness and warmth). In their empirical study, they found that male and female family therapy trainees did not differ significantly on the rates of these kinds of behaviors. An interesting finding, however, was that fathers responded more positively to therapy than did mothers when therapists used instrumental behavior—active, goal-directed behavior appealed to the men—and that all family members expected gender-stereotypic behavior of male and female therapists. (If the therapist does not carry the gender bias into the session, the family will!)

Green and Herget (1991) provide further support for the therapist combining instrumental and expressive behaviors. Their empirical study indicated that families improved more when their therapists were warmer and more actively structuring. It would appear, therefore, that the therapeutic alliance is enhanced when the therapist combines interpersonal warmth and assertive, directive behavior or, in other words, displays both male and female role behaviors.

Combining traditional gender role behavior is easier said than done, however, because to one degree or another, we are all influenced by socially constructed gender roles. For example, female family therapists might struggle in balancing the power of a professional expert directing family members' behavior with a woman's more traditional role of nurturer and caretaker (Walters et al., 1988). Also, because women are taught to influence men indirectly, female therapists might have difficulty being assertive and challenging dominant male family members (Bogard, 1990). In contrast, a male family therapist could compete with the dominant male family member while falling into a paternal, protective mode with female clients (Worden & Worden, 1998).

Worse still, the subtle influence of gender roles could bias our clinical evaluations. After reviewing the literature on therapist attitudes and sex-role stereotyping, Sherman (1980) found that male therapists stereotype clients according to gender roles more than female therapists do. In Sherman's findings, when a client's behavior deviated from that person's gender role, he or she was judged more maladjusted by male therapists than by female therapists. "Again, what is normal and what is abnormal would seem to be at least partially dependent on one's sex and fulfilling one's gender role, even for therapists" (Worden & Worden, 1998, p. 51).

To return to the Martin family, gender issues play a large role in the treatment process. For example, the family's chief complaint was the conflict between the stepmother and stepdaughter. From one perspective, Mrs. Martin could be seen as intrusive and controlling, and Cindy could be seen as vying for her father's attention and in competition with her stepmother. With this hypothesis, the therapist would focus on disengaging Mrs. Martin and allowing Cindy more time with her father—changing the family's structural patterns.

Walters and her colleagues (1988) offer another perspective. They argue that because women are acculturated to move toward emotional issues and not away from them, stepmothers and stepdaughters are drawn together as the family undergoes this transition and new beginning. Moreover, women are socialized to assume responsibility for the family's emotional life. Thus, if the transitions are not going smoothly, women blame themselves and are blamed by others for their supposed failures.

Within this context, Mrs. Martin's behavior is readily understandable. She bore the responsibility for making this new stepfamily work and moved to make it happen. At the time of the first interview, she bore the shame and guilt for the family conflicts. Clearly, in this situation, the therapist only compounds the family's problems by focusing on Mrs. Martin's "overinvolved and controlling" behavior. She would feel increasing blame and frustration, and this would not bode well for change.

Therapist's Family of Origin and Life Cycle

In addition to the development of a conceptual model and the problems of gender bias, the therapist's own **family of origin** strongly influences the engagement process. Therapists, for better or worse, carry with them the paradigm of their own family of origin. This is neither bad nor good; it is a simple fact. Therapists are not immune to the very thing they treat: family systems.

With some families, engagement is relatively easy, with commonalities permitting an immediate rapport. These shared elements can be quite diverse—similar ethnic or religious upbringing, value systems, interests, and life cycle stage—but they are quickly recognized, overtly or covertly, by both the therapist and the family. Subsequently, the therapist "knows" the family and the family members feel comfortable with someone they believe will understand them and the style they all share.

There can be too much of a good thing, however. Although commonalities between the therapist and family increase the probability of engagement, if the family's dynamics mirror the therapist's issues concerning family of origin or life cycle, therapeutic change might be difficult to achieve. For instance, a therapist with an alcoholic father might experience difficulty working with a family in which the chief issue is the effect of the father's alcoholism on the mother and children. Although readily understanding what the children are experiencing, the therapist might have difficulty empathizing with the father. Consequently, lineal causality could enter the picture: "Everything would be better in this family if the father quit drinking." Unfortunately, in this scenario, the father might believe he is being blamed for the family problems and unilaterally terminate therapy.

A similar situation occurs when a young therapist works with a family whose adolescent son is acting out and feels overcontrolled. In this situation, the therapist, recently out of a similar developmental time period, readily appreciates the adolescent's request and works toward changing the parents. With this agenda in the room, the parents sense the blame being sent their way, do not feel understood, and cancel the next appointment.

Family therapy theories differ in their emphasis on therapists' need to explore their own family-of-origin issues. Proponents of Bowen's family systems theory strongly believe that the therapist's own extended family work is a key to his or her developing therapeutic neutrality, while supporters of structural and strategic models do not believe it is relevant to becoming a successful family therapist (Titleman, 1987).

Despite these differences, some knowledge and understanding of their own family paradigm facilitates the engagement process and keeps therapists from falling into the trap of linear causality. Also, it is unrealistic for a therapist to believe that he or she can engage any and all families. For instance, a clinician easily engages a teenage victim of incest but has great difficulty working with the abusing father. In these types of situations, when the therapist has difficulty engaging a family member because of a conflict in value systems, therapy will quickly bog down as the therapist fails to engage the entire family. At this time, a referral elsewhere is needed.

Therapist's Role

In forming a therapeutic alliance, is the therapist an outside expert who diagnoses the family and directs the family into new behavior? Does the therapist need to merge with the family to fully appreciate the family's dilemmas? Are family therapists guilty of fitting families into defined theoretical models? What, precisely, should be the therapist's role?

Overall, the therapist's model strongly influences the therapy process. Moreover, each model's assumptions, at the very least, broadly define parameters of the therapist's role. For example, a behavioral family therapist would be an objective observer outside the family system who serves as a "consultant" to parents who, in turn, serve as primary change agents (Falloon, 1986). With a quite different perspective, experiential family therapists would use all their personal reactions to both nurture and confront families (Whitaker & Bumberry, 1988). A consistent theme in the field is to view family therapists as experts who "see" the "real" family dynamics and who "do" things to families. Recently, however, this theme has been challenged.

In a review, Nichols and Schwartz (1991) point out that in the past, family therapists too often made the mistake of believing that their models (theories) were describing and identifying "real" family interactions—for instance, that families were highly undifferentiated, that children's symptoms implied marital conflict, and so on. Instead, a social constructionism position views family therapy theories as a consensually agreed-to, coherent group of propositions used as explanations. That is, each model is a metaphor attempting to illuminate family behavioral patterns.

Family therapists strongly influenced by social constructionism argue that what therapists "see" is a product of their particular assumptions about families and their interactions with families (Efran, Lukens, & Lukens, 1990; Keeney & Ross, 1985). Consequently, therapeutic reality is co-constructed by the family and therapist through mutual participation and sharing (Goolishian & Anderson, 1987, 1990). The meaning of the problem, its meaning to the family, and potential solutions are all products of the interaction between the therapist and the family. The therapist is not standing outside the family as an expert, ascribing theoretical concepts to the family's functioning or "doing" something to the family. Instead, the therapist is involved in a thoroughly collaborative enterprise: a search to discover meaning in the family's problem. (To explore further the philosophical underpinnings of constructivism, the reader is referred to Watzlawick's 1984 book, *The Invented Reality: How Do We Know What We Believe We Know? Contributions to Constructionism.*)

This collaborative enterprise is reflected strongly in the current popularity of narrative therapy. Seeking the structure and meaning of one's life or family through stories involves both an understanding of the connections between life events and the affective component attached to those understandings. Narrative therapy emphasizes the co-construction of meaning between the therapist and family members as a central concept and goal of therapy. Metaphorically, the therapy process is seen as an evolving text.

Narrative change in therapy is associated with the therapist's role of "not-knowing" (Anderson & Goolishian, 1992). The "not-knowing" stance is akin to that of an anthropologist encountering a new culture. Although the anthropologist possesses knowledge of other cultures, he or she approaches the new culture without preconceived notions or attempts to fit the new culture into prescribed categories. Simply put, the anthropologist approaches it with an open mind. Moreover, following specific methodology, the anthropologist embraces or joins with the culture to discover its patterns and meanings.

From this perspective, the family therapist is not the all-knowing expert assessing and telling the family members what to do. Instead, the therapist's not-knowing approach opens up a conversation concerning the family's "problems" so that new meanings and narratives can emerge. The not-knowing stance does not mean the therapist abandons prior knowledge; instead, "it refers to what I do with what I know—that what I know stays in front of me and is always open to question, is always tentative" (Andersen, 1993, p. 160).

The challenge, therefore, is in what ways the therapist uses his or her knowledge and experience to enrich the family's narrative, helping the family "see" the problems in new ways that enhance the members' choices and options. To do this, the therapist moves within and with the family's reality and language toward understanding and changing the assumptions that the family members have about their problem (Goolishian & Anderson, 1987, 1990; White & Epston, 1990). This takes place as the therapist and family members are in "conversation." Consequently, the therapist is a conversational expert.

The purpose of introducing the social constructionist, narrative perspective is to alert you to the field's ongoing discussion of this issue and to point out that there is not a universally accepted role for the therapist. Role prescriptions vary as theories vary; they range from viewing the therapist as an outside expert who does things to families to seeing the therapist as co-investigator with the family, seeking meaning in the family's "reality."

Beginning family therapists, more often than not, start their careers as relative purists, following the model they were exposed to in graduate school and training; with increasing experience, however, most gradually become more eclectic (Nichols & Schwartz, 1991). Consequently, the approaches that therapists ultimately develop are frequently amalgamations of theory, experience, their personalities, and their personal preferences.

In recognition of this diversity and in keeping with the tone of the book, the rest of this chapter addresses in pragmatic terms the role of the therapist in building a therapeutic alliance: "What do I do in the therapy sessions?" To further this discussion, the role of the therapist is viewed from the perspective of establishing and maintaining therapeutic boundaries and the therapist's use of self in the treatment process. Before discussing these issues, however, I should define my personal view (or biases?) of the therapeutic role (Worden, 1991):

1. The therapist is responsible for promoting an atmosphere conducive to change.

2. In so doing, the therapist actively forms a therapeutic alliance in collaboration with the family. Therapy is a joint effort between the therapist and family, with the therapist as a participant, observer, and facilitator.

3. The therapist may lead or show the way to change through supporting, questioning, challenging, or provoking the family, but he or she must give utmost respect to the family's capacity or willingness to change.

4. Change is ultimately the responsibility and choice of the family.

Case Presentation

Having agreed to begin family therapy, the Martin family tentatively stuck a toe into the water. Mr. Martin (Peter) worried that the sessions would be too hot to handle. He had actively sought to avoid confrontations at home and was fearful that therapy would be very confrontational. Mrs. Martin (Donna) covertly believed she was to blame for the family's unhappiness but projected the blame onto Cindy. Cindy assumed the therapist was going to be just one more adult trying to control her. Robert clearly stated he did not want to be there and sought to be excused from future meetings. Karen's behavior regressed as the tension in the room built.

One of the most difficult things for anyone to do is go to a therapist for the first time. Expectations are colored by cultural stereotypes: "Will she be able to read my mind? I am so vulnerable. Will I be blamed for the problem? Will I discover something I am afraid of?" To go with your family, however, is even more unpredictable: "Why are we all going? What will be said? Will they blame me? Will I say more than I should? Will I say something I will pay for later?" This unpredictability raises anxiety and causes reluctance in all the family members.

Underlying these fears is frequently a nagging sense of shame, failure, and blame, particularly for parents with a "troubled" child: "Where have we gone wrong? Why can't we handle this ourselves? Why do we have to go to a shrink? They always blame things on parents. I don't buy any of this psychology stuff."

For these families, therapy is a double bind encounter. "We (parents) want help for our son or daughter, but we fear we will be blamed. If the therapist succeeds, that means we are failures as parents. If therapy does not work, then even an expert was unable to change our child and we truly have done the best we could, given how difficult our child is." This ambivalence colored by both hopes and fears can make the engagement process particularly difficult with some families.

As for the Martins, Cindy's and Mrs. Martin's arguments threatened the very existence of the family. Both Mr. and Mrs. Martin did not know how much more stress they could take. The stepfamily as a unit was still in its infancy and needed nurturing to grow, not strife.

As a means of summarizing, the following points highlight many characteristics that are common to stepfamilies with adolescents and are seen in the Martin family:

1. At the time of divorce, the authority structure of the family is disrupted during the very period the emerging teenager needs clear and firm limits (Keshet & Mirkin, 1985). Cindy had entered early adolescence at the height of the conflict that led to her parents' divorce. During this time, each parent was absorbed in the dissolution of the marriage, and Cindy lacked consistent limits. To compound the matter, Cindy learned to exploit the differences between her parents to her advantage. She became increasingly manipulative in her efforts to hide the fear of a scared little girl watching her parents' marriage end.

2. In the post-divorce living arrangement, the adolescent has a more intense involvement with the parent he or she lives with; a typical way of increasing the intensity is through angry exchanges (Keshet & Mirkin, 1985). Cindy originally lived with her mother following her parents' divorce, but their arguments frequently escalated to the point where Mr. Martin was called by his ex-wife and told, "You have got to do something with your daughter. She is out of control." For Cindy's part, during her visits with her dad, Cindy complained of her mother's "screaming and yelling." Finally, after a particularly heated exchange, Cindy's mother blurted out, "If you don't like it here, then go live with your father." To which, Cindy countered, "I will; any place is better than this!" Angry words and stubborn pride are a lethal combination in families. Cindy left the next day for her father's home.

3. Girls have greater difficulty than boys following a remarriage (Clingempeel, Grand, & Ievoli, 1984; Wallerstein & Kelly, 1980). Cindy liked Donna when she and her father were only dating. She felt that her dad was lonely much of the time and was glad there was someone with whom he was comfortable. The direct time Cindy spent with the future Mrs. Martin was minimal because her father usually took Cindy out alone. When her father first brought up the idea of marriage, Cindy experienced a sickening feeling in her stomach. Dating was one thing; marriage was something else. Cindy would now have a stepmother! Boszormenyi-Nagy and Spark (1973) identify loyalty issues as a key ingredient in family life. In their framework, a family member is viewed as embedded in a multiperson loyalty network that demands compliance with the expectations and obligations of the group—a responsibility, in other words, to act in prescribed ways toward others. Despite their differences, Cindy felt a loyalty to her mother. She was her mother, and no one would take her place! Cindy could barely tolerate the idea of a stepmother, and when Donna attempted to parent (discipline, instruct), it was akin to throwing down the gauntlet. Cindy would have none of it.

4. Adolescents have a particularly difficult time with the stepfamily's new discipline structure (Lutz, 1983). In the process of individuation—the movement from a childlike dependency state to increased autonomy and a sense of self—the adoles-

cent's chief tool is testing the family's limits. Any parent of an adolescent or a professional who works with adolescents will tell you that testing limits is the teenager's breakfast of champions. To emerge into adolescence in an intact family is difficult enough—"They still treat me like a child; I want some freedom"—but to have to adapt to a whole new set of rules in a new stepfamily is intolerable. One of Donna's fundamental rules was that all the children had to be home on time. For Donna, this was a simple matter of respect and consideration. Cindy, on the other hand, was accustomed to coming and going as she pleased. She believed the curfew times were attempts to control her. Because she felt Donna's curfews were for Karen and Robert but not for her, Cindy violated her curfew times at every opportunity.

5. Of all the possible relationships, the stepmother-stepdaughter relationship is the most difficult to develop in a stepfamily (Clingempeel et al., 1984). Moreover, traditional gender roles requiring women to take responsibility for the emotional well-being of the family pit stepmother and stepdaughter against each other (Carter, 1988). Cindy was bound by loyalty to her mother. Equally significant, Cindy felt a rivalry with Donna, a competition for Peter's attention but also a struggle for control. Cindy would not allow Donna to control or influence her. Subsequently, at every opportunity, Cindy was more than happy to ignore or respond with passive-aggressive behavior to Donna's requests. Cindy's passive-aggressiveness took the form of procrastination, "forgetfulness," and negativity. Cindy would look Mrs. Martin directly in the eye and say, "Okay, I'll do it later" knowing full well that she had no intention of honoring Mrs. Martin's request. When confronted later by Mrs. Martin for not completing a task, Cindy would say, "I told you I forgot, so get off my back." Cindy knew exactly how to get the veins to pop out on her stepmother's forehead.

6. The adolescent and stepfamily exemplify conflicting periods in the life cycle. The adolescent is seeking to break from parental, dependent bonds, whereas the stepfamily is seeking to create bonds and establish new parent-child relationships (Visher & Visher, 1988). Mr. Martin hoped that Cindy would join his new family and that they would all become close. Still guilty over his divorce, he hoped to make amends to Cindy with the new family. Moreover, he saw the opportunity to make a successful second family. Cindy, on the other hand, wanted to be out with her friends.

7. Forming a stepfamily with young children is different from forming a stepfamily with teenagers because of developmental needs. Parents and young children in stepfamilies need close, cohesive family relationships, whereas the adolescent is at odds with the developmental push of the new stepfamily for closeness and bonding (Bray, 1995). Karen welcomed the marriage of her mother to Peter. She would now have a "Daddy." Robert and Cindy, in contrast, each spent as much time out of the house as they could. They had no desire to become the Brady Bunch. They tolerated family dinners but, when home, Robert and Cindy stayed in their respective rooms as much as possible.

Treatment Notes

Therapeutic Alliance

In forming a therapeutic alliance, the therapist accommodates to the family norms while also drawing the therapeutic boundaries needed for treatment to progress.

For example, in engaging the Martin family, the therapist found three issues to be paramount: the fragile nature of the newly formed stepfamily, the need to avoid gender bias or scapegoating in focusing on Mrs. Martin or Cindy, and the need to understand the family's narrative.

Recognizing the Fragility of Newly Formed Stepfamilies

The shared history is between the parents and their children and not between the spouses or steprelationships. Consequently, a stepfamily is the merging of two distinct family narratives. As the stepfamily begins to construct its own distinctive narrative, the newest and weakest bond in the family is between the spouses. Consequently, it is important for the therapist to give a great deal of attention and support to the couple bond (Carter, 1988).

The triangle involving Mr. and Mrs. Martin and Cindy threatens the stepfamily. Mrs. Martin wants to be close to her stepdaughter, but Cindy's behavior is a direct affront to her. Mr. Martin loves his new wife but he also loves his daughter. Their conflicts hurt him greatly and he hopes to avoid choosing one or the other. In this mismatch, both Mr. and Mrs. Martin are wondering secretly and silently whether getting married was such a good idea. Thus, in the engagement phase of treatment, the marital dyad is supported and not challenged.

> **Therapist:** It is never easy trying to blend two families together, particularly with teenagers. During these difficult times, how do the two of you [Mr. and Mrs. Martin] support each other?

Here the therapist is emphasizing the ways in which the parents positively interact and not what is driving them apart.

> **Therapist:** I was wondering, before the wedding, when all of you were talking about being a new family, what hopes did each of you have?

The therapist is exploring from a "not-knowing" position to sketch the early outlines for the stepfamily's narrative.

Avoiding Gender Bias and Scapegoating

From a linear perspective, Mrs. Martin's actions toward Cindy could be labeled as intrusive and controlling, making her a "wicked stepmother." Mrs. Martin, however, is being true to her ethnic tradition and could proudly point to her two children as examples of the correctness of her approach.

Furthermore, she is assuming a great deal of the emotional responsibility for making the stepfamily work. Mr. Martin is colluding with her by encouraging her to make many of the decisions concerning the children while he avoids taking a clear stand in any of the arguments.

Consequently, the engaging process would be threatened if the therapist challenged Mrs. Martin's mothering style or questioned the ethnic values behind it. Moreover, forcing Mr. Martin to take a stand in these arguments at this early stage of treatment would be coercing him to do something he dreads and has been studiously avoiding. These issues might be confronted later in treatment, but in the engagement phase, putting them at center stage would threaten the family even more.

Therapist: Before you were married, did the two of you discuss how you would parent your three children? Is it what you had thought it would be? What has surprised you?

The therapist opens up the issue of parenting styles. The open-ended questions are designed to put the issue on the table without focusing specifically on one parent or the other.

Understanding the Family's Narrative

The emotional distance between Cindy and her stepmother is respected. Early attempts to reconcile the two of them or suggestions that this would be a goal of treatment would only serve to isolate Cindy.

Therapist: Boy, Cindy, it must be hard remembering the house rules for both your mom's and dad's homes. On top of that, you're probably giving some thought to your own future when you move out of both these homes. How do you manage these things?

Cindy is invited into the treatment process as an adolescent/young adult. The therapist communicates to Cindy that her opinions are as valid as anyone else's and that the focus is not merely on "fixing" her. Although the therapist's query is guided by his knowledge of adolescent, developmental behavior, the question is asked from a "not-knowing" stance. Cindy is offered the opportunity to tell her narrative.

These three clinical concerns are based first on exploring and understanding the family's paradigm or narratives. In doing so, the therapist is not only gathering valuable information on the family's functioning but is also building the therapeutic alliance by listening to the family members and trying to capture what it is like to be "in their shoes." The family members, in turn, feel that the therapist is genuinely trying to understand them and is not judging them.

Apart from understanding the individual family members and establishing rapport, the therapist, in the engagement phase, is also establishing the therapeutic boundaries that will be reinforced throughout treatment.

Therapeutic Boundaries

Boundaries, as we saw in Chapter 1, refer to demarcation lines within a system that reflect the rules and limits defining patterns of interaction: Who is responsible for what? Who interacts with whom and in what way? Who is closer to whom? And so forth. Similar to boundaries within the family, **therapeutic boundaries** define the interactions between the therapist and the family. And just as in a family, the clearer the boundaries, the more defined are the rules of participation. Finally, the boundaries are defined through interaction; they are therapeutic norms the therapist shapes through interacting with the family.

A key issue in drawing therapeutic boundaries is how much responsibility the therapist should take for therapeutic change. On a more personal level, the question can be put: "How much responsibility do I take for my clients?" In the process of therapy, determining who is responsible for change and who should change can become visceral issues. The fights between Mrs. Martin and Cindy had greatly escalated by

How much responsibility does a therapist have in therapist + client change?

the time the first session was held. Cindy was the scapegoat and Mrs. Martin, in particular, wanted the therapist to "fix" her.

With all parts of the system calling out for help, a therapist would feel compelled to act. First, however, the central question is the responsibility boundary: Which family members need to change? Will they take responsibility for the change? How much responsibility will the therapist assume?

> **Therapist:** Mr. and Mrs. Martin, I know Cindy will probably object to my saying so, but I agree with both of you that the situation is quickly going downhill. I also agree that each of you is part of the problem but also part of the solution. For me to work individually with Cindy, therefore, would be a waste of time and money. All she would do is try to convince me that both of you are wrong and, at some point, determine that I was also. Instead, I recommend that all five of you come to the sessions. If this family is to work well, it will need everyone trying to make it better.

Who will participate in the sessions and what is the first therapeutic boundary to establish? Families frequently present the scapegoat for the therapist to fix. The notion of coming in together is both foreign and threatening to the family members. Even more confusing for the parents is the involvement of their young children in therapy.

Zilbach (1986) argues that young children serve critical functions in family therapy. First, they might carry the family symptom. For example, school problems in a young child could be symptomatic of deeper family issues. Second, depending on their age, young children often express family concerns in unsophisticated clarity. A simple statement, "I want Mom and Dad to stop fighting," cuts directly through the adults' obfuscations. Finally, involving young children enables the therapist to understand whole family interactions while highlighting potential problems.

In the Martin family, Karen was quiet and withdrawn. She sat and played with her doll throughout the initial interview, sharing a seat with her mother. Performing well in school, Karen was recently experiencing sleep difficulties and frequently wanted to be in bed with her mother. Although not displaying any overt symptoms that concerned her parents, Karen needed attention. At the very least, she was experiencing stress symptoms that largely coincided with Cindy's moving into the house.

In spite of the benefits, objections for including young children come from three sources: therapists, parents, and the children themselves (Zilbach, 1986). Unless they are the ones exhibiting the symptoms, young children in therapy can serve as a powerful distraction. Parents, for example, may expend considerable energy managing the child in the session. A 5-year-old pulling books off a shelf demands attention. Likewise, the 4-year-old who is tired whines, "When are we going home?" as he tugs on the mother's sleeve, focusing everyone's attention on the time. Because of their potential ability to distract the group from more salient issues, young children are frequently excluded from treatment by family therapists.

Parents might object to involving young children for a number of reasons. Sometimes they believe the younger children should not be exposed to family problems. At other times, the parents believe the content of the discussions is inappropriate for young children. Finally, the parents fear that family secrets kept hidden from the younger children will emerge in therapy.

[margin handwritten note: Why to include/or not young children.]

Children themselves sometimes voice objections to coming to therapy. In these cases, a safe assumption is that the young child has an intuitive grasp of the parents' doubts and is voicing their concerns (Zilbach, 1986).

Obviously, there is not one established guideline for involving young children in family therapy. Zilbach (1986) argues that if therapists wish to engage children in family therapy, they must appreciate and participate in play, a young child's medium for expression. Most therapists, however, are reluctant to include young children, because they haven't been trained in play therapy and are generally uncomfortable with it.

Ultimately, each family therapist weighs the pros and cons of involving young children in therapy. The following guidelines are offered as a starting point for your own formulation:

1. *Include all family members initially.* The therapist cannot truly appreciate the family patterns without knowing the full "cast of characters."
2. *Include the young child when his or her symptoms are the presenting problem.* Doing so offers the therapist immediate access to the family patterns and an opportunity to intervene directly in the interactions.
3. *Exclude young children if their presence dilutes the focus of the sessions.* As an example, if a young couple who are experiencing marital problems brings their 2-year-old to the session, they will spend the entire session with one set of eyes on the therapist and one set of eyes on their child, who is systematically pulling all the leaves off the office plant.
4. *Establish the flexibility to involve various combinations of family members as you decide this is important.* For example, parents have sought therapy for the behavioral problems of their 6-year-old. After meeting with the entire family for several sessions and having gained an appreciation of the dynamics, the therapist schedules several sessions alone with the parents. In those sessions, strategies are formulated and the parents decide to try new parenting skills. After several weeks, the therapist invites all the family members to return for a session to both observe and modify the new patterns, if necessary.

[handwritten margin note: Who to include in the family session.]

As discussed in the following section, the therapist decides that all the Martin family members need to attend the sessions, including Karen. Also, the therapist seeks to expand the boundaries of participation.

Therapist: At some point in the future, I will probably want to bring Cindy's mother in for a few sessions. I am not sure when that might be, but we will discuss it thoroughly beforehand.

The therapist is introducing the participation of Cindy's mother. Although that could raise the family's anxiety level, it is better to bring up the topic in the engagement phase than to surprise the family with it later. Note that the therapist attempts to reduce any anxiety by stating that the decision will first be thoroughly discussed.

Establishing the Boundaries with the Family

With the Martin family, the therapist is drawing boundaries for several reasons. First, from a systems perspective, he has decided that both Mr. and Mrs. Martin and

Cindy's mother must assume an active role in treatment. One explanation for Cindy's behavior is that it was a delayed reaction to the divorce and her father's remarriage. Thus, individual therapy for her is needed to work through these past issues. Another argument is that Cindy is experiencing a sense of displacement because of her position between two families. Consequently, the therapist is emphasizing that blending families is never easy, and for it to work well, everyone must participate.

At first glance, the unilateral therapist-established boundaries appear to be a gamble on the therapist's part: What if the family rejects the boundaries and terminates treatment? On closer examination, however, the gamble seems to have been minimal. To see Cindy alone would certainly increase the number of contacts with the family. The parents would keep Cindy coming as long as they believed the therapist was trying to "fix" her, but the lack of change in her behavior over time would begin to scream out. Phone calls to the therapist would increase as Cindy continued to act out, and the parents, frustrated with the lack of change, would soon terminate therapy, concluding, "Well, *that* therapist was of little help!"

The therapist, therefore, had little to lose by drawing the initial boundaries. If the family agreed to the boundaries, then the prospects for success increased. If the family rejected the proposed boundaries, the therapist was in a position to refer them to someone else, with no hard feelings or frustration for anyone.

For example, if the Martins were to reject the proposed boundaries, the therapist might respond like this:

> **Therapist:** I am sorry we won't be working together. I respect your judgment concerning your needs at this time, but I also must be clear about how I would approach the problem and why. Only you can decide what would be right for your family. If you would like, I would be happy to give you the names of other therapists who use a different approach.

The Martins, however, accepted the therapist's boundaries—with one reservation: They wanted to exclude Robert and Karen from the sessions—"He doesn't want to come, and she's too young and not involved in all this." This reservation is frequently voiced in families experiencing difficulties with an older sibling. In these cases, the parents are most often motivated by their concern for upsetting a younger child. Some will even say they fear the older sibling will "contaminate" a younger brother or sister.

Although these fears may be justifiable, they also hint at a family's acceptance of secrets. By excluding information from various family members, the family's communication patterns could be facilitating covert alliances ("Now don't tell your father this") to promoting scapegoating ("Let's talk about her when she's not around"). Consequently, if the therapist goes along with the parents' reservation, the dysfunctional family patterns continue.

Again, the therapist is in the position to define the boundaries. He considered participation by Robert and Karen to be essential. Not only are they close in age to Cindy but they also have experienced many of the same life events that she has: the loss of a parent, a single-parent family, the struggle to blend families and accept a stepparent. Furthermore, while Karen is not exhibiting symptoms at this time, a preventive intervention alone would be to include her in the sessions. Also, Robert's and Karen's involvement in treatment lessens the scapegoating of Cindy and symbolically states that Cindy's problems are embedded in the family's struggles as a new stepfamily.

The responsibility for change and for who should be involved in treatment illustrates two therapeutic boundaries. Although boundaries vary from case to case, there is one rule of thumb: The therapist must decide what he or she needs to do to facilitate change. Sometimes, insisting on this is difficult for a beginning family therapist. The desire to keep a family in treatment can outweigh clinical judgment. The therapist might back off an initial boundary for fear of the family's termination. Bergman (1985) observes, however, that a clinician's fear of losing a family can keep a family system from changing, as the therapist accepts the family's norms and will not challenge them. Only when the family needs the therapist more than the therapist needs the family is change optimal. Implied in Bergman's observation is an element of timing. Every therapist works well with families who enter therapy on the verge of or motivated for change, just as even the most experienced therapist has difficulty with poorly motivated and highly ambivalent families.

Implied in this discussion is my bias that therapy is a collaborative effort. The therapist accepts 50% of the responsibility for change, recognizing that the family must contribute the other 50%. Although this is my personal belief, research outcome studies strongly support the beneficial impact of collaborative patient and therapist roles, with the crucial factors being the therapist's encouragement of clients' initiative and the clients' assumptions of an active role in resolving their problems (Orlinsky & Howard, 1986). In the end, the family works at maintaining therapeutic changes long after therapy has terminated.

Testing Boundaries

To reiterate, therapeutic boundaries are guidelines the therapist establishes through interaction with the family, which define how therapy will be conducted. Particularly in the engagement phase of treatment, the family will ask the therapist, "What's this therapy business all about?" Boundaries help answer this question. Some boundaries are overtly stated by the therapist, but many more evolve in the process of therapy. It is a reciprocal process in which the family and therapist are shaping one another and, thus, shaping the nature of the therapeutic alliance.

To draw up a list of boundaries applicable to every family one sees is not possible. Each case has unique aspects that call for flexibility from the therapist. However, regardless of the boundaries drawn, be assured that they will be tested, to one degree or another, by the family members. This testing is not necessarily an indication of opposition to treatment per se; it is better viewed as the family's attempt to explore the boundaries and find out where they are drawn. Accordingly, the active testing of boundaries can be a positive diagnostic sign of the family's vitality: The family is active in therapy, engaging the therapist and collaborating in shaping the treatment process.

The testing of boundaries, therefore, is an essential aspect of the therapeutic process. Through testing, the therapeutic norms are established. The question, though, is how to respond to the testing in ways that will further the family's therapeutic progress. The following list of common interactions that test the therapist's boundaries is certainly not inclusive, but it does give a flavor of the process.

Attendance Issues

Deciding who should attend the sessions is one of the first therapeutic boundaries established. The idea that the entire family or at least parts of the family should come to discuss a member's problems is understandably foreign to most people. Consequently, an initial challenge to including all family members is to be expected. Even after the therapist has made clear the reasons for this approach, this boundary is likely to be challenged periodically.

Although the therapist was clear concerning the involvement of Robert and Karen, in one of the early sessions Robert did not show up. The parents offered the excuse that Robert had a wealth of school responsibilities to finish. Although this was certainly a legitimate excuse, if the therapist failed to at least address the issue, the family might have assumed that it would be all right for Robert to miss future sessions.

> **Therapist:** I am sorry Robert was unable to attend tonight's session. This must be a busy time of the year for him, but I believe his help with this is essential. Next time, I would rather reschedule to a more convenient time than have him miss the session.

The therapist acknowledges that sometimes outside commitments need to be attended to, but he emphasizes, quietly but firmly, the initial boundary.

Although not present in the Martin case, a difficult but frequently encountered pattern is the refusal of one of the parents to participate in therapy. Most often it is the father who does not share the mother's concern that a problem even exists. He grudgingly tells his wife, "Do whatever you want to do, but I am not going!" In these situations, the therapist is presented with a dilemma: Do I go ahead and see the mother and children alone, or do I insist on the father coming in?

Several questions are weighed in resolving this dilemma. First, is the mother truly helpless in getting the father in? Does she not see or does she deny the power she has in persuading him? Second, can the family problem be adequately addressed without the father's involvement, or should the father's lack of involvement become the central focus, at least in the initial phase of treatment? Last, would the father come in if he were contacted directly by the therapist?

In the worst-case scenario, the mother is truly dominated by the father and fearful of him. He is central to the family's problems, and he refuses the therapist's direct request. At this point, another therapeutic choice is at hand. The purist might tell the mother that the father's involvement is absolutely necessary to address the problems adequately and refuse therapy until the mother gains the father's cooperation. If this happens, the mother is further defeated and left with the same problems. Instead, the following tack may be taken:

> **Therapist** (after the father's refusal of involvement): Well, after talking to your husband, I can see and feel what you are up against. I know you came here to get help for your children and I want to provide that, but it appears to me that the most dominating factor in the family is the relationship you have with your husband. I would like to talk to you first about that relationship before we discuss what we can do for your children.

Drawing this therapeutic boundary addresses the mother's conflicts and offers assistance with her specific problems, but also focuses the attention on systemic issues.

Parent Refuses to come in

Pushing Time Boundaries

One boundary the therapist is in absolute control of is the length of the session. Some therapists plan 90-minute family sessions. Others work on an hourly, or a 50- or 45-minute basis. The reasons vary from financial (the higher costs of longer sessions) to institutional (the need to document a certain number of cases per week). No absolute standard exists. With experience, therapists begin to establish time boundaries that best work for them.

The point, therefore, is not what time boundaries to draw but to draw them and then consistently maintain them. Although it is idealistic to want to continue working with a family as long as needed—an extra 15 or 30 minutes—doing so flies in the face of time demands on both the therapist and family members; also, it presents the family with an unclear boundary. "Last week we met for 90 minutes, and this week the therapist stopped after one hour. What gives?"

How people use time is an interesting discussion in and of itself, but in therapy it has particular meaning. An experienced therapist will talk of the "time process" of a session. The opening minutes are full of chitchat as the family and therapist reaccommodate to one another. Issues are likely to be brought up about a quarter of the way through the session. Finally, there is a need to begin closing the session before time runs out. Many therapists find that emotional bombs—issues not previously raised or emotional reactions not previously expressed—are typically dropped in the last quarter of a session.

In retrospect, there is wisdom in this behavior. Emotionally loaded issues are hard enough to express, much less elaborate on. By raising agendas at the end of a session, the family member is introducing a new topic to the therapist but is also signaling that this is a highly charged issue to be addressed later. Practically and protectively, the end of the session leaves little time for elaboration but has established an agenda for the next meeting and alerted the therapist to a threatening issue.

Clarity and consistency of time boundaries add predictability to the treatment sessions for both the therapist and family. This is a boundary that is initially stated by the therapist: "Each session lasts 60 minutes." Session length is established as a norm through interaction.

Testing this boundary occurs in several ways. The family arrives late for the meeting but expects to have the full session time. Someone brings up an emotional issue right at the end of the session, begging the therapist to continue. Family members linger in the office, hoping to speak to the therapist alone. Family members concretely ask for more time. Each of these is an attempt to seduce the therapist into extending the session, thus blurring the time boundaries.

[handwritten marginal note: examples of testing time boundaries. solidifying/ quit time boundaries.]

Telephone Calls

The telephone is frequently used in making alliances. Family members will call with information they "did not want to bring up in the last session but thought the therapist should know." Consciously or unconsciously, the family member in these situations is seeking an alliance with the therapist, frequently against another family member.

It is most important that the therapist establish a boundary on information outside the sessions. If the family members believe or know they can call the therapist between sessions to discuss other family members, this will happen.

The therapist can announce this boundary in the early phase of treatment.

> **Therapist:** I believe very strongly that what all of you have to say to one another is most important. Consequently, our sessions are the time to raise the issues each of you feel are important. If you have something to say to me, please do so in our sessions.

Even with this announcement, an inevitable test will occur. Sometimes, within the first few sessions, one family member will call with information he or she believes can be said only to the therapist. Such a call will have several meanings. For one, it is diagnostic; it hints at the use of secrets in the family. Second, the way the therapist handles the phone call will set the tone for the treatment. A simple but effective response over the phone is this:

> **Therapist:** Before you begin, please know that whatever you tell me, I'll assume I can bring up in our next family session. With this in mind, I would be happy to hear whatever you have to say.

The caller then usually expresses the need for secrecy and again appeals to the therapist, who responds:

> **Therapist:** I understand your concern that what you are about to say can't be said in the family session, but I've found openness to be the best approach with families. Consequently, you will be the best judge of whether to raise your issues at our meetings. I hope you will, but I'll respect your decision if you don't. I hope our meetings will reach the point where you will raise your concerns.

These are just a few examples of boundaries that are tested in the course of treatment. Again, the basic question the therapist asks is, "What do I need to do my job?" All boundaries flow from the answers to this question.

Therapist's Use of Self

The **therapist's use of self** refers to the ways the practitioner employs all aspects of his or her personality to further the treatment process. Certain questions are relevant to this discussion: "How much do I share about myself? How do I handle family members' personal questions about me? What does my own behavior communicate to the family? Should I reveal my strong personal reactions to what is occurring in treatment?"

Although falling under the rubric of therapeutic boundaries, the use of self is directly defined by a therapist's theoretical model, but it also reflects his or her comfort level and personal style. One therapist may feel quite comfortable answering the family's personal questions, whereas another will experience an elevated anxiety level when such questions are asked. To further this discussion, the therapist's use of self is subdivided into issues of self-disclosure and the use of personal reactions. Again, there are no universally accepted answers. With experience, therapists discover their own personal comfort level.

[Handwritten margin note: Families using the phone to test the boundaries.]

Therapist's Self-Disclosure

How much do I share with the family? How do I answer the family's personal questions? Where do I draw the boundaries on the family's questions?

Some families ask a series of personal questions of the therapist: "Are you married? Have you ever been divorced? Do you have children?" These questions can range from a legitimate request for information to defensive challenges: "Have you and your wife ever had marital problems?"

In the engagement phase of treatment, the family is evaluating the therapist as much as the therapist is evaluating the family. The family members might need additional information from the therapist to determine whether he or she is the one with whom they wish to work. To address this need and to clear the way for the family-focused therapeutic work, the therapist offers in the first session to answer any questions the family members may have:

> **Therapist:** To help you determine whether I am the right therapist for the family, are there any personal questions you wish to ask me?

By opening up the initial session for personal self-disclosure, the therapist addresses the family's concerns but also displays an openness and honesty, symbolically communicating that therapy will be a collaborative effort.

Typically, the family members will ask, if they ask at all, basic questions concerning academic degrees, marital status, number of children, and so on. Frequently, the way the therapist responds is more important than the answers to the questions. Is the therapist defensive or guarded? Is the therapist open and honest?

Paradoxically, the more open the therapist appears, the less need the family has for questions. The family members are assured through the therapist's behavior that he or she will be responsive to them.

Finally, whereas family members' personal questions of the therapist in the initial interview or the engagement phase of treatment represent legitimate requests for information, in the latter stages of treatment, 99% of the time these questions are resistance and defensive maneuvers. This behavior typically occurs when a heated family issue is surfacing, the family is at an impasse, or the therapist is pushing into sensitive family issues and the family is attempting to escape the spotlight. At these times, turning the question back to the process furthers treatment and not resistance.

> **Mr. Martin** (in a later phase of treatment and in the middle of a heated discussion): Have you ever had problems like this with your own wife?
>
> **Therapist:** Well, that is something for me to think about, but I think it is irrelevant to what just occurred. I think you and Donna have locked horns on this issue, and there doesn't appear to be any way out.

The therapist draws the therapeutic boundary and redirects the discussion back to the issue at hand.

Use of Personal Reactions

Experiential family therapists would argue that the heart of the therapeutic process is the therapist's use of self or, more concretely, the therapist's use of personal reactions

(Whitaker & Bumberry, 1988). Whatever the therapist's reactions are to the family process—anger, frustration, sadness, joy—it is reasonable to assume that family members may be experiencing similar feelings, even if they do not articulate them. Consequently, sharing personal reactions could strike responsive therapeutic chords in the family members and encourage faster change. The choices, therefore, are if, when, and how to use these reactions.

As a rule of thumb, the therapist's sharing of personal reactions is most beneficial when (1) the treatment process has reached an impasse, (2) the family asks for feedback, (3) the therapist assumes a defensive position, or (4) therapy is about to end.

At various times throughout the treatment process, impasses can develop. An impasse signals any number of themes: The family is avoiding a difficult issue, the family is struggling with an issue that precedes a positive breakthrough, the family members do not feel understood by the therapist, or the therapist has missed an important ingredient in the family's dynamics. Regardless of its interpretation, on the very concrete, experiential level, an impasse may leave all participants, the therapist included, feeling discouraged. The therapist's direct confrontation of the impasse could foster its resolution, particularly when the task is addressed as a cooperative effort:

> **Therapist:** I may be wrong, but does anyone else feel as stuck as I do? I feel like we have gone around this mulberry bush one too many times. Anybody have any ideas on how to get through this?

A variation of impasse occurs when the family asks for direct feedback. Typically, this request occurs in the middle phases of treatment, and although it has a strong defensive element—the family members are shifting the focus away from themselves and onto the therapist—it really is a request for feedback!

> **Mrs. Martin** (after several disagreements with her husband over establishing consistent expectations for Cindy): I don't think we will ever reach an agreement on this. The two of us come from such different backgrounds. Do you [therapist] see any point in all of this?

> **Therapist:** You may be right that you and Peter will never develop boundaries with Cindy and consistently reinforce them. However, for better or for worse, you are both parents to your children and will be for years to come. It's your decision what kind of parents you will be.

The therapist refocuses the discussion back to problematic issues.

In the course of treatment, the therapist is also responding to the treatment process. The individual personalities of the family members, content or process themes, and specific behavioral patterns all act as stimuli for both conscious and unconscious reactions within the therapist. At any point, the therapist can assume a defensive position by daydreaming or not fully listening to the family. This is not a flaw in the therapist but a human response. The issue, therefore, is how to use this reaction to promote change.

For example, Mrs. Martin will always be the first to bring up Cindy's misdeeds since the previous session. Mr. Martin will look perplexed and frustrated. Cindy will consistently demonstrate overt or passive-aggressive hostility. Confronted with the power and persistency of these patterns, the therapist could become as frustrated and annoyed as the family members.

Concretely, frustration and annoyance affect the ability of the therapist to listen. Therapists may find themselves attending less and less to the individual family members. If this pattern is allowed to continue, therapists become part of the problem. From another perspective, this annoyance and inattention are valuable feedback to a therapist:

> **Therapist** (to Mrs. Martin after she has related another incident of Cindy's disobedience): Mrs. Martin, I know that Cindy's behavior is intolerable and that she continues to violate your wishes, but in each session we have had, you bring up one violation after another. I have a feeling you are sending me, or your husband, a strong message, but I am not sure what it is. Tell us directly why you focus on these events.

The therapist is moving past Mrs. Martin's complaints to the message behind them. Is she trying to say how frustrated she is? Whom does she want to hear that message? How does she want the person to respond to her?

> **Therapist:** Mr. Martin, when your wife brings up her concerns about Cindy, you look to me as if you'd love to leave the room. Am I right or wrong in that impression? What do you want to say to your wife at those moments?

Mr. Martin's perplexed look is frequently a cue for the therapist to answer the wife's concerns. If the therapist responds in this manner, the parents can avoid dealing directly with each other and the therapist has inadvertently taken over Mr. Martin's role. The response above draws Mr. Martin back into the discussion in his proper role.

> **Therapist** (after Cindy interrupts the discussion with a hostile comment): Cindy, you have an amazing sense of timing. Not only do you choose to interrupt your parents and me just at a point where we might solve something, but you also have the capacity to make the blood vessels stand out in our necks. I must say, you are good at it because I have felt it in my own neck more than once. But I have a feeling there is something else you are trying to say. Do you want them to be at odds with one another? Are you trying to tell us that you are hurt and angry, too?

Here, the therapist is not only addressing Cindy's hostile comments but also defusing the impact of Cindy's hostility and suggesting that the teenager has feelings she would like others to understand.

As shown by these examples, the therapist's use of personal reactions can be a powerful diagnostic tool: What troubles the therapist might also bother the family members. It can also be an intervention technique, a personal and direct statement. Used as an intervention tool, however, it can harm as much as it helps. The question is one of intent: Is the therapist's use of personal reactions serving the needs of the family or the needs of the therapist (an acting-out of the therapist's own hostility and frustration)? As Shapiro (1981) points out, there is a thin line between the use of self to facilitate therapeutic process and the use of self to meet the therapist's needs.

For example, depending upon the therapist's predilections, any one or all of the family members could be confronted:

Therapist: Mrs. Martin, your complaints fall on deaf ears. I wonder why you persist in bringing them up?

Therapist: Mr. Martin, you play dumb like a fox. Why do you leave your wife out on a limb like this?

Therapist: Cindy, you have a one-note act. All you can do is interrupt in a hostile fashion.

Taken out of context, these confrontations are neither bad nor good. If timed properly and if the recipient is ready to "hear" the message, however, they can be surprisingly effective. On the other hand, if the therapist believes the confrontations are justified "because the person needs to hear what I have to say," an observer must wonder about the therapist's motivation. *Overall, the question is whether the therapy process will be facilitated or inhibited by the therapist's use of self.*

No therapist is immune to an abusive use of self. Family therapy, in particular, takes place in a very emotionally charged atmosphere. Remember that therapy touches the therapist as much as it touches the family. Family-of-origin and nuclear family issues can be stirred up, with each family seemingly tapping another aspect of the therapist's own emotional life: "Someone reminds me of one of my parents. This theme existed in my own family. I have always had difficulty with this type of person. I am always rushing to save someone."

Empathy, an invaluable tool of the clinician, is born of this self-awareness. Personal thoughts, feelings, and memories remind us that we too have felt similar things; that we too have been stuck in our own self-made box, unable to get out; that we too have felt emotions we cannot put into words.

It is not, therefore, the thoughts and feelings stimulated by the therapist's interaction with the family that inhibit or facilitate therapeutic progress. Thoughts and feelings will come and go throughout the treatment process. Rather, how the therapist uses them will either facilitate or hinder the therapeutic alliance.

Summary

As a means of summarizing the engagement process, Table 3.1 highlights the clinical concerns.

Glossary

Ethnicity A sense of cultural commonality (norms, values) transmitted over generations by the family and reinforced by the surrounding community.

Family life cycle A developmental concept referring to a family's evolution over time; transitional phases and crises are seen as inevitable with exits and entries from the family.

Family of origin A person's parents and siblings; usually refers to the original nuclear family of an adult.

Family paradigm A family's construct of the social world that guides individual family members' thoughts, feelings, and actions.

Fundamental attribution error Attributing personality characteristics to an individual's behavior while underestimating the influence of social role restraints.

Gender biases Overt or covert biases that support traditional views of male-female relationships; feminist theorists highlight the inequality of traditional sex roles and how these biases can be reinforced in therapy to the detriment of women.

Joining Therapeutic technique emphasizing the therapist's actions in accepting and accommodating to various families; types of joining techniques are:

    Maintenance Actively confirming and supporting the family subsystems.

    Mimesis Mirroring the family's communication style; for example, in terms of pace and use of humor.

    Tracking Encouraging and following the family's communications and behavior.

Therapeutic alliance Therapist and family form a new system to facilitate the treatment process; reflects a basic level of trust and a shared agenda.

Therapeutic boundaries Boundaries defining the interactions between the therapist and family; mutually co-constructed.

Therapist's use of self A concept that refers to the ways in which the therapist employs all aspects of his or her personality to further the treatment process.

Table 3.1	**Engagement Questions**

Therapeutic Alliance

Ethnicity
1. What ethnic patterns are operating within the family?
2. How do the ethnic patterns reflect the family's paradigm?
3. Do the ethnic patterns shape the family's defined problems?
4. How similar or different is the therapist's ethnicity from the family's?
5. What are the potential problems in engaging the family because of these differences or similarities?

Family Life Cycle
1. What is the family's life cycle stage?
2. Is the family experiencing difficulties in this particular stage?
3. Have earlier stages been successfully negotiated? Are past unresolved issues being carried into the present stage?
4. How does the therapist's own life cycle stage compare with the family's? Are there potential problems in engaging the family because of the differences or similarities?

Gender Bias
1. What are the gender roles within this family?
2. Do these roles reflect ethnic patterns, broader cultural, or idiosyncratic family-of-origin patterns?
3. Who will challenge the therapist's control of the sessions? How will this person do so?

Therapist's Family of Origin
1. What themes from the therapist's family of origin might affect the treatment process?
2. What strengths and vulnerabilities does the therapist bring to the treatment process?
3. What themes in the family are familiar or foreign to the therapist?
4. What family themes provoke an emotional reaction in the therapist? Can these reactions be channeled positively into the treatment process or will they interfere?

Treatment Notes

Therapeutic Boundaries
1. What boundaries are important to draw with the family?
2. Which therapeutic boundaries are non-negotiable with the family (boundaries the therapist deems essential for treatment) and which ones are more flexible?
4. How will the family test these boundaries?
4. What will the therapist's response be?

Therapist's Use of Self
1. How much do I share with the family?
2. How will I respond to personal questions?
3. What emotions of mine are frequently evoked while working with this family?
4. Will sharing my reactions facilitate or inhibit the treatment process? When should I share them?

4

Assessment: Diagnosis and Systems Models

Individual Versus Systems Assessment

Models of Systems Assessment

Case Presentation

Assessment Guidelines

Summary

Glossary

E ngaging the family, establishing therapeutic boundaries, and laying the foundation for treatment absorbs much of the first interview and possibly several more sessions. But unless the family establishes at least a tentative therapeutic alliance with the therapist, the first interview will be the last interview. Sometimes, with highly resistant families or those difficult to engage, the sole purpose of a first interview is have one more interview.

When the family agrees to further sessions, therapy then moves more formally into the assessment stage of treatment. It is in this stage that the therapist seeks to organize his or her observations into a coherent map of the family's functioning. This map not only orders the therapist's observations but also guides interventions. Why has the family sought therapy at this particular time? What are the family's strengths? What patterns underlie the family's complaint? Where should I intervene? What questions should I be asking?

The combination of the therapist's questions and the family interactions occurring rapidly in the room frequently overwhelms a therapist with data. How to pull data together into a coherent treatment plan is the focus of the following two chapters.

Specifically, in this chapter, three empirical models of family functioning are presented. Each of the models proposes a unique, global view of family patterns and is based in extensive research. (The process of identifying family patterns is outlined in the following chapter.) In addition, each model has developed measurement scales for both clinical and research needs. One model in particular, the Circumplex Model, is directly applied to the Martin family.

Before exploring these models, however, it is necessary to make the distinction between individual and systems assessment.

Individual Versus Systems Assessment

The medical model dominates the field of mental health. It is a model that identifies symptoms (patterns of behavior), categorizes these symptoms under a diagnosis, and, based on the diagnosis, recommends specific treatments. From the medical model perspective, pathology resides within the individual. Although external environmental events can precipitate or exacerbate dysfunctional behavior, the root causes of the behavior are intrapsychic, psychological, and biological in origin.

Notice the emphasis on pathology residing within the individual. The medical model pays lip service to external forces impinging on the individual, for example, employment, educational, or family stressors, but these are seen as forces exacerbating internal pathology. A therapist, for example, seeped in the medical model would give individual diagnoses to Mr. Martin, Mrs. Martin, and Cindy. The subsequent recommendation would be individual therapy for each of them.

In order for a therapist to function within the field of mental health, a working knowledge of individual assessment is necessary, specifically, a working knowledge of the **Diagnostic and Statistical Manual of Mental Disorders (DSM).** Some background is in order.

Intent on fostering international cooperative research by creating a common nosology (naming scheme), the United Nations' World Health Organization, in 1948, produced the International Statistical Classification of Diseases, Injuries, and Causes of Death (ICD). It included biologically based mental disorders. The American Psychiatric Association, however, dominated by psychoanalysts, did not adopt the ICD terminology. Instead, it produced its own *Diagnostic and Statistical Manual of Mental Disorders (DSM),* which stressed the psychological role of traumatic experiences (Schwartz, 2000).

Revised and expanded over the years, the current *DSM IV* (fourth edition) is the dominant form of communication within the field of mental health. It serves as a form of shorthand communication among mental health professionals and establishes guidelines for diagnosis that foster research efforts. For example, a researcher in California, studying depression, applies the same criteria in defining clinical depression as a researcher in New York. (*DSM V* is in the planning stages as of this writing and to ensure comparability of research data collected in different countries, the U.S. government, along with other members of the United Nations, agreed to maintain consistency between the *DSM* and the ICD.)

The *DSM IV* is also the language of clinical practice. As a shared reference source among professionals, the *DSM IV* summarizes a client's major symptoms, personality traits, medical problems, environmental stress, and highest level of functioning in the past year. The *DSM IV* is also the language shared with insurance companies and behavioral health maintenance organizations.

Family system assessment, on the other hand, places an individual within the family context. A fundamental premise of family therapy is that the individual family member presented as problematic is actually manifesting the stress of the dysfunctional family patterns. Instead of diagnosing the individual's symptoms, this member is seen as the **family symptom carrier.** That is to say, the family member presented as "having the problem" is the family member evidencing the symptoms of the family's dysfunctional patterns. Thus, his or her behavior is understood within the context of the family patterns.

The family systems perspective places individual behavior within the greater family context and thus avoids viewing pathology within any one family member. Cindy Martin, for example, is not diagnosed with a disorder, but instead, her behavior is seen as flowing out of her parents' divorce and the creation of her new stepfamily. Although her father and his new wife attribute their family's turmoil to Cindy's behavior, the family therapist is not assessing Cindy for symptoms of a disorder.

A family systems approach to assessment minimizes blaming and scapegoating within families. The Martins initially presented Cindy as the problem and their reason for seeking therapy. The family therapist, however, broadens the family's view of the problem to include the family interactions and makes those relationships the focus of treatment.

There are, however, drawbacks to blindly believing that an individual family member's behavior is caused by the family patterns. Although the family systems approach greatly expands the definition of the family's problems, it can underestimate individual pathology. In the early stages of family therapy development, each family member's behavior, even severe psychiatric disorders, was attributed to family dynamics. Schizophrenia, for example, was seen as a result of faulty communication and family projection systems. While family dynamics can play a role in the development and maintenance of schizophrenia, recent findings in brain imaging and behavioral genetics strongly point toward genetically inherited biochemical deficiencies as more significant causes of the disease.

A family systems approach to assessment can also confuse the question of causality. Are the family patterns causing the behavior, or is the family trying to cope with a family member struggling with a psychiatric disorder? We may err in blaming family dynamics for a member's behavior when in reality the family is trying to cope with a member's biological disease. For example, family dynamics comfortably explain Cindy's behavior. But, what if Cindy is experiencing a biological depression exacerbated by the onset of puberty? Maybe the family patterns are more influenced by Cindy's depression than the other way around?

Worse yet, family therapists sometimes subtly or not so subtly blame parents for a biological disorder. Until we understood attention deficit disorder with hyperactivity better, parents of these children would have easily been blamed for poor parenting. If the parents just would draw firmer and more consistent boundaries, then their child would be more in control. But then again, maybe the parents' boundaries are a result of coping with their child's hyperactivity? Frequently, in a two-way interaction, an individual is shaping the family as the family is shaping the individual.

Summary

To practice in the field of mental health that is dominated by the medical model, a family therapist should be familiar with the *DSM*. Besides being the language of psychiatry, the *DSM* offers diagnostic and assessment guidelines. Although these guidelines are narrowed to an individual focus, they alert a therapist to more severe, biologically based disorders, such as major depression and bipolar disorders. As a therapist, you would err in blaming the family system for a neurochemical disorder. Thus a *DSM* assessment is frequently part of the assessment process.

If Cindy's school or an insurance company wanted a *DSM* diagnosis after the initial interview, the following could be submitted:

Axis I (contains a person's primary clinical diagnosis): Conduct disorder, depression, or adjustment reaction

Axis II (describes any existing personality disorders): None

Axis III (identifies nonpsychiatric medical conditions that may play a role in a person's problem): None

Axis IV (indicates psychosocial or environmental problems that may affect the diagnosis, treatment, or prognosis of mental disorder): Problem in primary support group. Difficulty in school.

Axis V (ratings ranging from 100 [superior functioning] to 0 [inadequate functioning] are used to plan a treatment program, measure its impact, and predict treatment outcome) Global Assessment of Functioning: 52—moderate symptoms and serious impairment in social and school functioning

The remainder of this chapter is directed toward family assessment. This is not to minimize individual pathology. A family therapist should be well grounded in abnormal psychology. Each day new technology and research reveal more information concerning psychiatric disorders. Our understanding of the brain is expanding exponentially with the new tools of brain imaging. To believe all aspects of human behavior are based in family interactions is to ignore current literature on the brain.

In reality, behavior cannot be attributed solely to family dynamics or biology. Family patterns and biology interact in ways that shape the family's and an individual member's behavior. Even if Cindy were experiencing a biological depression, the family patterns can exacerbate or help to alleviate her symptoms. Thus, a family therapist's work would be an invaluable aid to Cindy and her family.

Models of Systems Assessment

As a treatment modality, family therapy shifts the focus away from individuals to the interactions among family members. This shift not only changes the process of therapy, but it is also a radical shift in assessment. Typically, a therapist's theoretical model guides his or her assessment. It is "as if" the theory becomes the lens through which a family is viewed. For example, a structural family therapist will focus on assessing the family's boundaries. A therapist trained in Bowen's Extended Family System Therapy will look for triangulation and a multigenerational projection system. A behavior-oriented therapist will look for the pattern of reinforcement underlying the family's behavior.

The advantage of basing assessment on a specific theoretical model of family therapy is that the applications of interventions also flow directly from the theory. The disadvantage of this approach is that one's assessment is limited to a narrow range of concepts. If there were one over-all, comprehensive model of family therapy and one way of doing family therapy, then textbooks would be very thin and very repetitive. Instead, as is true in most fields, theories and techniques endlessly compete for attention. Some theories complement one another while others emphasize distinct concepts. What one theory does not cover, another does.

There are, however, family models of functioning that stand apart from a theory of treatment: the Circumplex Model of Family Systems, the Beavers System Model of Family Functioning, and the McMasters Approach. These family systems models are based in empirical research and offer distinct lenses for viewing and conceptualizing family interactions. The assumption underlying each of the models is that family patterns are observable and measurable. Consequently, each of the models has developed self-report and clinical rating scales that conceptualize functional and dysfunctional ranges of behavior.

Because each model assumes family patterns are observable, they have more in common with problem-oriented, family systems therapies than with solution-focused, narrative approaches to clinical practice. The models are social constructions, that is, socially agreed-upon categories and these categories are "real" only to the extent we agree that they are. Still, Carr (2000) argues that even though the models are social constructions, they are useful for solving clinical problems. For example, woven into clinical practice, the models offer guidelines for assessment, suggest interventions, and provide outcome measures.

Each of the models differs in the degree to which it allows clinicians and researchers to conceptualize the status of family subsystems. One model highlights a particular area of functioning, for example, power, while another emphasizes communication. At the end of this chapter, the models are combined to provide guidelines for assessment.

In order to bring to life one of the models and demonstrate its usefulness for assessment, the Circumplex Model of Family Systems is used to assess the Martins.

Circumplex Model of Family Systems

Developed over 20 years, the **Circumplex Model of Family Systems** attempts to bridge theory, research, and practice (Olson, Russell, & Sprenkle, 1983; 1989; Olson et al., 1979; Olson, 1991; Olson, 2000) (see Figure 4.1). The model integrates three dimensions that "emerged from a conceptual clustering of over fifty concepts developed to describe marital and family dynamics" (Olson, 2000, p. 144). The dimensions are cohesion, flexibility, and communication.

Cohesion refers to a family's level of emotional bonding. It is the balance in the family between the separateness of members and their togetherness. For example, one family fosters individuality but at the expense of a sense of togetherness. In this family, members are involved in their individual pursuits while little attention is given to family relationships. Everyone typically eats at different times and family meals are few and far between. Another family, however, insists on family time, even at the expense of individuality. In this family, it does not matter what individual commitments exist outside of the family because family comes first. Everyone is expected for Sunday dinner!

The model conceptualizes a range on the cohesion dimension from disengaged (very low) to separate (low to moderate) to connected (moderate to high) to

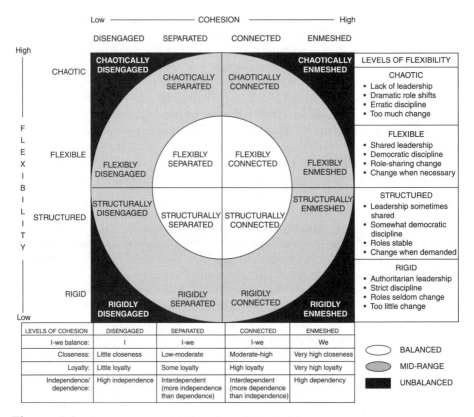

Figure 4.1   Circumplex Model: Couple and Family Map

Source: From "Circumplex Model of Marital and Family Systems," by D. Olson, 2000, *Journal of Family Therapy, 22,* Fig. 1, pp. 148. Copyright © 2000 Blackwell Publishers, Ltd. Reprinted with Permission.

enmeshed (very high). Disengaged and enmeshed are the extremes of the dimension. The family members in a disengaged family have little time for one another. The family members look outside the family to satisfy essential needs and wants. When you need someone with whom to talk, you look to friends not to family. On the other hand, enmeshed families place the family at the center of its members' lives. Family and family obligations always come first.

Separate and connected families represent balance points along the cohesion dimension. Each with a slightly different emphasis, separate and connected families foster in their members a sense of being both independent from and connected to their families. Family time and outside commitments are more easily balanced within these families.

Optimal family functioning results from a family's capacity to balance family members' needs for autonomy and belonging. It is hypothesized that families entering therapy more often than not fall into one of the extremes. For example, a rebellious teenager is fighting for a sense of autonomy in an enmeshed family. Tied in knots by the family's guilt system, this teenager struggles to find a place in his or her peer group. This family brings into your office battles for control. On the other hand, another rebellious teenager is angry because he or she feels rejected in a disengaged family. This teenager is running wild because the family does not care enough to stay involved in the teenager's life. A therapist working with this family would need to strengthen the emotional connections within the family.

Flexibility is a family's capacity to change its leadership, role relationships, and relationship rules as needed. It is the capacity to balance stability and change. For example, parenting practices for a child 5 years of age are different than those needed for a teenager 15 years of age. The protective parenting of a younger child gives way to the increased freedom granted to an older child. Parents who insist on treating their teenager as if he or she was 5 sow the seeds for family turmoil. Unfortunately, not only will the parents encourage in their teenager the rebellious behavior they fear, they will also inadvertently be stifling their son's or daughter's capacity to cope with the world outside the family.

The model conceptualizes a range on the flexibility dimension from rigid (very low) to structured (low to moderate) to flexible (moderate to high) to chaotic (very high). Rigid and chaotic are the extremes of the dimension. In the rigid family, one individual is typically in charge and highly controlling. What he or she says is the family law. Family rules are rigid and unchanging. Children are children no matter their ages. In contrast, the chaotic family lacks a leadership structure and consistent rules. Because decisions are impulsive and not well thought out, the family runs in a constant state of crisis.

Structured and flexible families represent balance points along the flexibility dimension. Structured and flexible families share stable roles and a democratic approach to decision making. In both types of families, rules can be changed and are age-appropriate.

Optimal family functioning is the capacity to balance stability and change. There needs to be a clear line of authority within the family but an authority hierarchy flexible enough to change when needed. It is hypothesized that families entering therapy more often than not fall into one of the extremes. For example, a teenager may rebel against a rigid, authoritarian figure. On the other hand, teenagers who are "out of control" may be exploiting the lack of leadership within their families.

Communication focuses on the family's listening skills, speaking skills, self-disclosure, clarity, continuity tracking, and respect and regard. Families balanced on the cohesion and flexibility dimensions tend to have very good communication. The family members listen with empathy, share feelings directly, effectively problem-solve by staying on the topic, and respect differences of opinions. Unbalanced families, on the extremes of the cohesion and flexibility dimensions, are more likely to be indirect in their communication by sharing feelings reluctantly, if at all, minimize or ignore differences of opinion, and problem-solve poorly.

Extreme Family Types

The Circumplex Model identifies four extreme family types: chaotically enmeshed, rigidly enmeshed, rigidly disengaged, and chaotically disengaged. Each type is in the extreme range on the cohesion and flexibility dimensions. As such, these families are likely to evidence a number of dysfunctional patterns and symptoms.

   1. *Chaotically enmeshed.* Extremely high on the chaotic range of the flexibility

dimension and extremely high on the enmeshed range of the cohesion dimension, chaotically enmeshed families are typically overwhelmed by change and lack clear interpersonal boundaries. Ineffective crisis management characterizes parental practices. Members struggle with gaining a sense of autonomy but ultimately are emotionally tied to the family through guilt. Without the capacity for establishing clear and consistent expectations for behavior, these families control behavior through guilt and mutual obligations. The lack of stability in the family creates a sense of anxiety that pervades the family.

2. *Rigidly enmeshed.* Extremely high on the rigid range of the flexibility dimension and extremely high on the enmeshed range of the cohesion dimension, rigidly enmeshed families fail to accommodate members' needs and employ rigid discipline and guilt to control individual members' behaviors. Any attempt at autonomous behavior is seen as a threat to the family structure. Children remain children no matter what their age. Parents always know best. The rigid and enmeshed qualities of the family structure tie individuals in emotional knots through a fear of authority and guilt. Children do not learn to master their environments and can be categorized as immature. They also tend to underachieve in school.

3. *Rigidly disengaged.* Extremely high on the rigid range of the flexibility dimension and extremely high on the disengaged range of the cohesion dimension, rigidly disengaged families employ inflexible discipline to control members but it is a discipline without a sense of warmth or belonging. Behavior is controlled through fear and punishment. In this family, it is "my way or the highway." Without a sense of connection to balance the rigid discipline, individual family members resent the parental authority and respond with passive-aggressive behavior or active rebellion. The lack of connection can fuel a sense of personal rejection that, combined with anger, can manifest itself in depression.

4. *Chaotically disengaged.* Extremely high on the chaotic range of the flexibility dimension and extremely high on the disengaged range of the cohesion dimension, chaotically disengaged families lack an effective parental hierarchy to address the rage family members feel at their emotional disconnection to the family. The rage at being neglected may be turned toward the family in terms of chronic arguments and battles for control or vented toward the environment via vandalism, acting-out, or even violence.

Clinical Hypotheses and Goals

The Circumplex Model predicts that families balanced on the cohesion and flexibility dimensions will generally function more adequately than unbalanced types. Specifically, families balanced on the cohesion dimension encourage a member's individuality while providing strong family support. In these families, members turn to the family for support but also maintain relationships outside the family. Families balanced on the flexibility dimension maintain a level of stability in the system but also are capable of changing when necessary.

The model, however, does not impose strict criteria for defining balanced and unbalanced family types. Recognizing the impact of ethnicity, religion, and race, Olson (2000) argues that these factors must be considered when assessing family types. Hispanic, Italian, or Southeast Asian families can be highly enmeshed, with the family the center of each member's life. Because of these cultural norms, what determines the functional or dysfunctional quality of the family patterns is the satisfaction of the individual family members. For example, a young woman who wishes to move out of her family home and live on her own may face great opposition from an enmeshed, ethnic family. The struggles in your office will be over the daughter's threat to her parents' control and her desire to explore a more autonomous lifestyle. While the rest of the family is quite satisfied with their enmeshed patterns, the young woman finds them suffocating.

The Circumplex Model endorses a family life cycle, adaptation approach. The model maintains that a family throughout its life cycle must adapt to both internal (e.g., an illness of a family member) and external (e.g., loss of employment or geographic move) forces. It assumes that changes can and do occur in family types over time. For example, when children are younger, the family needs to be more structurally connected; when the children are in their early teens, flexibly connected relationships are more functional. Likewise, with children in their late teens and early 20s, flexibly separated relationships are more functional.

More than 250 studies support the model's major hypothesis that balanced systems are more functional than unbalanced systems (Olson, 2000). The model implies that families experience difficulties and may seek treatment when family patterns fail to adapt to internal or external stressors. The family symptom carrier may be evidencing the stress of the family's inability to adapt.

The goals of family therapy based on the Circumplex Model are:

1. reduce presenting problems and symptoms by

2. moving the family system toward more balanced positions on cohesion and adaptability dimensions,

3. improving communication skills, and

4. increasing the family members' abilities to negotiate and change the system over time.

In summary, family therapy based on the Circumplex Model is not limited to reducing or interrupting dysfunctional family patterns. Individual symptoms are alleviated when the system moves to a more balanced position on the cohesion and flexibility dimensions.

Case Presentation

The Martin family faces a number of challenges: (1) blending two families at different points of the life cycle, (2) integrating distinct ethnic patterns, and (3) negotiating the developmental transition of adolescence.

Divorce, separation, or death of one of the parents throws a family into a state of disequilibrium and shakes the family's foundation. Who is the decision maker in the family now? Who is the disciplinarian? Who pays the bills? Even, who takes out the garbage? Roles shift in an attempt to fill the vacuum in the family patterns. Perhaps the oldest sibling now needs to come home directly from school to care for younger brothers and sisters. The single parent has to rely on the children in ways he or she never did before. A blow to family finances forces a realignment of priorities. The single parent is now the sole decision maker.

Still, through all the readjustments that must take place, the family can fall back on relationships that have been built over time. Asking a teenage girl to come home early and take care of her younger brother is less likely to be resented if the request is in the context of a long-standing, positive relationship. These long-standing positive relationships are the motivation for individual family members to sacrifice for the overall good. Unfortunately, a blended family does not have such luxury.

A blended family is formed because two adults choose it. It is not a decision of the children. Of course, the children are usually asked what they think. Mrs. Martin wanted Randy and Karen to like her future husband and their future stepfather. She carefully and slowly introduced Mr. Martin to her children and only after feeling a comfort level among all of them did she agree to marriage. Although Mr. Martin felt he was auditioning for the role of father with Mrs. Martin's children, he genuinely engaged her children and took an interest in their lives. Privately, Randy resented the new man in his mother's life, but his mother appeared happy and Randy believed he could put up with anything until he moved out of the house.

Mr. Martin told Cindy about his impending wedding one evening when they shared a pizza together. Cindy had met the future Mrs. Martin on several occasions, but her father had dated several women after the divorce and Cindy paid little attention to them. Because she lived with and was embroiled in her own drama with her mother, Cindy believed her father's remarriage would have little impact on her. When Mr. Martin asked Cindy what she thought of him remarrying, Cindy replied, "Whatever!"

As new stepparents, Mr. and Mrs. Martin wanted everything to go well. They wanted to create a family in the fullest sense of the word. They wanted the children to embrace the new family. They believed the love between the two of them would carry the day and that this love would be the bedrock of the new family. They were shocked and disappointed when that did not happen. They forgot or had not learned the key factor in a blended family: *The children do not choose to create a new family and more likely than not resent it.* This fundamental fact emerges when one spouse attempts to discipline his or her stepchild. When this occurs the child's lament is, "Why do I have to listen to someone I barely know tell me what to do?" Respect among family members is built up over time. Initially, a blended family lacks this shared history.

The blended family, therefore, represents two distinct family life cycles merging separate histories of relationships. Individually, old family norms and patterns of interaction must change and new patterns need to emerge. This is difficult under the best of circumstances.

The distinct ethnic family histories also carry the seeds for conflict in the Martin family. Borrowing from her Italian heritage, Mrs. Martin believed that obedience and respect go hand in hand. Mrs. Martin tightly controlled her children with love and discipline. And, although they did not like some of their mother's decisions, Randy and Karen complied with her requests. Randy, in particular, found his mother over-protective and restrictive, but he recognized she had sacrificed a great deal for him and he consequently rarely fought one of her decisions. Cindy's behavior was a blatant affront to all that Mrs. Martin held dear. Cindy's disobedience was a slap in Mrs. Martin's face.

Mr. Martin sympathized with his wife's feelings but had a long history of struggling with his daughter. Consequently, Cindy's "attitude" was barely a blip on her father's radar. Mrs. Martin found her husband's seemingly blasé attitude toward Cindy's rebellious behavior extremely upsetting. "He is my husband. He should back me 100% and demand Cindy respect me," she thought. For his part, Mr. Martin was confused by the intensity of his wife's reactions. "Cindy is being Cindy," he thought.

Finally, the Martins were being torn apart by two separate forces. On the one hand, Mr. and Mrs. Martin were trying to pull the family together while Cindy and Randy were developmentally exiting from the family. Adolescence is a time to shift away from one's family. It is the transition years from dolls and toy soldiers to young adulthood. Even in the best of situations, families with adolescents struggle to transform the relationships from parent-child to parent-teenager to parent-young adult.

The Martin family, unfortunately, had not established parent-child relationships before they were thrust into parent-teenager relationships. Mr. and Mrs. Martin did not have years of knowing one another's children and lacked the emotional bonds between parent and child that sustain and buffer the transition to adolescence. Mr. Martin struggled with being a stepfather. His wife and her children had well-established relationships and clear expectations among them. Following his divorce, when he moved out of his first home, Mr. Martin's relationship with his own daughter had consisted of an occasional weekend visit and a fast food dinner once a week. When Cindy came to live with him and his new wife, Mr. Martin found himself learning from scratch how to relate to and discipline Cindy. For her part, Cindy just wanted to be left alone.

In terms of the Circumplex Model, the Martin family, at the time of referral, was functioning at the chaotic end of the flexibility dimension. In blending two family histories, the family was struggling with its leadership, role relationships, and relationship rules.

Before Cindy moved into the household, Mr. Martin deferred all parenting responsibilities to his wife. Mrs. Martin and her children were comfortable with this arrangement because it continued their familiar patterns. Cindy's arrival, however, forced Mr. Martin into a parenting role that threw him into direct conflict with his wife. Mrs. Martin assumed she would parent Cindy as she parented her own children. But without any history with her stepmother, Cindy resented Mrs. Martin's attempts at disciplining and rebelled. Mr. Martin only wanted things to work out and reluctantly tried to mediate between his wife and daughter—a role he soon found out was a "no-win" position.

Besides the new leadership arrangement in the family, role relationships and rules were evolving in a hit and miss fashion. Randy, Cindy, and Karen, for example, now shared the same bathroom. Randy claimed Cindy monopolized the bathroom while Cindy delighted in 20-minute showers. Karen initially welcomed an "older sister" in the home, but was crushed when Cindy wanted nothing to do with her. Even putting a meal on the table was a challenge for the Martins. Who would set the table? Who would clean up? Who would talk? Who would eat as fast as possible and leave the table?

The cohesion dimension was more difficult to assess. Mrs. Martin's relationship with her children would be best categorized as enmeshed. After her first husband died, she pulled her children close to her. The children, in turn, were close to their mother. Karen loved it when her mother brushed her hair. Randy, in particular, felt protective of his mother.

After Mr. Martin and his first wife divorced, he moved out of the house. Cindy at the time was quite young. Mr. Martin tried to stay active in his daughter's life, but the tension between him and his ex-wife always exploded. Over time, it just became easier to let his ex-wife make the parenting decisions surrounding Cindy. In turn, Mr. Martin saw his daughter infrequently and their visits were usually strained. At the time of referral, the emotional bonding between Cindy and her father was disengaged.

As stated above, a blended family is a mix of two distinct family systems. The more different these family systems are from one another, the more likely conflict will occur. For example, before the wedding, the family of Mrs. Martin, Randy, and Karen would be categorized as rigidly enmeshed. Drawing on her Italian background, Mrs. Martin had clear rules for behavior while also being emotionally close to her children. The family of Mr. Martin, his ex-wife, and Cindy, ripe with conflict even years following the divorce, was chaotically disengaged. Because Mr. Martin and his ex-wife could rarely agree on disciplining Cindy, Cindy grew up without consistent rules. To compound matters, Cindy felt little connection to either of her parents.

Needless to say, communication in the blended Martin family was greatly limited. Discussions rapidly escalated to a conflict level. People accused one another instead of listening and trying to understand one another. Without basic respect and regard for one another, communication was guarded with a hint of suspicion. Within this context, it was very difficult if not impossible for the family to negotiate rules that would foster the movement of Randy and Cindy into young adulthood.

At the time of referral, the blended Martin family was functioning in the chaotically disengaged quadrant of the Circumplex Model. Flowing from the model, therapeutic initiatives would focus on:

1. Moving the family toward a more balanced position on the adaptability dimension. This would entail strengthening the leadership functioning of the parents.

2. Moving the family toward a more balanced position on the cohesion dimension. If emotional bonding was to be developed in the family, members would need to understand and respect one another's positions. In doing so, positive interactions would replace the negative ones and ever so slowly relationships could begin to build.

3. Improving communication skills. The family was a textbook on how-not-to-communicate. Members did not listen to one another and frequently interrupted one another. The therapist would need to be extremely vigilant in the family sessions by becoming a strict police officer directing communication traffic. Interruptions would not be permitted and members would be asked to paraphrase what one another said to ensure the message had been heard.

Summary

The Circumplex Model helps organize observations by identifying functional and dysfunctional patterns of behavior. A treatment plan flows from the assessment and is guided by the concept of moving a family from less extreme positions on the cohesion and adaptability dimensions to a more balanced position. It also provides research-based instruments for assessment that can be employed for pre- and post-empirical outcome measures. Briefly summarized, The Circumplex Assessment Package (CAP) (Olson, 2000) includes the following:

Family Adaptability and Cohesion Evaluation Scales—Second Edition (FACES II): On this self-report inventory, family members assess the family on the adaptability and cohesion dimensions.

Marital Adaptability and Cohesion Evaluation Scales—Third Edition (MACES III): Couples assess their relationship on the adaptability and cohesion dimensions.

Family Satisfaction Scale: Family members rate satisfaction with their family's position on the adaptability and cohesion dimensions.

Clinical Rating Scale (CSR): Clinicians or researchers observing the family are able to rate the family on the adaptability and cohesion dimensions as well as the family's communication style.

There are limitations to the model. It reduces a number of family concepts, for example, boundaries, power, emotional bonding, and authority hierarchies, to two chief dimensions: adaptability and cohesion. While simplifying the concepts is laudable, the subtleties of the individual concepts are missed. For example, the concepts of power and authority hierarchies can be quite different in a particular family. Also, there is a lack of evidence that any one symptom is specifically linked to a family type. Rigidly disengaged families, for example, may foster an angry, out-of-control, rebellious adolescent or a depressed, suicidal teenager who feels profoundly rejected and turns the rejection inward. Thus, the Circumplex Model captures a family from a global perspective but does not facilitate predictions regarding an individual's behavior.

Beavers Systems Model of Family Functioning

The **Beavers Systems Model of Family Functioning** also graphically portrays families along two dimensions: **family competence** and **family style** (Beavers & Hampson, 2000) (see Figure 4.2). Similar to the Circumplex Model, the Beavers Model emphasizes a family's capacity to respond and adapt to flexibly stressful situations. Specifically, the horizontal axis—family competence—evaluates the family's ability to change structures to meet internal or external needs. In high competence families, members intuitively understand the circularity of cause and effect and readily acknowledge their ability to influence one another. Thus, family members are not scapegoated or blamed for family difficulties. For example, instead of blaming a teenager, parents in a highly competent family will question what they are doing to help or exacerbate the situation. This willingness to look within the family relationships and change them if needed promotes a flexibility that is highly adaptive.

The vertical axis—family style—evaluates the quality of family interaction. It is a curvilinear relationship whereby healthy functioning falls between two extremes: **centripetal** and **centrifugal**. Centripetal families turn inward in times of stress. Relationships within the family supersede relationships outside the family. In the extreme, centripetal families possess poor boundaries and confused communication. Members in centrifugal families, on the other hand, turn outward, away from the family. In the extreme, the family is not seen as a nurturing environment. The family members have little loyalty to one another and look outside the family to satisfy individual needs and wants.

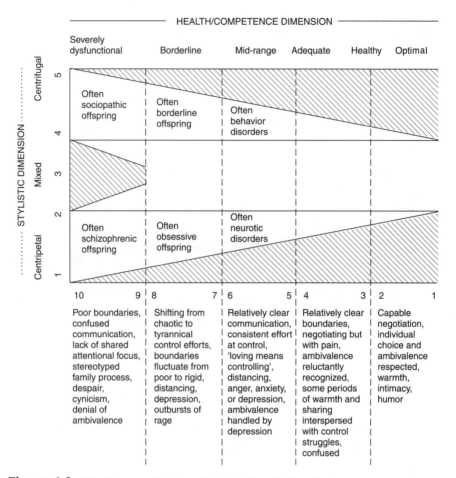

Figure 4.2 The Beavers Systems Model of Family Functioning

Source: From "The Beavers Systems Model of Family Structure," by R. Beavers and R. Hampson, 2000, *Journal of Family Therapy, 22,* Fig. 1, p. 129. Copyright © 2000 Blackwell Publishers, Ltd. Reprinted with permission.

Similar to the Circumplex Model, the Beavers Model recognizes that families need to change their style to adapt to developmental needs. For example, small children require more supervision and care; thus, the most adaptive family style would be centripetal. Late teenage children need the freedom to explore the greater world; thus, centrifugal family patterns are more adaptive.

Placing families on the competence and family style dimensions delineates six different family groupings: optimal, adequate, mid-range centripetal, mid-range centrifugal, severely disturbed centripetal, and severely disturbed centrifugal. The six family groupings are based on both clinical observation and empirical research (Beavers, 1977).

1. *Optimal:* Optimal and adequate family types are characteristic of healthy families. Both promote individual responsibility for feelings, thoughts, and behavior. Unresolved conflict is minimal compared to mid-range and severely disturbed fam-

ilies. The hierarchical structure is clear in these families, but flexible. The family listens to and respects each member. Within this supportive atmosphere, negotiations help produce desired changes.

2. *Adequate:* Adequate families are more similar to mid-range than to optimal families. Although dominant/submissive parental roles may be evident, both parents are consistent in their behavior and committed to the family. Controlling can be equated with caring and result in conflict, but children in these families know they are loved and protected.

3. *Mid-range centripetal:* Interpersonal boundaries are tentatively maintained in these families. Power struggles, particularly in the parental subsystem, are covert or overt. One parent may dominate and rigidly attempt to control family members' behavior. Because of power struggles, particularly for both connection and autonomy, the family turns to an external "family referee" to judge right and wrong. The "referee," for example, might be a formal religious code. Guilt can also be used to control behavior. With its emphasis on controlling behavior through guilt or blame, the offspring of these families are restricted in emotional expression and behavior. They struggle to develop a personal sense of identity apart from the family. They, in turn, are likely to blame their families for the disappointments they experience in life. The anxiety they experience fuels a pattern of neurotic behavior.

4. *Mid-range centrifugal:* Resolving conflict through negotiations is difficult for these families. One parent is typically more dominant than the other. Inconsistent discipline is a consequence of the unbalanced parental coalition. Because of the underlying conflicts, this family also turns to outside authority to judge right and wrong. Family members seek nurturing relationships outside the family. Without a close emotional bond to parents, the children of mid-range families can fail to internalize the family rules and consequently develop behavior disorders.

5. *Severely disturbed centripetal:* This family fights against all individuation. Closeness is defined as all family members thinking and feeling alike. Conflict is covert and avoided. There is a profound absence of warmth and trust. Offspring of this family may be categorized as process schizophrenic, borderline personalities, and "well" siblings who struggle with gaining a sense of autonomy.

6. *Severely disturbed centrifugal:* Family members are disengaged in these families. Conflict is open and never-ending. Parents lack the ability to effectively parent because of their constant conflict. The lack of attachment in these families leaves family members with a profound sense of disconnection. These families are fertile soil for shaping antisocial personalities who fill the emotional emptiness they feel with a rage directed at the outside world.

Clinical Goals and Implications

Although not as explicitly stated as in the Circumplex Model, the goals of treatment based on the Beavers Systems Model would also seek to improve the family's balance on the health/competence and stylistic dimensions. On the health/competence dimension, a therapist would first and foremost aid the family in viewing their relationships as interconnected and mutually influencing one another. Scapegoating is addressed and the cause of the family symptom carrier's behavior is placed within the web of family relationships. Individual responsibility and accountability are promoted.

On the stylistic dimension, a therapist seeks a balance between the centripetal and centrifugal extremes. The therapist attempts to address the fears of separation in centripetal families while promoting individual responsibility for thought, feeling, and behavior. Working with centrifugal families, the therapist seeks to build trust and warmth within the families. The roots of the centrifugal family's fear of closeness are explored.

Two outcome studies are reported using Beavers rating scales. The first study, which was based on 434 families who entered therapy at a sliding-fee clinic, investigated the variables that best predicted outcome following treatment (Hampson & Beavers, 1996b). Families who received the most benefit from therapy were more competent with a more centripetal style. They formed a good therapeutic alliance with their therapist and attended at least six sessions. The demographic variables of family income, family size, single- versus two-parent households, race of the family, and gender of the therapist had little effect on therapeutic outcome. Thus, families who are rated higher on competency and who form an alliance with their therapist are more likely to stay in treatment and to receive more benefit from therapy.

The second study investigated the degree to which the outcome of therapy was related to the match between family type (as defined by the Beavers interactional scales) and therapist style (Hampson & Beavers, 1996a). Following three sessions with a family, therapists rated their style on three dimensions: (1) degree to which they disclosed their therapeutic strategy to the family; (2) degree to which they shared power with the family; and (3) how close and cooperative or distant and directive the therapeutic alliance was. Families more competent with a more centripetal style benefited most when the therapist was more open about strategy, shared power equally, and created a therapeutic partnership. The more dysfunctional and more centrifugal families benefited if the therapist was less open about strategy, and fostered a therapeutic alliance more hierarchical, direct, and distant.

The results from both studies demonstrate the importance of establishing a strong therapeutic relationship by matching therapeutic style with family type. The more dysfunctional and more centrifugal the family patterns, the more the therapist needs to be an authority figure directing the course of treatment. It is as if the therapist is providing the necessary leadership and direction lacking in a highly dysfunctional, conflicted family. In contrast, the more competent and centripetal the family, the more the therapist needs to collaborate with the family by being open about possible therapeutic strategies and moving away from the "expert telling the family what to do" position.

Summary

Of the three models, the Beavers Systems Model is most closely allied with the individual assessments of the *DSM IV*. Within the model, family patterns are associated with specific psychiatric disorders (see Figure 4.2). For example, severely dysfunctional centrifugal families are more likely to produce sociopathic offspring.

The model also identifies family types, from optimal to severely dysfunctional. These family types describe a range of family patterns incorporating the key dimensions of structure, mythology, goal-directed negotiation, autonomy, affect, and global health. These dimensions offer both assessment and treatment guidelines. Besides moving a family toward more adequate or optimal functioning, treatment goals also include balancing the family on the centripetal and centrifugal dimensions.

Similar to the Circumplex Model, the Beavers Model has also developed measuring instruments that include:

Beavers Interactional Competence Scale (Beavers & Hampson, 1990)
Therapists and observers use this scale to assess a family's overall level of health and competence on the following subscales: structure of the family, mythology, goal-directed negotiation, autonomy, family affect, and global health pathology.

Beavers Interactional Style Scale (Beavers & Hampson, 1990)
Therapists and observers use this scale to assess a family's style, which may range from centrifugal to centripetal.

Self-report Family Inventory (Beavers & Hampson, 1990)
Whereas the interactional competence scale and interactional style scale offer an outsider's view of the family, the family inventory provides an insider's view. The 36-item, self-report instrument can be completed by family members 11 years of age and older.

McMaster Approach to Families

The **McMaster Approach to Families** is also based on systems theory (Miller, Ryan, Keitner, Bishop, & Epstein, 2000). It is more clinically oriented than the above models in its focus on specific family patterns and is a treatment approach flowing directly from the assessment of those patterns.

The McMaster Model does not focus on any one dimension, such as the Circumplex's cohesion and flexibility dimensions, but argues that many dimensions are needed for assessing families. The model selects the following dimensions because of their relevance in clinical settings.

1. *Problem solving.* Problems and differences in opinions are inevitable in family life. Some problems are easily solved while others fester and threaten the stability of the family. Ineffective problem solving is frequently seen in families experiencing difficulties.

2. *Communication.* Concerned that nonverbal communication is difficult to measure, the model assesses the verbal communication patterns in the family on four variables: (a) instrumental (b) affective, (c) clear or masked, and (d) direct or indirect. Instrumental communication refers to the family's ability to function in day-to-day problem solving. For example, who will pick up the children after school is clearly understood by all. Affective communication is the capacity for emotional expression. Masked communication as opposed to clear communication distorts the exchange of information. Family members are typically left wondering what the "real" message being sent was. Direct communication is the family members' ability to speak directly to one another. In these families if you have something to say to someone, you say it directly to him or her. Dad does not give a message to mom for her to give to their daughter.

3. *Roles.* Roles define who does what in the family. Who takes out the garbage? Who makes sure homework is completed? Who do family members turn to for emotional support? To whom do the family members turn for a decision?

4. *Affective responsiveness.* Emotional responsiveness ranges from anger at one end to tender intimacy at the other. Families experiencing difficulties may be restricted in their emotional expression. For some families, anger is easily expressed compared to tenderness, while in other families, anger is a taboo emotion that is held inward and never expressed.

5. *Affective involvement.* Emotional involvement is more than the ways family members respond to one another. It is the degree to which family members show interest and value the activities of one another. It is value placed on family time as well as individual activities outside the family.

6. *Behavior control.* Behavior control is specifically assessed in three situations: (a) physically dangerous situations; (b) situations that involve meeting and expressing psychobiological needs or drives; and (c) situations involving interpersonal socializing behavior. In general terms, behavior control refers to the standards or norms for acceptable behavior that the family establishes and maintains.

Impairment on one or more of the above dimensions is considered a dysfunctional transactional pattern. These patterns are seen as defensive reactions decreasing the anxiety levels in the family, but at the expense of overall family functioning. For example, because open and direct expression of anger threatens the family, anger is masked and indirectly expressed through passive-aggressiveness. The teenage son in this type of family "forgets" to take out the garbage on time, knowing full well his dominating father will go through the roof when he sees the trash cans still sitting on the back porch the next morning. In another example, a father gives his teenage daughter permission to attend a concert without informing his wife, knowing she would oppose the daughter's plans.

The McMaster Model does not identify, as the Beavers Model does, specific family patterns producing specific pathology. Instead, the McMaster Model argues that dysfunctional transactional patterns are associated with family impairment and that changing these patterns is necessary for improving family functioning. Similar to the Circumplex Model, the McMaster Model recognizes that some transactional patterns are dysfunctional for one family while adaptive for another. Without directly acknowledging the connection, the McMaster Model is endorsing the viability of diverse racial and ethnic family patterns. Thus, there are no absolute dysfunctional patterns assessed in each and every family. Variations in family patterns on the above six dimensions may or may not be adaptive for the individual family.

Family Treatment Approach

Unlike the Circumplex and Beavers Models, the McMaster Model has evolved a highly structured, multidimensional, and systems-oriented treatment approach called the Problem Centered Systems Therapy of the Family (PCSFT) (Epstein et al., 1990). The PCSFT is a short-term, cost-effective model that emphasizes collaboration between the family and therapist based on open, direct communication; builds on the family's strengths; believes the family is responsible for change; and focuses on behavior change needed to address the family's current problems.

The PCSFT approach divides treatment into four major stages: (1) assessment; (2) contracting; (3) treatment; and (4) closure. Each major stage is further divided into a sequence of substages addressing specific goals. For example, in the assessment stage a therapist would establish an open, collaborative relationship with the family, identify all current problems, prioritize the problem list, and begin to hypothesize concerning the relationships among the problems.

A therapist employing the PCSFT would be highly active in implementing the structure of the approach. Following the assessment stage, in the contracting stage, the therapist and family prepare and sign a written contract that delineates the mutual expectations, goals, and commitments regarding therapy. This contract serves as the blueprint for the treatment stage whereby the therapist produces behavioral change in the family through a series of assigned tasks. The family is to accomplish or at least attempt the tasks between sessions while using the treatment sessions to evaluate the success or failure at accomplishing these tasks. The overall goal of treatment is to promote cognitive and behavioral changes that will increase the family's ability to successfully address their problems.

Summary

The McMaster Model is a comprehensive approach to assessment and treatment. It provides self-report and clinical scales as well as a structured interview for assessment. A brief treatment model flows directly from the assessment of a family's functioning in the areas of problem solving, communication, roles, affective responsiveness, affective involvement, and behavior control. Although the model identifies clinically significant patterns, it says little regarding normal or optimal functioning.

McMaster (Miller et al., 2000) does not report outcome studies similar to Beavers (Hampson & Beavers, 1996a, 1996b). It is reasonable, however, to hypothesize that the model best serves clinicians who prefer a highly structured therapeutic approach and families who are able to commit to and follow a prescribed course of treatment.

Finally, the McMaster Model also has measuring instruments for research and clinical purposes:

Family Assessment Device (FAD) (Epstein et al., 1983)
> The FAD is a self-report instrument measuring individual family members' perceptions on the six dimensions of the McMaster Model. In 20 minutes, all family members over the age of 12 can complete it.

McMaster Clinical Rating Scale (MCRS) (Miller et al., 1994)
> The MCRS is designed for researchers and clinicians. It consists of a seven-item rating scale (1—most ineffective or disturbed functioning; 7—most effective or healthy functioning) of each of the six dimensions of the McMaster Model.

McMaster Structured Interview for Family Functioning (McSiff) (Bishop et al., 1980)
> Simultaneously employed, the FAD and MCRS provide insider and outsider assessments of a family. Each, however, provides a single score for each

dimension. The McMaster Structured Interview is designed to specify particular areas within each dimension that further differentiate family patterns.

Is One Model Better Than Another?

Is there a difference among the models? Which one is more appropriate for clinical use? Is one model more advantageous than another? To address these questions, Drumm, Carr, and Fitzgerald (2000) compared the Beavers, McMaster, and Circumplex clinical rating scales in terms of their ability to discriminate between families that require therapy and those who do not. Videotapes of 60 families engaging in a standard family task interview were rated using the three clinical scales. Unknown to the raters using the scales, the 60 families included 20 containing a child with an emotional disorder, 20 containing a child with a mixed disorder of emotions and conduct, and a control group of 20 families in which none of the children were diagnosed with clinically significant difficulties.

The results highlight the relative strengths and limitations of each of the models. The Beavers clinical rating scale was the best of the three scales in identifying families containing children with emotional problems (65% for Beavers, 60% for McMaster, and 55% for Circumplex). The McMaster scale was the best of the three scales in classifying families containing children with mixed disorders of emotion and conduct (90% for McMaster, 80% for Beavers, and 70% for Circumplex). All were similar in their abilities to correctly classify non-clinical cases (90% for Beavers and Circumplex scales and 85% for the McMaster clinical rating scale).

Individual shortcomings were identified for each scale. The centripetal–centrifugal dimension of the Beavers scale added little to the scale's ability to discriminate among the three types of families. The competence dimension was the better indicator of family functioning. Although the best of the three in identifying clinical cases, the McMaster clinical rating scale was slightly poorer than the other two in correctly classifying the normal, control families. Finally, the Circumplex clinical scale was strong in identifying normal family patterns but poorer in classifying emotional and mixed disorder cases.

Drumm et al. (2000) conclude that any one of the scales is clinically useful. Integrated into one's practice, the scales can be used with confidence for assessment and to measure the progress of therapy as well as therapeutic outcome at termination.

Assessment Guidelines

Although you may wish to employ one of the above models in your practice, the following integrates the three models to provide assessment guidelines useful for beginning family therapists. (See Table 4.1 on p. 100 at the end of the chapter for a summary.)

Interpersonal Boundaries

Families are made up of individuals connected through family ties. Each family via interpersonal boundaries defines for itself what it means to be a member of the family in terms of the dynamic tension between satisfying individual needs and satisfying family needs. *Centripetal, highly enmeshed families* place the family before the individual. In times of crisis the family members turn toward one another. Family loyalty is demanded or coerced through guilt. Interpersonal boundaries are blurred in these families. Parents, for example, may live vicariously through their children's accomplishments. Individual needs are sublimated to the family group. An individual's decision is always influenced by family expectations. Finally, although the family provides a sense of belonging and satisfies dependency needs, each family member possesses little sense of autonomy because individuality threatens these families.

Centrifugal, disengaged families emphasize individual needs over family needs. Each family member looks outside the family to satisfy wants and needs. Emotional relationships are more likely formed with those outside the family. Interpersonal boundaries are disengaged. Closeness is feared in these families because the relationships are filled with a history of anxiety and rejection. Family time is avoided and even when all the family members are home, they are each more likely than not isolated from one another. The family is a family in name only. Finally, although the disengaged interpersonal boundaries foster a sense of autonomy, each family member has little sense of belonging.

At the time of referral, the Martin family was spinning outward in centrifugal, disengaging motion. Cindy wanted no part of a Brady Bunch. She actively resisted pulls to be more involved in the family and looked outside the family to get her needs met. Although he was protective of his mother, Randy wanted no part in the family battles. At 17 years of age, it was easier for him to stay out with friends than to go home. Mr. and Mrs. Martin's interactions were less and less loving and supportive and more confrontational. They were starting to avoid one another, fearing any interaction would result in an argument.

Stability and Change

Families are living organisms adapting to the world around them. Although systems seek homeostasis, change is an inevitable part of life. Sometimes the need for change is generated within the family. An illness, for example, can force a family to change its structure. If one of the parents becomes ill and cannot fulfill his or her typical duties, other family members need to assume some or most of those responsibilities. Likewise, a divorce radically changes the family structure; family members are forced to create a new structure if the family is to survive.

Sometimes external stressors force a family to change. A geographic move pulls a family from familiar ties and forces it to create new support structures in a new environment. Sometimes unemployment and financial difficulties force changes within a family. There is now less money to go around and the family must make difficult choices regarding its priorities.

As children and parents age, all families face the challenges of the stages of development. From the time their children enter kindergarten through high school graduation, parents are continually letting go of their children so that they might find their way in the larger world. At one extreme, some families deny or ignore these developmental changes. Kids are kids whether they are 5, 10, 15, 20, or 25. At the other extreme, families are overwhelmed by the need to change. The parents second-guess themselves and in turn are so inconsistent in their discipline that they relinquish control and the children run the household. In these families, a child of any age soon learns that if you throw a big enough fit you will probably get your way.

A continuing challenge for a family is maintaining stability while adapting to change. *High competence, flexible families* successfully maintain their integrity while making needed changes in their structures to meet internal or external demands. These families possess a stable parental subsystem that clearly guides the family's decision-making process. Although the parents view themselves as authority figures, they listen to and respect each family member. Furthermore, the family is willing to look within the family relationships and change them if needed.

There are two types of low competence, inflexible families: low competence, rigid families and low competence, chaotic families. *Low competence, rigid families* deny or resist the need for change. They apply the same old solutions to new problems with limited success. For example, even though punishments have had little effect on rebellious teenager's behavior, parents in these families, instead of wondering what needs to change within the family, would increase the severity of their punishments. In the ensuing escalating conflicts, the parents become more restrictive and the teenager more out-of-control. *Low competence, chaotic families* are overwhelmed by change. Lacking stability, these families are inconsistent with discipline or completely lack it. Poor decision-making skills throw the family into one crisis after another.

Rather than look to change family patterns, low competence, rigid or chaotic families are more likely to blame one or more family members for the family's conflicts. Over time, the blaming process evolves into a family scapegoat pattern. These families try to convince therapists that everything would be fine if the scapegoat would only change. They hope a therapist will see it their way and work with them to change the problematic family member.

The Martin family had just begun building the foundation to their new blended family when the hurricane named Cindy hit. At the time of referral, they lacked a foundation of stability. Mrs. Martin fell back on pulling her children to her and parenting them the way she always had. Mr. Martin was clueless about how to parent Cindy. Unfortunately, conversations with his wife quickly deteriorated into Mrs. Martin telling her husband what he should do. Mr. Martin silently resented what he believed was his wife's authoritarian approach but feared arguing with her. Scapegoating Cindy was the outgrowth of Mr. and Mrs. Martin's unspoken fear that they each had made a terrible mistake in getting remarried. It was easier to blame Cindy, although in fairness Cindy gave them plenty of ammunition, than address the differences between them.

Feeling Tone

In the first interview you begin to sense the feeling tone within the family. Are the family members guarded in their speech? Do they look at one another before they speak, or are they more likely to address you, the therapist, without looking at other members? Is the family playful or deadly serious? Does sadness pervade the family? The feeling tone of a family is best assessed along two dimensions: optimism versus pessimism and the range of emotional expression from warmth and caring at one end to anger and negative emotions at the other.

Even though they are presenting their problems, *optimistic families* are animated in their speech. They actively engage a therapist and all members are free to speak. The first interview flows easily with this type of family because of the family's optimism. They are seeking therapy at this time and likely stuck in dealing with a problem, but these families also have belief in their own abilities to address their problems. They openly care for one another and are anxious to make things better.

A cloud of resentment, anger, and depression hangs over *pessimistic families*. Unresolved conflicts over years have sapped the family's ability to cope with stress. It is as if each conflict has diminished the family's strength and they are left feeling helpless in dealing with the next problem. The first interview with these families seems to last forever. Sometimes the only family member to speak is the family spokesperson, typically the family member who has brought the family into therapy. Unfortunately, the family spokesperson usually begins the interview by listing the problems the family is experiencing with one of its members. While the spokesperson is listing the problems, the other family members sit silently, not wishing to bring the spotlight onto themselves. Even when the therapist actively tries to have the other members speak, the rest of the family members respond with a "yes," "no," "maybe," or "I don't know."

In the first interview, or within the first few sessions, the family's range of emotional expression is readily apparent. Does the family easily express warmth, or is there a cold reserve to their interactions? Can the family members be playful with one another, or is everything deadly serious? Do family members easily smile or laugh, or sit with rigid, downturned corners to their mouths? An expression of warmth between family members and their ability to laugh with one another hint at possible strengths and flexibility. The inability to laugh with one another and easily express caring can be the tip of an iceberg of anger and resentment.

Warmth, laughter, and caring represent one end of the emotional expression dimension. The other end of the expressive dimension is the family's ability to express negative emotions such as anger. An assumption throughout this book is that family life consists of individual wants and needs balanced by the needs of the family. As such, conflict is an inevitable part of family life. Conflict is neither bad nor good; instead, its effects are determined by the family's capacity to manage conflict, specifically the emotion of anger.

For example, one family easily expresses warmth but represses anger. Parents who repress anger between one another quickly teach their children that anger is taboo in their family. Because anger is forbidden in these families, the members learn to swallow their feelings or don't even know they are angry. Because conflict threatens to unleash anger, it is avoided at all costs. Problem resolution is next to impossible if conflict cannot be faced.

Another family has difficulty expressing warmth but is all too familiar with anger. Anger is readily expressed in these families but without an expression of warmth to soften the blows. The expression of anger, however, does not mean it is managed well. In some families, conflict ignites a string of firecracker anger. The anger can explode between two or more family members until all parties are exhausted and withdraw from one another. Individual family members retreat to privately lick their wounds. Unfortunately, effectively resolving the cause of the anger cannot occur in these families because their emotional volatility overwhelms their problem-solving skills.

Again, the lack of shared history between Mr. Martin and Cindy on one hand and Mrs. Martin, Karen, and Randy and Cindy on the other limited the expression of warmth and fostered an atmosphere of anger. The expression of warmth and good humor is built up over time and mixes elements of caring, acceptance, and a sense that even though we are angry with one another at this particular moment, we still know we love one another. When love is present in a relationship, rarely do confrontations spiral downward into going for the jugular vein. And even when hurt is inflicted, two people who love one another evolve ways of apologizing and even consoling one another after the dust has settled. The Martin family was too new to have evolved strong connections of love among its members. True, Mr. and Mrs. Martin loved one another but it was a love that had not been tested until Cindy moved into their home.

Leadership

The power hierarchy in a family refers to the parents' ability to lead. Parents should involve the children in the discussion of the rules, but ultimately the parents decide on them and see that they are followed. Although there can sometimes be exceptions to the rules, overall, the children know where the lines are drawn. Because the expectations for behavior are clearly communicated and reinforced, children and adolescents in these families minimally test the rules. They also characteristically accept the consequences for violating their parents' expectations.

Leadership can be conceptualized on a dimension from authoritarian to laissez-faire. *Authoritarian leadership* lays down the law and rigidly enforces the rules. Unfortunately, the rules are decided unilaterally (usually the most powerful person in the family) and do not consider individual needs or developmental changes. Authoritarian leadership breeds compliant children and the occasional bully. At school, the bully, for example, mimics his father's harsh leadership. As the children enter adolescence, authoritarian leadership actively shapes passive-aggressive and rebellious teenagers who fight the oppression of the family's leadership.

Laissez-faire families appear incapable of establishing and maintaining rules and expectations. They react to minimize pressure or conflict. Children and adolescents in these families know that you can get what you want if you just keep arguing, or, even if the parents do say no, just go ahead and do what you want to do because there will be no consequences. You will probably get a lecture, but that is about all.

Laissez-faire leadership may be a consequence of a dysfunctional parental subsystem. Covert conflict between the parents diminishes their ability to effectively lead. Instead of supporting one another, each parent subtly or not so subtly undercuts the other. Children soon learn that even if one parent says no, the other parent will say yes. Laissez-faire leadership is also a consequence of parents wanting to be their children's friends or to make their children happy. In both cases, parents abdicate their leadership position, and their decisions are more influenced by their children's moods and reactions instead of what the parents judge to be in the best, long-term interest of their children.

Laissez-faire leadership can be indicative of a parental subsystem that is overwhelmed by internal or external stressors. A severe physical illness diminishes a parent's ability to function. Parents are less involved in the family because financial pressures force them to work longer hours or multiple jobs to provide basic needs for their family. Finally, the parent in a single-parent household is exhausted from just trying to hold everything together.

Mr. Martin's laissez-faire leadership style contrasting with Mrs. Martin's authoritarian leadership style was at the heart of the family conflict. Both Mr. Martin and Mrs. Martin believed their respective styles were right for the family and actively tried to convince the therapist of the correctness of his or her approach. The therapist will need to be careful not to praise or blame one style over the other. If the family is to survive, the parents will need to find a common, middle-ground leadership style that accents the best of both of their approaches.

Solving Problems and Managing Conflict

An effective problem-solving process draws on the family resources to identify the problem, propose solutions, and implement change. All family members participate in the process and different points of view are respected. Problems are seen as an inevitable consequence of family life and do not threaten the structure of the family. Discussions are open to all, but in the end the parents decide the course of action.

There may be irresolvable problems in the family. For example, the family members may agree to disagree regarding key topics. The wife may not like her in-laws but, knowing it is important to her husband, she will cooperate and attend important extended family events. Although the husband would like his wife to get along better with his family, he does not force the issue or blame her for her feelings.

Managing conflict differs from problem solving because it possesses an emotional component. Some families easily solve day-to-day problems such as who will do what chores. These families run fairly smoothly until strong, negative emotions emerge. These negative emotions—anger, jealousy, hurt, or rejection—test the family's strength. In some families, negative emotions fester and build until they explode and run out of control, while other families repress anger at all costs.

Managing conflict challenges a family to recognize and accept that there are negative feelings in the family. Accepting this fact, families draw these feelings out through direct, open, and honest communication. In these families, conflict is not seen as a threat to the family but as a signal that something or someone in the family needs to be addressed.

How the parents address their difficulties with one another frequently sets the tone for the rest of the family. If parents constructively manage their conflicts with one another, they model effective conflict management. If they bury their conflict, they communicate the importance of keeping negative thoughts to oneself. Either way, the children will absorb the family's style.

Mr. and Mrs. Martin did not anticipate the problems in blending two families. They were poorly equipped to define their problems, much less to solve them. Cindy's entrance into the family highlighted the deficiencies in solving problems. At the time of referral, the family was reduced to mutual blaming and scapegoating. Unfortunately, without time to develop a history of positive interactions and a sense of mutual caring and respect, the family was caught in a whirlpool of negative feelings that threatened to destroy the family.

Communication

Communication is the glue that holds the family together and permits the family to adapt to internal or external stressors. Without basic communication skills, such as listening, self-disclosure, and clarity, it is very difficult to establish and maintain consistent rules, respect individual opinions, keep conversations on track, effectively problem-solve, and manage conflict.

Families experiencing difficulties characteristically possess poor communication skills. Members do not typically speak directly to one another; when they do, they constantly interrupt without fully listening to one another. In these families, members speak for one another or assume they know what the others are going to say before they even say it. Families may be competent in day-to-day problem solving but have difficulties expressing both positive and negative emotions.

Because of their brief time together, the Martin family had not yet had the opportunity to develop and refine effective communication patterns. To be fair, the family may have, with time, evolved such patterns. But the addition of Cindy overloaded their communication skills. Family members actively blamed one another and in so doing were unable to listen to one another. That said, their brief history together was also an opportunity for the therapist to help the family members develop the necessary skills. It would be a challenge in which the therapist would need to be extremely active in monitoring and modeling effective communication, but, on a positive note, the therapist was not faced with the task of dismantling years of dysfunctional communication patterns.

Summary

The Circumplex, Beavers, and McMaster models organize complex family data and observations, create working hypotheses of family functioning, guide interventions, and provide outcome measures. Each offers a roadmap into a family's dynamics. Each, however, places a family within the parameters of its model. The Circumplex Model, for example, focuses on three key dimensions: cohesion, flexibility, and communication. When a therapist employs this model, he or she is looking at a family through the lenses of cohesion, flexibility, and communication. The family's behavior is made to fit within the conceptualized dimensions of the model. Thus, while something is gained from employing the model, for example, organizing the family's structure, something may also be lost, for example, the family's unique narrative.

Although the models provide a formal structure for assessment, a therapist must explore more closely the family's unique patterns. The following chapter presents the next stage of assessment, that is, the process of identifying specific and unique family patterns. Working in concert with the family's expressive style, constructing a genogram, understanding and respecting the family's paradigm, and assessing the family's resilience leads to specific intervention priorities tailored to the individual family.

Glossary

Beavers Systems Model of Family Functioning An assessment model of family functioning based in research and clinical practice that highlights the following dimensions:

Family competence A family's ability to change structures to meet internal and external needs.

Family style An assessment dimension evaluating the quality of family interaction from centripetal to centrifugal style.

Centripetal style A description of a family that turns inward in times of stress and emphasizes family loyalty.

Centrifugal style A description of a family that turns outward in times of stress and emphasizes relationships outside the family.

Circumplex Model of Family Systems An assessment model of family functioning based in research and clinical practice that highlights the following dimensions:

Cohesion An assessment dimension referring to a family's level of emotional bonding.

Communication An assessment dimension referring to a family's communication skills.

Flexibility An assessment dimension referring to a family's capacity to maintain stability while also adapting to change.

Diagnostic and Statistical Manual (DSM) A diagnostic, classification system of the American Psychiatric Association based on a medical model of individual pathology.

Family symptom carrier A family member who exhibits symptoms of the dysfunctional family patterns.

McMaster Approach to Families An assessment and treatment model of family functioning based in research and clinical practice evaluating families on a series of dimensions.

Table 4.1	Assessment Guidelines

Interpersonal Boundaries

1. Centripetal, enmeshed boundaries. Family needs come before individual needs. Members possess little sense of autonomy because individuality threatens these families.
2. Centrifugal, disengaged boundaries. Members look outside the family to meet basic needs. Keeping one's distance and avoiding intimacy are perpetuated by these boundaries.

Stability and Change

1. High competence, flexible patterns. The family is capable of maintaining its structural integrity while making needed changes to address internal or external demands.
2. Low competence patterns.
   a. Low competence, rigid patterns. The family denies or resists change when it is needed. The family typically applies old solutions to new problems with limited success.
   b. Low competence, chaotic patterns. The family is overwhelmed by change and runs in continual crisis. The family is devoid of effective leadership.

Feeling Tone

1. Optimistic patterns. The family draws upon inherent strengths to manage stressors. Feeling tone is upbeat and family members believe they can make things better.
2. Pessimistic patterns. The family has a history of unresolved conflict. The tone is a predominant feeling that nothing will get better.

Leadership

1. Authoritarian patterns. These patterns reflect "It's my way or the highway" school of parenting.
2. Laissez-faire patterns. Consistent rules and discipline are lacking. The patterns promote one crisis after another.

Solving problems and managing conflict

1. How effective is the family's ability to solve problems? Does the family have a history of effectively solving problems? Are certain areas of family life easier to address than others?
2. How is conflict managed in the family? Does family address and deal effectively with negative emotions such as anger and jealousy? Are negative emotions permitted in the family?

Communication

1. Effective patterns include the ability to listen, offer feedback, self-disclose, and express the full range of emotions.
2. Ineffective patterns are deficient in the above areas and lead to chronic misunderstandings, repressed anger, and hurt feelings.

5

Assessment: The Process of Identifying Family Patterns

Assessment Process

Case Presentation

Treatment Notes

Summary

Glossary

Powerful human themes are at the heart of family life: love, acceptance, rejection, hate, compassion, sacrifice, cruelty. To approach the family from a systems perspective, however, it is helpful to first think of a family as a social group. Having worked in groups, led groups, and participated in groups, therapists become familiar with the issues that frequently emerge: leadership, status hierarchy, power channels, supportive behaviors, task behavior, and communication patterns. Above all, most therapists are struck by the predictability that evolves in a group's interactions.

Formal groups, for instance, establish overt patterns through bureaucratic procedures and policy. Even a small group meeting can follow *Robert's Rules of Order.* Some groups develop such clear, consistent interactive rules that the parts (people) can be replaced and the group will continue to operate smoothly. Other groups have far looser boundaries and emphasize egalitarian procedures. The interactive patterns of these groups are less procedural and more a function of the personalities of the group members; self-help groups are an example.

In family therapy, each family evolves its own predictable patterns or **norms**. For instance, can you predict the sequence of events at your next family get-together? Who talks to whom? Who will correct whom? Who will tell the jokes? Who will listen the best? Who will talk the most? Who will be the most problematic? How will this person be "managed" by the group? Overall, is there a consistent pattern to these family gatherings?

Just as all family groups evolve norms of interactions, some are more functional than others. For example, some people welcome holidays as a time to reconnect with family members and receive nurturing and support; others dread the thought of family gatherings because of what they are pretty sure will occur. As one person put it, "Getting my family together is a recipe for heartburn."

Of course, what is functional for one family member can be dysfunctional for another. A parent wants the children to do exactly as they are told as a sign of respect. An older adolescent, however, bristles at this restriction of autonomy imposed by the parent and rebels through passive-aggressive behavior.

Besides being the time when clients and therapists are building a therapeutic alliance, therefore, the beginning phase of treatment is also the time to identify and understand family patterns. Treatment and intervention strategies evolve from this firm grasp of the family dynamics. As a means of discerning these patterns, a therapist is continually forming hypotheses and testing them out. These working hypotheses serve to guide the therapist's questions. For example, the therapist working with the Martins initially hypothesized that one factor fueling the arguments between Mrs. Martin and Cindy was Mr. Martin's inconsistent support of one against the other. The therapist's questions, therefore, test the hypothesis:

> **Therapist:** I am a little confused on something. Mrs. Martin, how do you get support from your husband when these arguments erupt? Cindy, how do you get support?

If both Mrs. Martin and Cindy responded that Mr. Martin always supports his wife, the hypothesis would be discarded in favor of a new one: Cindy is angry because she believes her father has chosen his new wife over her.

> **Therapist:** Cindy, in the middle of these arguments, when your father steps in to support your stepmother, how do you react? What are your feelings?

If the original hypothesis was confirmed, the therapist would then explore Mr. Martin's thoughts and motivation:

> **Therapist:** Mr. Martin, both your wife and daughter appear confused about when you will support one or the other. Would you tell me how you decide what to do?

Identifying patterns is a process of forming working hypotheses, testing them out with questions, and either confirming or discarding them. Whichever the case, the therapist is led to further hypotheses.

As the patterns are being identified, the individual and family narratives are also revealed. How do Mr. and Mrs. Martin each view the family? Do their narratives overlap with one another or diverge at critical points? What are the children's narratives? Again, do their narratives overlap or diverge from one another's and also from their parents'?

To formalize and clarify the assessment process, the chapter is divided into three sections: assessment tools, case material, and treatment notes. Assessment tools combine techniques for engaging and assessing a family's expressive style, formal procedures such as genograms and kinetic family drawing, and guides to interviewing. The case presentation follows the Martin family through the assessment phase of treatment. Finally, the chapter concludes with treatment notes highlighting four tasks that are performed before therapy moves into the middle phase of treatment.

Assessment Process

Family's Expressive Style

Some families are open and answer the therapist's questions directly. Some are guarded and volunteer little information. Others regularly explode in anger. Others sit in depressed silence. One way to conceptualize this distinction is to imagine an emotionally expressive dimension ranging from retentive silences at one end to explosive outbursts at the other. Silences beg for the therapist to fill the void, while arguments draw the therapist into the role of chief negotiator. These two extremes challenge any clinician's engagement skills; even so, the therapeutic task is to work within these styles in hopes of understanding the dysfunctional patterns. Because silent families and argumentative families are particularly difficult for beginning therapists and are among the most common family types seen, they are highlighted here.

Silent Families

At one extreme, silent families present their own distinct challenge to the therapist. Does the silence hint at a coiled spring of resentment and anger waiting for a release, or does the silence reflect a depression and resignation that dominates the family's mood? With these two possibilities, therapists might feel as if they are entering a minefield: "Will I stumble onto an explosion or not?" Although he or she may speculate on the dynamics behind the silence, the therapist must address this behavior and facilitate the uncovering of family patterns.

First, the silence itself has a message. Instead of actively engaging the therapist and defining their problem, the family sits in relative silence. Adults will answer with brief responses; adolescents will blankly stare and say, "I don't know"; younger children will giggle or shift uncomfortably in their chairs, anxiously looking toward one of the parents. In these situations, possible initial hypotheses are these:

1. The family is waiting for its spokesperson to lead.
2. Blame dominates the family, and members are sitting anxiously waiting for the accusations to begin.
3. The family's anger is barely contained, and silence masks repressed rage.
4. The family was coerced into coming and resents being here.

As a way to address this silence, three methods are helpful: allowing the spokesperson to emerge, attempting to draw in other members, and acknowledging silence during the engagement phase and inviting participation.

1. Allowing the spokesperson to emerge In the first session, after defining the purpose of the meeting (see Chapter 3) and asking why the family decided to make the appointment, the therapist sits back and waits for the patterns to emerge. In meeting silence with silence, the therapist nonverbally communicates that therapy will be a 50-50 enterprise and that nothing will be accomplished without the family's cooperation.

As the silence and accompanying anxiety in the session grow, the family will move to fill the vacuum. The first to speak is the family's spokesperson. This may or may not be the most dominant parent. He or she is, however, the one parent who does most of the liaison work between the family and authority figures (teachers, ministers, therapists). A key observation to make is whether the spokesperson continually glances toward the other parent and how that parent responds nonverbally. For example, a mother, speaking of the difficulty she is having with one of her children, continually shifts her focus between the therapist and her husband. The husband, in turn, either nods or stares evenly at his wife. In this situation, a significant family pattern is being revealed: The father is the dominant parent, and the mother operates within his sphere of control.

In contrast, consider the same initial behavior—the mother discussing her children's problems. In this case, however, the mother stares directly at the therapist the entire time (she has the power to define the problems in the family). Furthermore, she fails to acknowledge her husband but implies he is part of the problem. "My son does nothing around the house, and his father just sits there!"

2. Attempting to draw in other members After listening to the spokesperson but being careful not to let this parent dominate the entire session, the therapist turns to other family members to ask their impressions. The therapist does this by either building on what the spokesperson has said—"Billy, your mom says you help very little around the house; I wonder if you see it the same way"—or moving back to the broader question—"Well, your mother has her point of view of why the family came in today, and I'd like to hear from each of you what your own point of view is."

3. Acknowledging silence and inviting participation In the early sessions, particularly in the first session, attempting to draw out other family members may be less than successful. Here, therapists should remind themselves that this difficulty has less to do with their clinical skill than with the recognition that they are entering a powerfully retentive, repressed, and controlled system. Silence is an ultimate form of control: "You cannot make me talk."

Family therapists first cut their teeth on this issue when dealing with passive-aggressive adolescents. In comes the family and right away the adolescent makes for the corner, slouches in a chair, and stares at the floor. The behavior speaks volumes and leads to many working hypotheses: What is adaptive in this young person's style? Why, in this family, does the teenager need to pull away in silence? What is he or she protesting?

In addition to creating hypotheses, therapists may also respect and acknowledge the silences. Regarding the Martins, Cindy would at times lapse into silence:

> **Therapist:** Cindy, it appears that you have decided not to talk today. I respect your choice because there must be strong reasons for your decision. At any time, if you feel like jumping in, I would appreciate your help in figuring this out.

Notice that the therapist has redefined Cindy's uncooperative behavior as a form of decision making over which Cindy has control. Furthermore, eliminating the threat that she will be made to talk opens the door for Cindy to decide to participate, on her own terms.

For the therapist, silence of family members in the engagement phase is accepted and not challenged. By his or her behavior, the therapist communicates a respect for the family's style. As therapy progresses, however, silence takes on a much different, more defensive posture and calls for alternative responses from the therapist. (This topic is addressed in the following chapter, under the heading "Resistance.")

Argumentative Families

At the other end of the spectrum are the families ready to do battle. Sometimes these families begin arguing in the waiting room. More often than not, the family members have their clear villains: It is always the other person! When the tension can be felt as the family enters the office, a simple greeting—"So how did things go this week?"—can touch off a broadside exchange.

From the individual perspective of the family members, each one knows other family members are causing the problems. Their arguments are demonstrations to the therapist of the correctness of their views. For the therapist, there is a hint of fleeting terror as the session seems completely out of control. The anger is palpable, and a therapist typically enters the fray in an attempt to negotiate a truce. More often than not, the negotiations fail to work because the therapist has missed the point: The family members are trying to demonstrate who is wrong and find out whose side the therapist is on, not seek a solution.

Rather than negotiate, the therapist has alternative responses: maintaining neutrality, letting the anger run its course until the family's patterns emerge, intervening by moving from the emotional to the cognitive, and above all, avoiding an emotional trap.

1. Maintaining neutrality Initially, the family members are presenting their cases to the therapist, assuming that he or she will be as judgmental as the family members are. Consequently, there is nothing new in their behavior, at least as they see it. In fact, that is the very nature of the problem: Their patterns consistently lead to accusations and polarization, with their anger a by-product of these dysfunctional patterns.

This is not said to minimize the family's suffering. The members are continually inflicting a tremendous amount of pain on one another. Rather, the point is that nothing new is occurring in the therapist's office and that the family has been existing at this level of anger for quite some time. To attempt to rescue the family from these arguments is the therapist's wish, not the family's. At this early phase of treatment, who is right and who is wrong is the family's foremost issue.

Furthermore, the therapist has not stirred up these conflicts with questions; they probably began in the waiting room or on the ride to the office; he or she will also not be able to stop them in one or two sessions. As a result, rather than feeling that the situation is out of control, the therapist should welcome the opportunity to witness the family's fighting style and, in the process, observe the patterns.

2. Letting the anger run its course until patterns emerge By not rushing in to put out the fires, the therapist allows the patterns to evolve. Who accuses whom of what? How does that person respond? How do other family members respond to this dyadic exchange? What underlies this exchange: hurt, jealousy, attempts at control? When and how do the other family members become involved in this conflict?

Once the initial patterns have been acted out, the therapist intervenes to block the patterns from escalating and dominating the session. Usually in the first half hour, the family has revealed many of its basic patterns. If the therapist is passive throughout the entire session, the risk is that the patterns will continue to recycle in a downward spiral, resulting in increased anger and frustration. In these situations, the family members understandably leave the session thinking, "What do we need the therapist for? We do this at home by ourselves."

Consequently, a therapeutic intervention is required, but it must be timed well: The therapist must allow the family to portray their patterns but intervene before the session becomes counterproductive.

3. Intervening by moving from the emotional to the cognitive In an emotionally charged atmosphere, simply asking someone to perform a learned behavior—for example, "Blow your nose"—interrupts the firecracker-hot chain of dysfunctional patterns. In an emotionally charged family interview, shifting away from exchanges between members to dyadic exchanges with the therapist and moving the content of the discussion from emotionally laden to more cognitive issues defuses the situation.

For example, after the patterns have been initially demonstrated, the therapist enters the discussion by engaging the family members one on one:

> **Therapist:** Mrs. Martin, I know you have been trying to get a message through to your daughter, but I am confused as to what that is. Would you tell it to me?

> **Therapist:** Cindy, it looked to me that when your stepmother said certain things, they really bothered you. Am I right? What were some of those things?

> **Therapist:** Mr. Martin, at first you were listening to your wife and daughter but at some point, you entered the discussion. What did they say to bring you in? What were you hoping to accomplish when you entered?

Moving the discussion from the emotionally laden to more cognitive issues, the therapist asks:

"Is this what happens at home?"

"How often do these fights occur?"

"Do the same issues start the same fights?"

"What brings each of you into the arguments?"

Such questions force the family members to disengage from the emotional argument, reflect on what is occurring, and interact in a problem-solving mode with the therapist.

With these questions, the therapist begins to assume control of the session and provides the family with a simple but powerful therapeutic experience: They can all be in the same room together discussing their problems without constant explosions. By engaging members one on one, the therapist subtly, without requiring it, induces the members to listen to one another. They are in the same room together, and unless they put cotton in their ears, they are bound to hear something of what another family member is saying.

When engaging individual family members, the therapist must not permit the discussion to turn into a gripe session about a third party. The therapist has already heard those complaints in the first half hour. Rather, the therapist is asking the individual family member to talk about his or her personal frustrations, hurts, beliefs, and attempts to remedy the family problems.

> **Therapist:** Mrs. Martin, I am quite clear about your concerns for Cindy, but I'm worried about what these continual fights do to you.

> **Therapist:** Cindy, your anger at your stepmother is clear to me, but it must be hard on you to be continually angry.

> **Therapist:** Mr. Martin, it looks like you try to put an end to the fights between your wife and daughter, but to no avail. What is this like for you?

As a note of caution, some families will actively resist the therapist's assuming control of the exchanges, particularly when he or she attempts to defuse the exchanges by establishing one on one relationships. Here, the family is not only demonstrating the power and compulsions of their conflicts but also testing the therapist: "Will you be strong enough to manage us? Our conflicts feel overwhelming to us; will they overwhelm you?"

These situations call for a clear message to be sent that the therapist is in charge. Sometimes it requires only a simple: "Please Cindy, I know you have a point of view and I would be happy to listen to it, but right now I am talking to your mother, so please don't interrupt." Other times, however, a forceful stand is required: "Look, for these sessions to accomplish anything, people need to be able to complete what they have to say, and I need to listen to what they're saying. Whether the rest of you want to listen or not, that is your choice, but I do."

4. Avoiding an emotional trap Family patterns possess a powerful whirlpool effect that can sweep a therapist up in their currents. The trap is becoming emotionally bogged down in the family drama.

Clinicians, in these cases, find themselves agreeing that the scapegoat is the family problem, believing that someone does need to be rescued, or taking sides in the conflict and, in the process, falling into a linear definition of the problem. When any of these occur, it is an indication that the family dynamics are powerful enough to skew the therapist's perceptions.

As discussed in the previous chapter, the therapist uses these personal reactions to understand the system. In taking a step back, the therapist may find these emotional pulls to be quite diagnostic: "Why do I feel like rescuing Cindy? Why do I feel the need to support Mrs. Martin? Why am I angry at Mr. Martin's ambivalence?" Answering these questions helps put the family patterns into clearer perspective and, equally important, alerts the therapist to the personal pitfalls of working with the family.

As a matter of course, specific emotional pulls will occur again and again throughout the sessions. As a rule of thumb, when a therapist begins to shift to a linear definition of the family's problems, it is a clear sign that the family's definition of the problem is dominating the session. When this is the case, the therapist risks becoming as lost and as stuck as the family in attempting to implement change.

Genograms

The **genogram** is a format for drawing a type of family tree showing at least three generations (McGoldrick & Gerson, 1985). Much more than a family tree, a genogram graphically portrays complex family patterns across several generations and places the problem behavior in a larger family systems context. With its origins in Bowen's family systems theory (Bowen, 1978; Guerin & Pendagast, 1976), the use of the genogram is accepted practice for many family therapists.

Genograms are co-constructed with the family members in the engagement phase of treatment. The therapist is not only gathering valuable biographical data but also engaging the family in a collaborative therapeutic effort. Moreover, the genogram offers a means of broadening the family's focus. For example, in constructing the Martins' genogram, Cindy's place in the broader system became graphically clear: She was between two separate families.

Briefly, creating a genogram involves three levels: (1) mapping the family structure, (2) recording family information, and (3) delineating family relationships (McGoldrick & Gerson, 1985).

In mapping the family structure, the therapist delineates the basic family relationships. Figure 5.1 presents the Martins' three-generational tree. Family information involves demographic information and critical family events. Demographic information includes ages, dates of birth and death, geographic locations, occupations, educational levels, and the like. Figure 5.2 adds the muscle to the family skeleton mapped in Figure 5.1.

The genogram in Figure 5.2 expands our view of the Martin family: Mrs. Martin is the oldest of three siblings (she has a younger sister and brother). Both her parents are still living and reside in the same town. Mrs. Martin's first husband died five years before her second marriage. Mr. Martin is the younger of two brothers. Both his parents had died in the previous 10 years.

Besides the basic information contained in Figure 5.2, many more details can be added. For example, each family member can be asked to use adjectives to describe the other family members. In the process, not only would each person be more fully described but conflicting views would be quickly revealed. For example, Mr. Martin described his older brother (Sean) as distant and uninvolved. Mrs. Martin, however, pointed out that Peter and Sean had had several arguments over the years, all revolving around Sean's alcoholism. Sean, she related, had been divorced twice, and alcohol played a strong role each time. Mr. Martin admitted that he and Sean rarely saw eye to eye on many things.

The most inferential level of genogram construction is delineating the relationships among family members. This is done using a combination of clinical observations and family members' self-reports. For example, Mr. Martin describes his relationship with his brother as distant, but as he speaks, it becomes clear that the relationship is highly conflicted and causes him much pain. His denial of the pain then becomes a working hypothesis to test later in treatment.

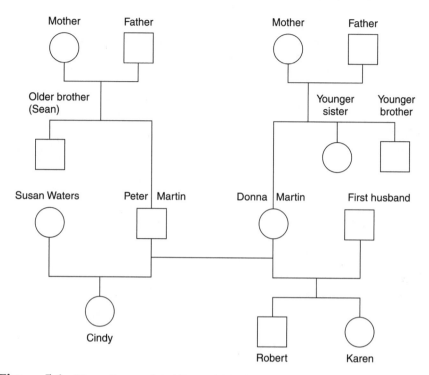

Figure 5.1 Three-Generational Tree of the Martin Family

Figure 5.3 illustrates the family relationships based on the members' self-reports and the therapist's observations. From this genogram, many working hypotheses begin to emerge:

1. The central triangular relationship in the family conflict involves Mr. and Mrs. Martin and Cindy. This conflict is what brought the family into treatment and will need to be addressed first.

2. The next central triangle involves Mr. Martin, Cindy, and Cindy's mother (Susan Waters). As the only child, Cindy has moved back and forth between her parents during their separation, divorce, and post-divorce periods. These relationships have shifting alliances that change rapidly. Cindy's behavior, therefore, could be a consequence of these circular interactions.

3. One is left to speculate on the possible triangles among Susan Waters, Mrs. Martin, Mr. Martin, and Cindy. Do Cindy's biological parents cooperate in raising her? What has their post-divorce relationship been like? What does Mrs. Martin think of her husband's ex-wife?

4. Mr. Martin's conflicted relationship with his brother remains to be explored. How has this relationship affected him? Does Cindy know her uncle? Does Mr. Martin fear Cindy might be like her uncle?

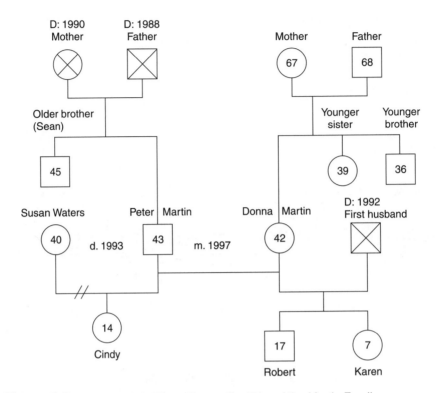

Figure 5.2   Demographic Three-Generation Tree of the Martin Family

5. Although not directly explored, one wonders about the marital patterns: When asked, both Mr. and Mrs. Martin described their relationship as "fine" but said they were experiencing significant stress in parenting Cindy. Still, they appeared guarded in their responses.

6. The triangle involving Mr. Martin, Mrs. Martin, and her parents is an area to question. How have his wife's parents received Mr. Martin? Is he comfortable with the closeness to them? Does he mind or support his wife's involvement with her parents?

7. Finally, what is the quality of the relationships involving Mr. Martin, Robert, and Karen? What role does Mr. Martin take in his stepchildren's lives? What role does Mrs. Martin want him to take?

In summary, besides the shorthand in describing complex family relationships, a genogram provides a practical, nonthreatening way of engaging the whole family (McGoldrick & Gerson, 1985). Because the task of constructing a genogram is one step removed from the threatening issues that brought the family into treatment, the members' anxiety is decreased, fostering a therapeutic alliance. As each family member begins to express his or her point of view regarding the other members, differ-

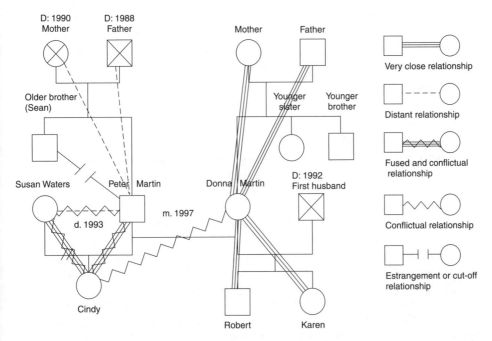

Figure 5.3 Three-Generational Tree Relationships of the Martin Family

ences are highlighted in a nontoxic way. In conclusion, the graphic portrayal of the family system is a picture worth a thousand words to both the therapist and the family. The black-and-white diagram offers a way to view family patterns and places the problematic behavior within a broader context—a systemic context in which all members influence one another.

The Interview Process

Besides observing, the therapist, through both verbal and nonverbal behavior, is facilitating the interaction and uncovering the family patterns. Focusing on the therapist's verbal behavior, one sees a balance being struck between questions and statements. Statements set forth positions or views, whereas questions call forth positions or views. The balance between the two varies with different schools of therapy (Tomm, 1988). For example, the Milan systemic approach relies heavily on questions—clinical hypotheses openly shared with the family; the structural and strategic approaches emphasize statements defining the therapist's view of the family's problem and giving directions for the family to follow. A therapist using the Milan model might speculate with the Martins:

> **Therapist:** Cindy, do you wonder whether your father favors you or your stepmother?

The therapist is questioning whether Cindy is in competition with her stepmother. The question invites Cindy to comment. However, although posing the question this way is nonthreatening, it also invites a simple "no" that would close the discussion.

A structural-strategic therapist might say this:

Therapist: Mr. Martin, I believe your daughter is trying to figure out where you stand. These arguments are a test to determine whose side you're on because Cindy is trying to determine whether you still love her.

In stating an opinion, the therapist is challenging the family. If Mr. Martin agrees with the statement, the therapist builds on this agreement. If Mr. Martin or Cindy disagrees with the statement, he or she must then defend that opposition. However, although certainly challenging the system, the therapist is also running the risk of increasing the family's defensiveness.

These two approaches reflect the differences between the role of the therapist in systems family therapy and his or her role in narrative family therapy. The structural-strategic therapist assumes an expert position with a distinct view of the family's reality. In contrast, the Milan-influenced therapist reflects a social constructionist view in asking the question from a "not-knowing" stance.

As discussed in the previous chapter, a "not-knowing" position does not imply an absence of theory or training on the therapist's part. Indeed, theory and training are guiding the therapist's questions. The difference is that the therapist does not assume his or her view of the family is necessarily true or real but uses it only to generate questions for the family members to ponder. It is within this conversation that the therapist and family members construct new meanings and solutions to their dilemmas.

The systems and narrative approaches to family therapy can complement one another in the assessment phase of treatment. Systems theory highlights family patterns, whereas narrative theory generates a number of questions for exploration. From a narrative perspective, rather than viewing the therapist as an expert telling the family members what their patterns are, the therapist becomes an expert at questioning the family about their patterns. It is through this questioning process that the family narrative is revealed in the individual members' cognitions, emotions, motivations, and behavioral patterns.

A number of different types of questions, discussed later in the chapter, can be used in this therapeutic technique.

Depending upon their ages and verbal abilities, young children may or may not be able to respond to the therapists' questions. As discussed in the previous chapter, however, their view of family furthers a therapist's understanding of the family patterns and narratives. To access this information, a therapist approaches young children through their medium of expression: play and drawing.

Types of Questions

In a series of articles, Tomm (1987a, 1987b, 1988) examines the process of family interviewing and makes several points about assessment and engagement issues. Specifically, focusing on therapeutic questions, he defines four major types: linear and circular questions (which serve to orient the therapist to the family members' perspectives, a process essential to both engagement and assessment) and strategic and reflexive questions (which serve to influence therapeutic change).

Linear Questions

The **linear question** is investigative in nature and assumes a linear cause and effect:

"Why did all of you decide to make this appointment?"

"What problems does Cindy have, Mrs. Martin?"

"How long have these problems persisted?"

"What have you tried to do to change the problems?"

"What has worked; what hasn't worked?"

"Cindy, what has made you so angry?"

Linear questions focus on identifying a problem in the family: Who has it? What has been done about it? How often does it occur? Moreover, they serve to orient the therapist to the family members' views of their problem.

Typically, the family expects such questions, and individually oriented or beginning family therapists are most likely to ask them. Therapists' common sense, steeped in linear causality, leads them to ask these questions.

Circular Questions

Circular questions also orient the therapist to the family's point of view, but they are based on circular causality and explore the interconnectedness of the family members:

"Cindy, which of your parents is worried most about you? Why?"

"Mr. Martin, you've been watching these battles between your wife and daughter for a long time. Would you please tell me what you have observed?"

"Mr. Martin, when these struggles start, what would you like to do, and what do you do?"

"Mrs. Martin and Cindy, how do you let the other person know that you are tired of fighting and want to break off contact?"

"Mrs. Martin and Cindy, if the two of you didn't fight with each other, in what other ways would you seek contact?"

Circular questions draw out the connectedness of family members and the recurrent patterns in their relationships. Rather than attempting to define the family patterns—who does what and when—the therapist uses circular questions to further explore the patterns while also raising the possibility that the family members are interconnected concerning the "problem." Circular questions, therefore, hint at circular causality and subtly expand the definition of the problem.

Strategic Questions

Questions directed toward change are **strategic questions**. The therapist has determined what needs to be changed in the family and uses questions to challenge the family:

"Mr. Martin, what would happen if you backed up your wife 100% in these arguments?"

"Cindy, how will you determine whose side your father is on?"

"Mrs. Martin, how will let your husband know that he must support you in these battles?"

"Cindy, how long are you planning to test your parents?"

"Mr. Martin, how long have you feared that Cindy is just like your brother?"

Strategic questions imply a strong and clear message from the therapist and are based on the therapist's assessment of what needs to change in the family. With these questions, the therapist moves right to the heart of the dysfunctional patterns and challenges the family to confront them.

For these questions to have the desired effect, a therapist must strongly assert the correctness of his or her assessment and move vigorously on the issues. When a therapist times these questions just right, the family members openly acknowledge their truth. Just as often, however, the family member opposes the therapist's implied message. As a response, the therapist, strongly convinced of the accuracy of his or her perception, further questions and challenges the family:

Therapist: Cindy, how long are you willing to test your parents?

Cindy: What do you mean? I don't test them.

Therapist: Well, from what I have observed, you use every opportunity to argue with your stepmother in hopes your dad will support you.

Cindy: You are crazy! She is always on my back. Nothing I do is good enough, but her kids don't do a thing.

Therapist: Then maybe I have got it wrong. You aren't testing them. Instead, you're angry at them and are protesting how unfair the rules are.

Notice that although the therapist's first hypothesis was denied, the therapist persevered in confronting Cindy on what she is thinking or feeling.

Reflexive Questions

Finally, **reflexive questions** are formulated to move family members to reflect on their behavior and to consider new options. These questions assume that family members are autonomous individuals, cannot be instructed directly, and will make their own decisions about changing. Consequently, the therapist is more like a guide or coach facilitating the family members to mobilize their own problem-solving resources:

"Mr. and Mrs. Martin, what is Cindy accomplishing by her behavior?"

"Cindy, how else would you get your dad's undivided attention if you did not fight with your stepmother?"

"Mr. Martin, what do your wife and daughter want when they fight with one another?"

"Cindy, these arguments appear to be a way you and your stepmother can make contact. Are there other ways besides fighting?"

"Mrs. Martin, is there no other way to show Cindy that you are hurt by her behavior?"

Reflexive questions, as opposed to strategic questions, presuppose that the therapist does not have all the answers and instead is co-constructing the nature of the family's problem and the nature of the change needed *in conjunction with the family*. Tomm (1988) believes that even though these types of questions are intended to influence the family (to facilitate the family members' reflection), they are more neutral than strategic questions because the therapist is more respectful of the family's autonomy and assumes all perceptions have validity.

In conclusion, Tomm (1988) argues that asking specific questions never guarantees any specific effect on the family, but that circular questions, as opposed to linear ones, will be more likely to engage the family and that reflexive questions, as opposed to strategic ones, reduce the sense of blame in the family.

Borrowing from Tomm's classification, in assessing family patterns and attempting to engage the family, a therapist employs a combination of linear and circular questions. (Strategic and reflexive questions are addressed in Chapter 7, on interventions.) As we have seen, family members typically enter treatment with a linear definition of their problem. Linear questions, therefore, not only explore this initial definition but also facilitate engagement: The therapist is attempting to understand the family members' initial presentations. At the same time, circular questions further orient the therapist to the family patterns while facilitating the movement to a circular or systems definition of the problem.

In the first several sessions with the Martins, the therapist first employed linear questions to understand the family members' perception of their problems: Mrs. Martin believed Cindy was to blame for the problems, Cindy thought her stepmother was too strict, and Mr. Martin thought the arguments caused the pain in the family. Circular questions were also intermixed in these sessions as the therapist began introducing the notion of circular causality to the family—that is, everyone has a part to play in the family drama.

To further specify, linear and circular questions can be broken down into four categories:

1. Questions directed toward family members' cognitions
2. Questions directed toward affective responses
3. Questions exploring members' motives and behaviors
4. Questions asking the family members to make predictions

Individual Members' Cognitions

Focusing on what people have been thinking accomplishes several therapeutic steps. First, the questions gather more data on the interactive patterns: Who was thinking what, and why? Second, angry family exchanges can explode quickly, with one angry remark eliciting another. By asking people what they have been thinking, the therapist disrupts the emotional chain reaction. Finally, the engagement process is enhanced as family members are asked what they think, allowed to finish what they are saying (the therapist blocks interruptions), and are listened to (at least by the therapist). For example:

> **Therapist:** Mrs. Martin, you have used the word *bad* several times when referring to Cindy. I was wondering if you can tell me what you mean by that.

> **Therapist:** Cindy, certain topics appear to set you off. What are some of them, and what is particularly irritating when your stepmother brings them up?

> **Therapist:** Mr. Martin, I was wondering what you were thinking when your wife and Cindy were arguing? What actions have you thought of taking?

> **Therapist:** Robert, you look like the family observer. What do you think is going on here?

Affective Responses

Exploring affective responses helps the therapist reveal the degree to which family members are aware of what they are feeling—that is, is there a great deal of denial?—and offers an opportunity for those feelings to be voiced. As examples:

> **Therapist:** Mr. Martin, it looked as though you were uncomfortable watching your wife and daughter argue. Would you tell me what you were feeling at that time?

> **Therapist:** Mrs. Martin, what do you feel when Cindy sleeps late in the morning?

> **Therapist:** Cindy, what hurts you in the family, and who recognizes your hurt?

> **Therapist:** Karen, at certain times you look upset in these meetings. What bothers you?

Besides the cathartic effect of letting people voice feelings, these questions present an opportunity to go beyond the raw surface reactions to underlying emotions:

> **Therapist:** Sometimes, behind anger, there is a sense of hurt or disappointment. I wonder if any of you have felt that after these battles.

> **Therapist:** I know in the heat of battle it is hard to feel anything but the anger, but I was wondering if there are other feelings after these arguments.

As a word of caution, beginning therapists frequently make the expression of feeling an end in and of itself. Certainly, it is a powerful effect when bottled-up emotions surface and appear as tangible evidence that the therapy is working. However, the expression of emotion may not accompany a change in behavior; in fact, if it remains the sole focus of treatment, it could result in no change.

For example, in working with the Martins, a therapist could have a field day with all the anger floating around the room: "What do you feel now? How did that make you feel?" The session would move from anger to silence to anger to silence. At this point, one might believe the session was being productive—"People certainly are expressing what they are feeling"—but in reality, the family patterns are merely being reinforced and exacerbated. The Martins are fully capable of expressing anger; *changing* the anger is what the therapy should be about.

Moreover, continually asking for feelings—"How did that make you feel?"—can be counterproductive to feelings actually emerging, particularly in the give-and-take of family exchanges. Asking people what they are feeling stops them from feeling. Such a question asks people to stop, reflect, and cognitively label what they were experiencing. Not only does this hamper the emotional spontaneity, but it also inhibits the family interaction.

Exploring Motives and Behavior

Frequently, in the process of family interactions, a person is acting and reacting based on known or unknown motives and the assessment of other people's motives. For example, Mrs. Martin believes that because her husband is so ineffectual and laissez-faire, she is the parent who must watch over and discipline Cindy. Similarly, she views Cindy's behavior as out and out rebellion. Cindy, on the other hand, views her stepmother's motives as purely controlling. Mr. Martin, for his part, believes his wife is too hard on his daughter because that was how Mrs. Martin was raised.

By and large, however, people never fully articulate these reasons to themselves or others. It remains, therefore, for the therapist to bring to light and explore these motives.

> **Therapist:** Cindy, your stepmother said that there are times when you are out of control. Have you given her any reason to think this?
>
> **Therapist:** Mr. Martin, your wife said she felt Cindy needed discipline. Do you agree?
>
> **Therapist:** Mrs. Martin, if you didn't try to guide Cindy, would your husband take over? Why?

Involving other family members in the discussion of individuals' motives aids in assessing family patterns, but it also hints at the prognosis for treatment. For example, it would be encouraging if the family members were able to listen to and comment on one another's observations without being provocative. It would be extremely positive if family members were willing to entertain another's point of view. At the other end of the spectrum, however, are families whose individual members rigidly maintain their positions, are unwilling to entertain alternatives, and continually attempt to triangle the therapist into an alliance.

Finally, exploring motives with family members present is therapeutic in and of itself as it exposes the family to new behavior. Not only does each person have the opportunity to look at his or her own motives and speculate on the motives of others, but family members have the opportunity to listen to others—even though there are no guarantees that they will. Whether or not this examination of themselves and others promotes change, it is a novel experience for many families.

Making Predictions

Another way of identifying patterns is to ask whether family members are capable of making predictions about behavior within the family:

> **Therapist:** Mrs. Martin, after you and Cindy have an argument, can you predict what will happen next?

Therapist: Mr. Martin, can you predict what will provoke an argument between your wife and daughter?

Therapist: Cindy, what could you do that will definitely set your parents off?

Therapist: Mrs. Martin, when will your husband attempt to intervene between you and your daughter? What signals does he look for?

Asking members to predict one another's behavior further details the family patterns and also explores the family's awareness of its own patterns. Suggesting that behavior can be predicted also suggests that it can be controlled and modified. Likewise, asking members to predict patterns plants a seed for change: They may have far more control over interactions than they realized.

Young Children: Play and Drawing

The questions discussed thus far require a certain level of emotional and cognitive maturity from the family members at whom they are directed. A question asks a person to reflect on an event or internal state, evaluate his or her own as well as another person's responses, and put his or her conclusions into words. This emphasis on verbal facility is often beyond the abilities of young children in a family. Asking many of these questions of young children would probably result in blank stares accompanied by "I don't know." By including young children in the therapy process, you are challenged to enter a child's world. Two means of doing this are through play and drawing.

Zilbach (1986), after tracing the history of play therapy, concludes that adults do not understand that play is children's work. Through play, children express themselves, struggle with feelings of mastery, and attempt to understand the world surrounding them. Therapists cannot rely on verbal expression when working with young children, and to do so imposes an adult world on them (Gil, 1994). Instead, Gil proposes play as a means of entering young children's worlds and engaging other family members. To this end, she recommends that you make available to the family members simple play materials such as paper, magic markers, crayons, modeling clay, and dolls.

For example, although Karen brought her favorite doll to the session, she quickly noticed a table in the corner of the office on which she saw paper, magic markers, and modeling clay. Asking her mother if she could play with the clay, Karen left her mother's chair and began kneading and shaping the material. Satisfied with her finished product, she proudly showed it to her mother who stroked her daughter's hair and praised her work. Karen returned to the table and began dividing the clay into four balls. Carrying each ball, she gave the first one to her mother, then one to her brother, Robert, and finally one to Cindy.

With these simple gestures, Karen revealed more of the family dynamics. Karen goes to her mother for approval and praise, which she readily receives. Also, she includes Robert and Cindy in her play. A striking note is that Cindy accepts Karen's offering with a smile: Cindy may not be as insulated from the family as she first appeared. As is often the case, what does not occur is more telling than what does. Karen did not include Mr. Martin in the play. Equally important, he did not ask to be let into the family interaction.

The therapist observes this sequence of behavior and watches the family members nervously twisting the clay in their hands; he builds on this spontaneous episode and seeks to further engage Karen and her family.

Therapist: Karen, what are you making there? That looks like fun; can I have a piece of clay, too?

Karen offers the therapist a piece of clay.

Therapist: What do you think would be fun to make?

Karen: A cat.

Therapist: Great; you make one and I'll make one.

It is interesting that Mrs. Martin, Robert, and Cindy also begin making cats, but Mr. Martin sits watching.

Therapist: Mr. Martin, you don't have a piece of clay. Would you like one?

Mr. Martin: No, that's okay.

Therapist (sensing that Mr. Martin was not resisting but rather needed encouragement): Oh, come on. Everyone has one. Karen, would you give a piece of clay to your father? (She does and he readily accepts.)

On a content level, this episode appears quite trivial, but from a process perspective, it revealed additional family dynamics and allowed the therapist to further engage the family members. The clay not only keeps nervous hands occupied but also serves as the medium to engage everyone in the room in the same activity.

Drawings also offer an opportunity for play; with a minimum expenditure of time and effort, they provide a wealth of assessment data. A simple structured technique that can be used with young children is the Kinetic Family Drawing test.

Since the early 1970s, Burns and Kaufman (1970, 1972) and Burns (1982) have refined the Kinetic Family Drawing (K-F-D) test. Briefly, the K-F-D asks the young child to "draw a picture of everyone in your family, including yourself, doing something" (Burns & Kaufman, 1972, p. 5). The unique feature of the K-F-D test is the portrayal of movement in the depiction of the family members. Burns and Kaufman (1970) contend that when this kinetic factor is added, family interactional patterns are more likely to surface.

For example, Figure 5.4 is Karen's initial K-F-D. She places her mother in the center of the picture, performing nurturing tasks. Her stepfather is outside the house working on the car. Robert is listening to his CDs, and Cindy is on the phone with friends. Noticeably, family members are not interacting with one another. Whereas the mother is involved in nurturing activities, everyone else in the family is absorbed in personal areas of interest. Also, each family member, other than Mrs. Martin, is looking away from the center of the picture.

At first glance, Karen's drawing reflects a typical family with adolescents, with both teenagers absorbed in their own worlds. Karen's self-portrait also reflects her current interest in dolls. Mr. and Mrs. Martin are engaged in stereotypic gender roles. However, the absence of interaction is clearly evident. One wonders if the family strife is forcing everyone to turn away from the family. (For further interpretations and research findings, see Burn's 1982 *Self-Growth in Families: Kinetic Family Drawings [K-F-D]: Research and Application.*)

Karen's drawing offers another view of the Martin family. It is not the only view but still the legitimate one of a 7-year-old. Developing the themes in the drawing, the therapist further engages the family:

Karen

Robert

Mother

Cindy

Stepfather

Figure 5.4

Therapist: Karen, I like your drawing. Would you tell me what each person is doing?

Therapist (following Karen's explanation and addressing the other family members): Does this fit each of your views of the family. Why?

At this point, each family member's opinion is elicited, with similarities underlined and differences highlighted.

Case Presentation

In the first several sessions, the dysfunctional triangle involving Cindy, her father, and her stepmother stood out. The arguments were consistent and predictable:

- Cindy violates a house rule—curfew, smoking, swearing, forgetting to do her chores—that particularly irritates her stepmother.

- Donna is offended by Cindy's behavior and believes that it is a direct affront to the family and a clear lack of respect.

- Confronted directly by her stepmother, Cindy is evasive and makes a series of excuses.

- Donna is hurt and offended by Cindy's obvious "lies" and begins to point them out to Cindy.

- Cindy becomes angry and yells at her stepmother, "Leave me alone," and then leaves the house or retreats to her room.

- Depending on the seriousness of the offense, Donna Martin may follow Cindy to her room or try to call her back into the house.

- Cindy then swears at her stepmother and cuts off any contact. If Peter is in the house, once the argument escalates he enters the picture, whereupon both Cindy and Donna present their cases to him.

- If he is not home, Peter will be told later of Cindy's offense by his wife and asked to do something.

- Approaching Cindy, Peter is met with her anger and her explanation.

- Unsure of what to do, Peter listens and returns to talk to Donna, who is disappointed by his lack of action.

As the presenting problem, this sequence is likely to be reenacted several times during the engagement phase of treatment. Besides the seemingly automatic repetition of these patterns, they are also played out as members try to establish blame and to seek alliances.

For example, Donna believed Cindy was to blame for the family's problems. Cindy knew her stepmother was to blame. Peter switched back and forth between the two. Robert agreed with his mother. Karen sheepishly nodded in agreement with her mother.

Closely tied to the blaming was the seeking of an alliance with the therapist: "Whose side are you on?" In the divided, conflicted Martin family, there was little sense of wholeness and much taking of sides. As a new player in the game, the therapist is the neutral agent to be wooed, a potentially powerful ally.

In the engagement phase of treatment, the appeals for alliance can range from emotional ("Help, I am a victim here!") to the logical ("I have tried and tried my absolute best in the face of all this irrationality"). The emotional appeals seek out the therapist's compassion, whereas the logical argument works on her or his neutrality and intellect.

Active from the beginning of the first session, these appeals seek to sway the therapist. Because these overtures are covert, family members look for signs of alliance in all aspects of the therapist's behavior: Does the therapist allow the session to be dominated by one family member's complaints? With whom does the therapist agree? (Does he or she appear to listen more to one of the members?)

In the Martins' second session, for example, a conflict erupted between Cindy and her stepmother. The argument was over restrictions Donna had imposed on Cindy. After the established pattern repeated itself, Peter pointed out to his wife that perhaps her restrictions were unfair. At this point, Donna began to cry, saying, "I have done all I can to make this family work. I just cannot do it anymore." Donna's implied possibility of withdrawal threatened the family and raised the tension in the session.

Silence gripped the room. Robert and Karen looked anxiously at their mother; Cindy, although still steaming, stared down at the floor; and Peter pleadingly looked to the therapist. The moment begged for someone to do something. A series of questions rushed through the therapist's head: Is Donna expressing a sincerely felt pain or crocodile tears? Is this a familiar pattern for the family? Whether this is old or new behavior, should I step in and respond to her? If I did, would this be reassuring, supportive, effective engagement, or playing into the dysfunctional patterns?

As with many family therapy situations, when in doubt, wait five minutes. It is highly unlikely that any behavior that occurs within the first several sessions is novel; rather, a conservative premise is to assume that the family is testing the therapeutic boundaries. Furthermore, from a systems perspective, the family is bringing into your office their established patterns that have evolved to manage a variety of scenarios. Mrs. Martin's threat of emotional withdrawal is not the end of the cycle, a contradiction in terms, but rather an escalation to a more damaging level of interaction—threats of family disintegration.

By waiting, the therapist is also permitting the cycle to complete itself. For the Martins, it is a dysfunctional homeostasis, but it is all the family has at this time. They sought therapy because the patterns felt endlessly frustrating and threatening. Again, however, the therapist is performing a balancing act. If he responds to the tears, he runs the risk of reinforcing the patterns—"Mrs. Martin, what are you feeling right now?"—and could be seen as creating an alliance with her. If the therapist remains passive and nonexpressive, the cycle reverberates until the end of the session and the family members leave more frustrated than ever—a poor predictor for a second appointment. Consequently, the therapist needs to respond. The question is, how?

One possibility for the therapist is not to be drawn into the patterns but to turn to other family members:

Therapist: Mr. Martin (or any of the children), I wonder what you are feeling at this time? What choices do you have at this moment? What do you think you should do? What do you want to do?

Therapist: Mrs. Martin, what do you want from your family right now?

With this response, the therapist not only explores the family dynamics but also communicates the belief that the family members have the capacity to nurture one another. For the therapist to assume the nurturing role in the therapeutic system robs the family members of the opportunity to develop it themselves. Moreover, therapy runs smoothly as long as the therapist has assumed and is fulfilling a critical role in the family—nurturing—but little learning or change is taking place. The family members are not developing the critical new behavior they need.

Besides the blaming and dysfunctional father-mother-daughter triangle, other patterns are also evident and explored via the genogram. Although briefly touched on in the first several sessions, the triangle involving Mr. Martin, Cindy, and her mother (Susan) possessed a consistent pattern.

Through her biological parents' bitter separation and divorce, Cindy grew adept at playing one parent against the other. If one refused her something, she sought it from the other. When one became strict with her, she went to the other and complained—a complaint that each parent was all too ready to hear about the other. In arguments with one parent, Cindy would threaten to move in with the other.

Although this pattern could be seen as more evidence of Cindy's "bad" behavior, from a systems perspective, the pattern developed and continued because of the roles the parents played. Their continual anger with each other several years after their divorce was highlighted by Cindy's behavior. Unable to resolve or move past their anger at each other, the parents were, unfortunately, unable to co-parent in any effective manner, and Cindy's manipulative behavior flourished.

On another level, Peter's brother, Sean, was a ghost who loomed in the sessions. While constructing the genogram, Peter described his relationship with his brother as conflicted and troublesome because of Sean's alcoholism. After seeing Sean through several difficulties throughout the years, Peter had quit trying to help his brother and cut off the relationship. Although Cindy did not remember her uncle very well, her father secretly feared that she might possess many of Sean's traits. This fear paralyzed him. He wished to guide his daughter firmly and to protect her, but he feared that if he did so, she would reject him and return to her mother.

Mr. Martin's ambivalence regarding Cindy was an area of conflict in his marriage. Mrs. Martin believed Cindy needed a strong hand and urged her husband to take a stand with his daughter. Choosing not to share his secret fear, Mr. Martin excused much of Cindy's behavior, which only served to increase the marital conflict.

For her part, Mrs. Martin did not feel strong support from her husband in the conflicts with Cindy. Moreover, after a disagreement over Cindy, Mr. Martin would emotionally withdraw from his wife. Thus, Mrs. Martin also walked a tightrope. She believed she knew what was best for Cindy, but feared pushing the issue with her husband because of his subsequent withdrawal.

Compounding the marital stress was the relationship between Donna and her parents. Donna had always been extremely close to her parents, sometimes visiting them four times a week. As the oldest daughter and with her parents aging, Donna felt a responsibility to watch out for them.

Peter initially enjoyed Donna's family. Having lost both his own parents and being cut off from his brother, he bathed in the warmth of his in-laws. However, what was nice on an occasional holiday became brutal when it was repeated every Sunday. He experienced the couple's obligations to Donna's parents as burdensome, but being newly married and having experienced one bitter marriage breakup, he wanted with all his heart for this marriage to work. Consequently, he rarely raised any objection to visits with her family, but he became increasingly silent at these gatherings and withdrew to watch television.

A final issue between Mr. and Mrs. Martin was the relationships with Robert and Karen. After her first husband died, Mrs. Martin became mother and father to her children. The support from the extended family helped, but still she felt all the responsibility for her children. Thus, not only did she love Peter and want to marry him, but she also saw the possibility for her children to have a second father. Unfortunately, with all the problems, Donna felt her husband was completely absorbed with Cindy, to the neglect of her own children. Whenever she brought up the subject with him, he said he would try, and the issue was dropped.

Treatment Notes

Engaging the family members and assessing their interactive patterns are the focus of the beginning phase of therapy. We have considered the general outline for achieving these goals by adapting to the family's expressive style, using the genogram, forming questions that guide the interview process, and including young children in the treatment process. Each family, however, is unique and as such presents new challenges. A therapist is therefore constantly weighing what will facilitate or inhibit the engagement and assessment process with a particular family. To simplify the discussion, we examine four tasks that are performed before therapy moves into the middle phase:

1. Engaging individual family members
2. Understanding and respecting the family's paradigm or narrative
3. Assessing family resilience
4. Focusing on what needs to change and establishing intervention priorities

Engaging Individual Family Members

It is one thing to speak of engaging a family, but in concrete reality, the therapist is engaging individual family members. Consequently, the therapeutic question involves whom to engage first while avoiding polarizing another family member. This juggling is particularly difficult when a family that enters therapy is strongly divided.

The Martins are a prime example of a family polarized along family loyalty lines as well as generational ones. The therapist's task is to engage these various factions without alienating others. The first issue is deciding the sequence in which to engage them.

Mrs. Martin brought the family into treatment. It was only at her insistence that all the members attended. Consequently, the therapist first focuses on engaging Mrs. Martin by listening to her and asking clarifying questions to ensure an appreciation of her position. If instead the therapist focused on Cindy's complaint and attempted to negotiate more freedoms from her parents, Mrs. Martin would probably pull the family out of treatment: "Why go to this therapist when he's obviously being duped by Cindy?"

Because of the conflict between Mrs. Martin and Cindy, Cindy would appear to be the next person to engage. In this case, however, the therapist chose Mr. Martin. By engaging him, the therapist underlines the boundary between the parents and children. More important, to be drawn to Cindy immediately might inadvertently have reinforced the dysfunctional patterns in the family. By pursuing a more logical tack—parents to oldest child through youngest child—the therapist communicates an order to therapy and a sense that he has a plan.

As for the children, Cindy is the most problematic for the therapist. She needs to know that she will be listened to and that her opinion will be respected but also that the therapist realizes there are always two sides to a story. Additionally, the therapist communicates that he does not sit in judgment, and that who is right and who is wrong is not his concern. Rather, all family members are contributing to the problems, and all will be involved in the change process.

Understanding and Respecting the Family's Paradigm or Narrative

As mentioned earlier (in Chapter 3), a family's paradigm reflects the family's capacity to construct its own view of reality. This view of the world guides the behavior of family members and serves as a set of unacknowledged but powerful family rules (Reiss, 1981). With the Martins, the issues of gender, ethnicity, life cycle, and step-family transitions shape the behaviors of the family members.

Mrs. Martin believed that the responsibility for the family's emotional life sat squarely on her shoulders. This cultural bias burdened her unnecessarily but also reinforced her husband's frequent noninvolvement: "I let Donna handle the kids." Moreover, this unstated agreement between Mr. and Mrs. Martin intensified the conflict with Cindy. If the turmoil in the family was Mrs. Martin's fault, it was up to her alone to solve it. It is no wonder she looked to the therapist to help her with the task of changing Cindy.

Consequently, if the therapist also shared the cultural bias, a chief focus of therapy would be either changing Cindy or Mrs. Martin, or both. By recognizing the cultural bias operating within the family, the therapist does not reinforce it and avoids increasing Mrs. Martin's guilt and frustration. Instead, he offers an alternative view: Mr. Martin is also contributing to the family's emotional life, as are Cindy, Robert, and Karen. Therapeutically, emphasizing this theme lessens the tension in the stepmother-stepdaughter conflict and opens up other options for behavior.

Raised in a traditional ethnic family, Mrs. Martin endorses many Italian family values:

1. A value system is organized primarily around protecting the family.
2. Respect for older family members is a strong norm.
3. Publicly disgracing the family is a powerful taboo.
4. Independence and individuality may be interpreted as selfish and neglectful of the family (Rotunno & McGoldrick, 1982).

With these values in mind and a wish to foster a therapeutic alliance, a therapist would err by condoning or excusing Cindy's behavior. Her disrespectful behaviors are affronts to Mrs. Martin. The therapist must acknowledge this.

Therapist: Mrs. Martin, Cindy's behavior must be terribly upsetting to you. It flies in the face of everything you hold sacred. Clearly, we must find a way for the family life to improve.

With this statement, the therapist is acknowledging Mrs. Martin's point of view without concluding that Cindy must be changed. Instead, he keeps the family life as the focus.

Furthermore, as the therapy progresses, the therapist remains sensitive to the issue of autonomy and family loyalty. Change will take place as Mrs. Martin begins to view Cindy's behavior as a form of adolescent maturation and realizes that she cannot expect Cindy to act like her own children do because of the differences in their backgrounds. Also, the relationship between Mrs. Martin and her parents is approached very carefully. Challenging this relationship early in treatment would jeopardize the therapeutic alliance because one of Mrs. Martin's most sacred values, loyalty to parents, would be questioned.

Even though he was third-generation Irish, Mr. Martin reflected many attributes of Irish culture particularly relevant to therapy:

1. Traditional fathers are frequently uninvolved in the emotional lives of their children.

2. Husbands deal with wives primarily by avoidance.
3. Emotional distancing characterizes interpersonal relationships.
4. Repression of feelings is not a sign of resistance but a reflection of blocked-off inner emotions.
5. Hostility in families is generally dealt with by silently building up resentments, culminating in cutting off relationships (McGoldrick, 1982).

Following these ethnic patterns as guidelines, some hypotheses regarding Mr. Martin's role in the family can be made:

- Mr. Martin may believe that he is a very involved father, based on his cultural norms.

- Marital tension may exist because of a contrast between the spouses' definition of intimacy. Mrs. Martin may be frustrated in her attempts to become close to her husband, and Mr. Martin may respond to his wife's overtures by distancing himself.

- The cut-off relationship between Mr. Martin and his brother hints at long-standing hostility between the two that was not openly expressed and resolved.

In building a therapeutic alliance with Mr. Martin, the therapist walks a fine line between trying to involve him more and respecting his need to distance himself emotionally. Moreover, the therapist could push the family out of treatment if the marital relationship became a focus in the initial phase of treatment. The marital relationship might be addressed later, but to raise the issue in the first several sessions would increase the family's anxiety and thus raise their defensiveness.

Finally, the Martins may be further understood by recognizing the family's stage in the life cycle and in the stepfamily transition.

Adolescence signals a transition from childhood to adulthood. Just as an individual goes through dramatic changes during these years, a family is also changing to accommodate the emerging young adult and to prepare to launch the person into adulthood. Both Robert and Cindy have little desire to invest in building a new family; they are busy with their own developmental task of individuating. Whereas Robert individuated by withdrawing from the family and becoming more involved with his peers and their activities, Cindy fought for her autonomy within the family.

In terms of treatment, it would be unrealistic and possibly counterproductive to attempt to increase Robert's and Cindy's bonds with the family. A therapeutic push to increase intimacy in the family would paradoxically shove Robert and Cindy away from therapy. If therapy instead offers an opportunity for them to be respected as young adults with their own wants and needs, the chance for their involvement in the treatment process increases. Accordingly, Mr. and Mrs. Martin need to be assisted in understanding this developmental process and in finding ways they can facilitate it.

Visher and Visher (1988) outline seven stages in stepfamily development: fantasy, pseudoassimilation, awareness, mobilization, action, contact, and resolution. When they came to therapy, the Martin family combined the pseudoassimilation and awareness stages. Both parents saw in their new marriage an opportunity to make amends for the past and to give their children a new future, a stepfamily in which everyone would get along and be happy. (It is surprising how many times stepfamilies will laughingly, but with a hint of disappointment, say, "We were going to be the Brady Bunch.") By the time the Martins contacted the therapist, they had moved past the fantasy stage and had begun to sense that things were not going well (pseudo-assimilation). As each parent felt pulled by the needs of his or her own children and the new spouse, there was a growing sense that changes were needed (awareness).

Contacting the therapist signaled the stepfamily's transition stage and was a positive step. Reassuring the family that what it is experiencing is well within the norms for new stepfamilies helps reduce the blaming and facilitates the engagement process.

Assessing Family Resilience

Family resilience is a recently adopted concept representing a substantial shift in assessing families. Whereas systems theories offer ideal models that serve as measuring sticks for family functioning, the concept of **family resilience** shifts the focus from finding dysfunctional patterns to identifying a family's strength and capacity for self-repair. Rather than focusing on families as dysfunctional systems, the family resilience approach views families as systems that are challenged by current crises.

The origins of family resilience can be found in earlier studies of resilient children. Garmezy (1985) identified three factors that protect children in high-risk environments. First, a flexible and adaptable personality, defined as an "easy" temperament, permits the child to generate new responses in times of crises. Second, there must be at least one adult who takes a strong interest in the child. Finally, a well-defined social support network, such as school, church, or friends, cushions the child from the blows of the environment. Further emphasizing the role of social supports, worldwide studies of at-risk children found the most significant positive influence to be a close, caring relationship with a significant adult (Werner, 1993). This adult serves as a role model, advocate, and protector for the child.

In a family, resilience develops as the family masters or overcomes stressful or challenging situations. Resilience is analogous to strengthening one's immune system by overcoming mild infections (Rutter, 1999). The key, however, is that the family overcomes stressful situations without resorting to scapegoating one or more family members. The family scapegoat who bears the brunt of the family's criticism is at greater risk than family members caught in family discord (Rutter, 1999).

When misfortune strikes people, the meaning or interpretation (the socially constructed narrative) they attach to the event exacerbates or mitigates against the negative impact of the experience (Kagan, 1984). For example, the child's experience of a divorce depends largely on how the child interprets the situation: Did dad leave mom? Did he leave me? Did mom kick dad out for good reasons? Did mom kick dad out because of her new boyfriend? Was I to blame for the divorce?

The answers to these questions do not occur in a vacuum but reflect the child's social environment. For instance, the younger the child, the more the answers are borrowed from the significant adults in the child's world. In a bitter divorce, a child may adopt the custodial parent's narrative: "We got a divorce because your father was never home." Accordingly, from a child's or adolescent's perspective, choosing sides in a divorce makes cognitive sense. "Once mom's or dad's side is chosen, at least I have a coherent view of the world and am not being bounced back and forth between opposite interpretations of the divorce." The child's narrative is coherent and consistent.

The interest in resilience coincides with the shift in the field from family pathology to a competency-based, strength-oriented paradigm (Walsh, 1995). From a family resilience approach, families are not damaged but are systems that are challenged by life stressors. Thus, a family is neither healthy nor dysfunctional, but a system attempting to adapt to both internal and external stressors. The advocates of family resilience seek to understand how families survive and even prosper in the face of stressors. As a familiar bit of folk wisdom says, "Fire melts butter and hardens steel." The hardening steel is the essence of family resilience.

Family resilience is the interplay of morphostasis and morphogenesis (Hawley & DeHann, 1996). As described in the first chapter, morphostasis is the system's ability to maintain its structure in a changing environment, while morphogenesis is the capacity to develop new structures to cope with change. The resilient family is able to maintain its structures, its coherency, and its competencies when faced with overwhelming stresses but at the same time can change its structures to adapt to environmental demands. A resilient family therefore is neither rigidly inflexible nor loosely flexible. The family possesses basic core values and beliefs that maintain its integrity in a hurricane, but it also knows when to bend to accommodate a strong wind.

The Martin family lacked a secure sense of itself or an agreed-on core belief system. As a stepfamily, they were attempting to unite two separate systems into a coherent whole, but the family members were more influenced by their previous family histories than the brief history they shared.

The Martins, however, were not without strengths. Mr. and Mrs. Martin loved one another and were determined to make the new stepfamily work. Additionally, they shared similar visions of the family they wished to create and supported one another's parenting styles. Still, they were writing their narrative from scratch. Even the best intentions were found wanting in the struggle to create a new family.

Focusing on What Needs to Change and Establishing Intervention Priorities

Having built a therapeutic alliance and developed working hypotheses concerning the dysfunctional patterns in the family, the therapist, by the end of the initial phase of treatment, is in a position to establish intervention priorities. Before examining the specific priorities for the Martin family, several guidelines bear mentioning.

It is one thing to be ahead of the family in conceptualization; it is quite another to be ahead of the family in interaction. Specifically, from the first contact, a therapist is formulating working hypotheses concerning the family's functioning. Guided by theory, the therapist begins to place the family's behavior within conceptual categories. In doing so, the therapist orders the clinical data, which then guides engagement and intervention strategies.

The drawback to this approach is that the therapist might begin to establish agendas separate from the family members' understanding of their problems or needs. With a family that presents a child-focused problem, for example, the theory says the child is caught in a dysfunctional triangle with the parents and that this pattern strongly suggests marital conflict. Although ongoing therapy might prove this view correct, the family does not initially share it. Consequently, the therapist errs by focusing on the marital relationship before the couple is ready.

Many families drop out of treatment in the initial phase for this very reason: The therapist is pushing agendas the family is not ready to address. Thus, in establishing intervention priorities, one rule of thumb is this: *Do not get ahead of the family; address the members' chief concerns first.*

The Martin family combines the developmental themes of adolescence with the losses experienced through death and divorce and the struggle to build a stepfamily. Research suggests that the primary goal of family therapy with adolescents should focus upon reconnecting adolescents and their parents by establishing flexible boundaries that fit the developmental needs of both parents and teenagers (Liddle, Rowe, Dakof, & Lyke, 1998). Establishing these boundaries, however, is difficult to do even in the best of situations. Divorce and marital transitions compound the problem by interfering with parents' ability to support and supervise their children (Hetherington, Bridges, & Insabella, 1998). "Dysfunctional family relationships, such as conflict, negativity, lack of support, and nonauthoritative parenting, exacerbate the effects of divorce and remarriage on children's adjustment" (Hetherington, Bridges, & Insabella, 1998, p. 179).

With this in mind, the following intervention priorities, in order, were established for the Martins:

1. Address the dysfunctional triangular patterns involving Cindy, her father, and her stepmother.
2. Clarify the relationship between Mr. Martin and his ex-wife, Susan Waters, particularly as it impacts Cindy's behavior.
3. Explore interaction among the three parents (Mr. Martin, Mrs. Martin, and Cindy's mother) and the consequences for Cindy's behavior.
4. Focus on the marital relationship—specifically, how Cindy's behavior has affected the couple and what other issues generate conflict.
5. Identify the extended family's influence on the Martins—in particular, Mr. Martin's estranged relationship with his brother and Mrs. Martin's allegiance to her parents.
6. Assist the family in building on their strengths and developing a narrative that better suits a new blended family.

Note that the list of priorities first addresses the issue that brought the family into treatment: Cindy's behavior. This issue, however, is the entry point into the broader family context.

In addition, remember that the list reflects the therapist's sense of priorities. In actuality, all these issues might not be addressed in the course of treatment. For example, focusing on points 1 and 2 may be sufficient to bring about reduction in conflict in the family. At that point in treatment, the family could be quite satisfied with what has occurred and be ready to terminate. Here again, the therapist is not ahead of the family. He could strongly feel that points 3, 4, and 5 should be addressed but recognize the change that has occurred and begin the termination process with the family.

This therapeutic balance of pushing for change but also respecting the family's limits is highlighted in the following chapter. Sensing this balance point in the course of treatment and using it for therapeutic change is a chief ingredient in conducting psychotherapy skillfully. Although the guidelines for developing this skill are discussed in the following chapter, experience and supervision will be the ultimate teachers.

Summary

Family therapy is an active process. In contrast to most individual psychotherapists, a family therapist in the initial phase of therapy is proactive rather than reactive: engaging the family members, setting therapeutic boundaries, identifying dysfunctional patterns, and establishing intervention priorities. In the engagement phase of treatment, more than any other, the therapist uses questions to set the pace of the interview.

For therapists trained in individual therapy, particularly the more reactive models such as client-centered, the assertiveness required of the family therapist can be disconcerting. However, with experience and supervision, your therapeutic skills will be enhanced by learning to use questions to assess and intervene in family patterns.

Glossary

Circular question An investigative question based on circular causality and designed to explore the interconnectedness of the family members.

Family resilience A concept emphasizing a family's strength in times of stress.

Genogram A graphic representation of a multigenerational family constellation.

Linear question An investigative question that assumes linear cause and effect.

Norms A set of expectations and restrictions guiding behavior of group or family members.

Reflexive question A question guided by the therapist's belief that family members will make their own decisions about change. This type of question asks the family members to reflect on their own behavior.

Strategic question A question guided by the therapist's assumptions of what needs to change in the family. This type of question is directed toward change by challenging the family.

6

Change and Resistance

J ust as approaching human problems from a systems orientation broadens assessment and intervention options, it also expands the concept of change. Specifically, a system can change in two ways: (1) Change is continuous, and the structure (rules governing behavior) is not altered—**first-order change**. (2) The system changes qualitatively; the structure rules are altered—**second-order change** (Watzlawick, Weakland, & Fisch, 1974).

For example, in response to Cindy's acting-out behavior, her parents became more restrictive; her punishments and limits were increased. Unfortunately, Cindy rebelled further. The family patterns became a deadly game: "You think you can control me; I will show *you*." It was after months of this impasse that the family sought treatment.

From a change perspective, Cindy's parents' responses were first-order: the parents tried more of the same restrictions. Even when confronted with their own ineffectiveness, they continued with the old responses. They were responding as the rules of the system dictated—children will be controlled. What was needed, however, was a change in the systems structure (second-order change). Because of their respective personal histories, Cindy would not respond to her stepmother as Robert and Karen did. Thus, what worked for Mrs. Martin in parenting Robert and Karen was not going to be effective with Cindy. Consequently, Mrs. Martin and Cindy's father were in need of developing more effective means (rules) of parenting Cindy.

Family patterns are powerful in their persistence: morphostatic forces maintain the family's status quo. When change is called for, first-order change is usually tried; that is, more or less of the existing patterns is employed. These commonsense reactions have worked in the past and are applied to new problems; but when first-order change tactics fail to alleviate the problem, pressure builds inside the family and the symptomatic behavior rapidly escalates. At the time of referral, Cindy was threatening to run away.

Despite the buildup of tension and the need for relief, however, change is still threatening. Giving up old patterns involves unknown risks for the family, yet family members are compelled to take these risks as their first-order attempts at change continually fail to reduce the tension in the system. Even so, they may resist therapeutic interventions. With some families, this dilemma is presented to the therapist as a double bind: "We want to make things better in our family, but we don't want to change."

This chapter discusses change and resistance by first conceptualizing change as an attempt by the family to balance morphostasis and morphogenesis forces (see the discussion of family resilience in Chapter 5) and by describing the "dance of change" that occurs in the therapeutic alliance. Next, the pros and cons of solution versus problem approaches are discussed. The second half of the chapter employs a case example to highlight a discussion of resistance.

Conceptualizing Change

Although all types of family therapy are concerned with the dysfunctional patterns in the family, the explanation for these patterns, goals for treatment, and conceptualization of change vary greatly among them (Gurman & Kniskern, 1991). For example, the models differ in whether the family must have insight into or understanding of the problem in order to change. For models at one end of the spectrum, family insight is essential, as in psychodynamic models and Bowen's theory. For the strategic model at the other end of the spectrum, the family gains insight, but only after their behavior has changed. Cognitive understanding is the key to change in one model, whereas behavioral reinforcement patterns predict and control change in another. The recent influence of social constructionism and narrative approaches emphasizes meanings and story construction.

In keeping with the tone of this book, rather than debate the merits of each theory, I address change within a broader perspective. Specifically, I view the family as a system moving through its life cycle while adapting to both internal and external demands. To maintain its integrity, the family must balance forces for stability (by supporting existing structures) and forces for change (by evolving new structures). Accordingly, the therapist works within the framework of the family's existing structures to facilitate the evolution of new patterns to help them adapt better to current needs.

Dance of Change: Balancing Morphostasis and Morphogenesis

From a systems perspective, families seek to balance forces for change (morphogenesis) and forces for stability (morphostasis). Family patterns evolve to regulate these two forces. Morphostatic forces act to maintain the status quo and help provide family members with a sense of sameness and continuity—that is, family traditions. This continuity offers stability: Roles are clear within the family and behavior follows predictable patterns. Even in a chaotic home wracked by alcoholism, patterns are predictable: husband abuses alcohol and becomes abusive to wife and children, wife takes children to her mother's house, husband sobers up, apologizes, and promises it will never happen again; wife returns home, setting the stage for a recurrence.

For healthy adaptation, families must grow and change—that is, learn or develop new behavioral patterns—in response to the changing members' needs and environmental demands. For example, parenting practices for a 2-year-old differ from those for a 5-year-old, are different for a 10-year-old, and are different for a 15-year-old. Likewise, environmental stress—for example, a death, illness, or loss of a job—demands new responses from the family. The family, therefore, sometimes through trial and error, learns new behaviors that facilitate adaptation and reduce stress.

Although these are complementary forces, one serving to balance the other, in families experiencing difficulties, one can outweigh the other. For example, morphostatic forces can dominate to the point of stifling all growth in the family. In these families, as long as the parents are alive, a child is always a child whether the child is 5, 15, 35, or 55. The mechanisms for stability are so strong that change from accepted norms is threatening and therefore resisted. Clinically, the family perseveres with old patterns despite the need for change. Symptoms evolve in one or more family members as pressure for change mounts within the family.

In contrast, families dominated by morphogenetic forces are constantly in flux. Nothing appears stable—it is uncertain whether food will be in the refrigerator, bills will be paid, and, more tragically, parents will parent. In the extreme, this void of leadership and structure leaves the family without a solid core; they appear chaotic, disorganized, and out of control. Chronic, severe stress—alcoholism, illness, the effects of poverty—has overtaxed the family's capacity to cope. These families operate in a continual state of crisis management.

Well-functioning families, however, can also be pushed into morphogenetic override. For example, death, job loss, divorce, or separation forces rapid changes in a family, changes that increase the family's stress past manageable limits. As a stepfamily, the Martins were attempting to blend two different systems with established histories into one new unit. In the process, old family structures were being applied while new patterns were also emerging. The family, at the time of referral, was undergoing great transition, with all the accompanying stresses and strains.

In more behavioral and practical terms, morphostatic forces are manifested in the family's existing interactive patterns. These patterns have evolved over time and regulate and maintain stability. Subsequently, the family is likely to respond to new internal or external demands with more of the same preexisting patterns. Mrs. Martin was attempting to parent Cindy as she had raised her own children.

This initial response is neither good nor bad; rather, the question is how effective the response is to morphogenetic requests for change. Existing family patterns might or might not be adequate to manage new demands (birth of child, remarriage, divorce, last child beginning school, first child entering adolescence, parents' midlife issues, last child leaving home, needs of elderly grandparents, illnesses, job loss, economic misfortune). If old patterns are able to respond effectively (first-order change), the family readily manages the new demands. If the old patterns respond ineffectively, however, and new patterns (second-order change) are not generated, the disequilibrium (stress) becomes a chronic condition and a precursor to symptom formation in one or more family members.

Steinglass, Bennett, Wolin, and Reiss (1987) have identified three ways in which families fail to maintain an adequate equilibrium between forces for stability and those for change:

1. Some families do not sense the need for change until the pressure builds past manageable limits—for example, the depressed adolescent attempts suicide.

2. Other families sense that something is wrong but mobilize either inappropriate or ineffective responses. In response to an acting-out, oppositional child, for example, the parents respond with harsh punishments, which only serve to increase the child's anger.

3. Some families have established an inappropriately narrow or wide range of corrective limits. That is, a family accepts little or no change, which inhibits growth; alternately, they have too wide a limit, which puts almost no restrictions on family members' behavior, leaving them with little sense of stability. In alcoholic families, for example, requests for change are threatening and are met with increased rigidity. Short-term stability is maintained at the expense of long-term growth and adaptability (Steinglass et al., 1987).

[handwritten margin note: 3 ways families fail to maintain equilibrium]

Regardless of how the imbalance has been created, the therapist's job is to assess and intervene to create a new equilibrium. Therapy, therefore, is the process of intervening and facilitating the production of new response patterns, which in turn help the family to accommodate to needed change. The motivation for therapy is the family's disequilibrium and its accompanying stress. As a family therapist soon discovers, however, there is a repetition-compulsion character to old, familiar patterns. The family rigidly clings to these patterns in the face of powerful demands for change.

Faced with the dilemma of accepting a family's existing patterns (so as not to threaten their remaining sense of stability), a therapist is also working with the disequilibrium to produce new patterns that will allow the family to develop more effective responses and to establish a new equilibrium point. *The dance of change, therefore, is the therapist's craft of facilitating the emergence of new interactive patterns that address morphogenetic needs without overloading the family's sense of stability (morphostatic needs).* Consequently, therapists are continually balancing a push for change with a respect for a family's capacity to change. Change, however, may be approached from two separate frameworks: problem versus solution.

Problem Versus Solution Focus

Until recently, family therapists were guided by a **problem focus**. In this approach, families present problems for the therapist to solve. The family's problems are then assessed from a systems perspective—for example, the Martins' difficulties could lie within dysfunctional enmeshed or disengaged boundaries. Based on this assessment, the therapist works to clarify existing boundaries and help create new, more functional ones. The problem-focused approach assumes that the family patterns are dysfunctional, particularly when compared with the therapist's theoretical model. Moreover, the therapist is an expert who will do something to the family.

Recent trends, however, are challenging the problem-focused approach. First, mental health practitioners find themselves in a rapidly changing health care environment. Managed care places a premium on the clinician's ability to provide effective, measurable, and brief therapy. In response, numerous books detailing "brief" treatment approaches have appeared. Second, the influence of social constructionism is seen in the paradigm shift away from the model of the expert therapist who does something to a family to one in which the therapist and family members are collaborators in the change process. Finally, along with social constructionism, multiculturalism highlights the diversity of family functioning. What is normal in one ethnic group can be abnormal in another. Thus, families are seen as unique cultural, historical entities that function in a variety of ways and do not easily fit within a specific theoretical model.

Psychotherapy that has a **solution focus** addresses the need for brief treatment techniques, highlights the collaboration between the therapist and family members, and works with the family's strengths. The Martin family, for example, is exhibiting any number of problems: Mrs. Martin is too controlling; Mr. Martin is too passive; Cindy is "out-of-control"; poor boundaries exist. With a solution-focused approach, the Martins are seen as two families with unique and distinct histories attempting to merge and create a new blended family. During this transformation, the family will need to mobilize all its available strengths. The Martins, therefore, are not a problem-filled system but a stepfamily seeking solutions to their challenges.

A solution-focused approach does not ask the family members, "What's wrong?" and "Why?" but "What is your request?" or "What do you want?" (Friedman & Fanger, 1991). Likewise, the therapist is not an expert doing something to the family but a partner or catalyst in the treatment process. This therapeutic role places a premium on learning the clients' assumptions and language (Fanger, 1993). The present and future are the focus instead of the present and past. The therapist helps the family to identify its own solutions (Norum, 2000).

The origins of brief, solution-focused psychotherapy are seen in the early work of Watzlawick, Weakland, and Fisch (1974) and formalized into brief therapy principles by Fisch, Weakland, and Segal (1982). Their basic premise is that the family's defined problem is not the problem but that the attempted solutions are what have created and maintained the problem. Mrs. Martin wanted Cindy to behave like her children behaved. Cindy's behavior, however, was an outgrowth of her own childhood environment and was quite different from Robert's and Karen's experiences. Unfortunately, Mrs. Martin's restricting and correcting Cindy's behavior pushed her into more and more defensive and oppositional behavior—the very behavior Mrs. Martin was seeking to change! It was this vicious cycle that first brought them into therapy.

DeShazer (1994), a leading proponent of brief therapy approaches, warns therapists against accepting the clients' definition of the problem and in making it the focus of treatment—for example, "Let's change Cindy." Instead, DeShazer (1994) first identifies exceptions—"When is Mrs. Martin pleased with Cindy's behavior?"— and moves to "How can we make this happen more often?" Therapy, therefore, moves from reinforcing problem conversations to generating alternative solutions.

Moreover, if changing Cindy or Mrs. Martin becomes the focus of therapy, unnecessary defenses and resistances are raised. Both Cindy and Mrs. Martin would resent the implication that one or the other must change, and either one would probably push the family out of treatment.

At first glance, you probably wonder whether the distinction between problem and solution focus is mere semantics. Instead of asking what is wrong, you ask what you want. Although seemingly a subtle shift in language, it represents a significant paradigm shift. Berg and DeShazer (1993), for example, draw a distinction between problem talk and solution talk.

Problem talk is problem-saturated: It continually reinforces the family's view of their problems. Many sessions could be conducted exploring the Martin family's problems. Why is the relationship between Mrs. Martin and Cindy so conflicted? What intrapsychic problems is Cindy manifesting? What is the quality of the marital relationship? Berg and DeShazer (1993) argue that such conversations concretize the family's difficulties even more—"One cannot solve the problem with the same kind of thinking that has created the problem" (Berg & DeShazer, 1993, p. 9).

Solution talk, on the other hand, is talking outside the problems. Just as continually talking about the "unsolvable" problems creates impasses in therapy, talking about solutions creates a new reality. The family members are no longer being victimized by problems but are seeking solutions.

Similar to solution talk, narrative therapy would argue that the family members' problems are based in their problem-based language or narrative. For example, family members agree on the facts of a situation: Cindy and Mrs. Martin frequently disagree. However, the "problem" is embedded in the meaning of these facts. For Cindy, her stepmother is a control freak. For Mrs. Martin, Cindy is disrespectful. As the therapist guides the family members in telling and retelling their narratives, change occurs in ways that allow new understanding and meaning to emerge (Hawley & DeHaan, 1996). The behaviors and solutions flow from these new understandings and meanings.

To summarize, brief, solution-focused therapy emphasizes these actions (Friedman & Fanger, 1991):

1. Focusing on what works rather than on what doesn't work.
2. Involving the family members as active participants in solution development.
3. Defining goals in concrete, solvable terms, not as abstractions, such as changing a "bad" attitude or improving communication.
4. Focusing on small changes in behavior so that the family can experience initial therapeutic success.
5. Developing the family members' resources and strengths.
6. Normalizing presenting complaints by placing them within a developmental perspective.
7. Employing language of change and possibility—"When these conflicts stop, what type of relationship do you wish to have?"

Summary

The dance of change involves the balancing of morphogenetic and morphostatic forces. The family is confronted with challenges that require new solutions. Still, change threatens the family's fundamental patterns and views of the world. Too much change throws the family into chaos; too little change inhibits their ability to adapt to internal or external stressors. The therapist works with both these forces by building on the family's strengths (existing patterns) to create new responses.

The paths to change depend on the theoretical model that is used. Problems might be identified and eliminated. In this process, the therapist is an expert exploring the roots of the problems and replacing dysfunctional interactions with more functional patterns. Or the therapist avoids "problem" talk and focuses on possibilities or solutions. Or the therapist collaborates in conversation with the family members to understand their views or narratives of their difficulties while rewriting these stories. The following chapter offers a variety of change techniques, including problem-focused, solution-focused, and narrative models.

Regardless of the theoretical model, during the course of therapy, you will undoubtedly run into obstacles to change—morphostatic forces attempting to maintain the status quo in the face of threatening change or morphogenic forces overwhelming the family. Regardless of the cause, the result is an impasse in treatment. When this occurs, the therapeutic alliance breaks down and the family members resist therapy. Successful treatment is based on recognizing and working with these resistances.

Resistance

With its roots in the psychoanalytic tradition, **resistance** is distinguished from a lack of motivation for change or a lack of interest in forming a relationship and instead is defined as an obstruction that evolves in the process of therapy (Mishne, 1986). From a traditional psychoanalytic perspective, clients will unconsciously resist therapeutic interventions because of the implied threat that these interventions will make unconscious material conscious. Consequently, the process of "working through" resistance and uncovering the unconscious material remains central to psychoanalytically oriented therapies (Anderson & Stewart, 1983).

At the other end of the spectrum are experiential family therapists who reject the idea of resistance and speak instead of a family's differential motivation for change or the absence of desperation (Whitaker & Keith, 1981). In a similar vein, DeShazer (1982) argues that resistance is only a metaphor for describing certain regularities of phenomena and that the concept of resistance places a boundary between the therapist and family, thus splitting the therapeutic system into imaginary oppositions and hampering therapeutic initiatives.

Regardless of one's theoretical position, family therapy is not a simple matter of telling family members what they need to do to alleviate their problem. (If it were this simple, family therapy books would be very thin indeed!) Rather, changing ingrained family patterns is often a difficult dance of two steps forward and one step back. For lack of a better term, resistance has been used as a global concept to identify the road blocks and impasses that frequently occur in therapy. As Anderson and Stewart (1983) point out in their classic work, "There appears to be almost universal recognition that resistance exists, if not universal agreement about what to call it, what it is, and what responsibility a therapist has for doing something about it" (p. 12).

Experiential family therapists argue that what has been defined as resistance is really the family members' convictions that their present solution is the best available and their insistence on continuing their patterns (Whitaker & Keith, 1981). To counter this persistence of patterns, each family member is encouraged to change, impelled by his or her own initiative (Whitaker & Keith, 1981). Along the same lines, extended family systems therapists, rather than working with strongly resistant family members, might work with the most motivated member in the belief that as one family member begins to differentiate, this change will begin to ripple through the family (Bowen, 1978).

Likewise, structural family therapists do not address resistance per se but emphasize the homeostatic rules that govern the way family members interrelate and thus maintain dysfunctional patterns. In contrast, the concept of resistance is at the heart of a strategic family therapist's approach: Families come to treatment because they are at an impasse in their attempts to resolve their problems and need therapeutic intervention precisely because they are resistant to change.

In their attempt to incorporate such diverse viewpoints, Anderson and Stewart (1983) operationally define resistance as all those aspects of the therapeutic system (therapist, family members, organizations) that interact to prevent the therapeutic system (therapist + family) from achieving the family's goals for therapy. From their perspective, families cling to familiar behavior patterns out of habits and fears that limit their perception of the alternatives open to them. Hence, families come to therapy in response to changes that they do not like or to which they have not adjusted, and they are asking the therapist to restore the earlier stability.

From another perspective, Will (1983) argues that symptoms are functional and arise when a family's coping mechanisms have been unable to deal effectively with current demands. Thus, even though symptoms are not completely effective in coping with the demands, they are a better solution than the earlier state of anxiety. Consequently, the therapeutic attempts to challenge the dysfunctional solutions (symptoms) are resisted because of the risk that the original problem and accompanying anxiety will reemerge.

For example, the triangle involving Donna Martin, Peter Martin, and Susan Waters was highly charged. Peter and Susan's bitter divorce still lingered in the air years later. Donna resented Susan's continuing requests of Peter and believed Susan undercut her discipline efforts with Cindy. Donna wanted Peter to be more assertive with Susan by drawing firmer boundaries. Peter wanted to avoid conflict. Susan felt that Peter had gotten the better settlement in the divorce and that his recent marriage was an indication of that fact.

Although this triangle was highly charged, it was covert. On the surface, all three adults presented themselves as reasonable people who had been wronged. What would spark anger, however, was Cindy's acting-out behavior. Cindy served as a lightning rod for the tension in the system. All three adults could readily argue over who should do what to change Cindy. Of course, Cindy had her own agenda, but for the adults, her behavior was an opportunity to express anger at one another. Intuitively sensing this, Cindy would play one end against the other by complaining to her mother about Donna, complaining to her father about her mother, and complaining to Donna about Susan.

Therapeutically, freeing Cindy from her role in the adult conflict would entail making the covert adult issues overt. This opening up had been studiously avoided by Donna, Peter, and Susan. It was easier for them to argue about Cindy than to confront their own issues. Consequently, resistance is expected when the therapist attempts to explore the adult triangle. The adults would be happy to discuss Cindy, but would be very guarded in discussing their own interpersonal relationships; the therapist's questions would be probing into a tender area. Opening up this area for discussion could be too risky for the family, and the therapist's probes would be met with defensiveness.

Will (1983) further points out that anxiety is the motivation for a family seeking therapy and that the anxiety exists because the stress generated by the symptomatic behavior or its consequences becomes greater than the anxiety the symptomatic behavior serves to avoid. In the Martin case, Cindy's acting-out behavior and the conflicts between Mrs. Martin and Cindy raised the family's anxiety and tipped the scale toward seeking therapy; the conflicts directly threatened the family's existence. Although confronting the tension in the adult triangle might also threaten the family, the stepdaughter-stepmother conflicts were a more immediate and tangible threat.

As part of the therapeutic alliance, the therapist can be a source of resistance to change. Blinded by his or her view of what the family needs to do, the therapist might confront and threaten the family's stability. A common way a therapist increases resistance to change is by trying to teach the family the therapist's model. The behavioral therapist explains reinforcement patterns to the family. The Bowenian therapist explains differentiation and the function of triangles in the family. The structural family therapist identifies the inappropriate boundaries in the family. These interventions in and of themselves can be quite therapeutic if the family understands and accepts the therapist's observations. In these situations, both the family and therapist are "on the same wavelength," and therapy progresses rapidly.

The reverse, however, is where problems arise. The therapist shares a conceptual view of the family but the family resists the viewpoint. The family might not understand what the therapist is saying, or the therapist's explanation of the problem could be too threatening for the family, or what he or she proposes raises too much anxiety in the family. Regardless of the reasons, the family resists or balks; in doing so, it sends a message or information to the therapist.

From this perspective, resistance is information sent to the therapist that the family's fragile morphostatic/morphogenetic equilibrium is being further overwhelmed. The message communicates that the new interpretations offered or new behaviors the therapist is seeking are more than the family is capable of integrating at this time. The family might be able to "hear" the information or perform the task at a later time, but not now!

Moreover, viewing resistance as information reduces its provocative nature (Worden, 1991). Resistance is not a threat to therapeutic progress but rather an intricate part of it. It is the family members' way of saying that they are being overloaded; therefore, it is a vital communication to the observant therapist. When seen as information, resistance does not have to be confronted or worked through but understood and responded to accordingly:

- What is the message the family is trying to send me?
- Am I pushing too much?
- Is the family as a whole overloaded, or only one of the members?

- Is the therapeutic relationship too weak to broach this topic at this time?
- Is the family's motivation too low to try the proposed behaviors?

Deciphering the Message

Deciphering the family's resistance message leads the therapist to several hypotheses. First, he or she is probing into an area that is highly threatening to the family. For example, if the Martins' therapist insisted that the problem was not Cindy's but was really Peter and Donna's marital relationship, the idea would be more than the parents could assimilate, not to mention the anxiety it would raise.

A second possibility is that the family does not understand the therapist's direction. This is a common occurrence in the early stages of therapy, when the family is confused about the therapist's reasons for wanting all the members to attend: "We came here because of Cindy's behavior. Why do all the family members have to attend?"

A third hypothesis is that the therapist is asking the family members to perform behaviors they do not have in their repertoire at the time. If Mr. Martin was asked to be assertive and firm with Cindy, his reluctance to do so might be resistance (fear?), but it might also be because he does not know how.

A final possibility is that the family members have not felt understood. While they have been busy trying to explain their problem to the therapist, the therapist has been busy explaining a theoretical model to the family. Consequently, the family members resist moving forward because they do not believe they have been understood or acknowledged in the first place.

Perhaps by now you have added a fifth or sixth hypothesis to the list. Regardless of the interpretation, however, the therapist first identifies resistance patterns and then responds to them in ways that facilitate therapeutic goals. To aid in this process, the next section returns to the Martin family and highlights resistances encountered in the middle phase of treatment. Following the case presentation, several examples of frequent resistance patterns are discussed in the Treatment Notes section.

Case Presentation

To summarize the resistance issues faced in the middle phase of treatment, this section outlines the dance of change that occurred as the Martins' therapist worked through the intervention priorities established in the initial phase of treatment (see the final section of Chapter 4). Each priority is briefly summarized, and the therapist's responses are highlighted.

1. Triangle Involving Cindy, Her Father, and Her Stepmother

In seeking treatment, Mr. and Mrs. Martin hoped the therapist would be able to change Cindy. Consequently, they consistently presented evidence both in and outside of the sessions that she needed to be changed. For example, in the initial sessions, Cindy would pull her chair into a corner, slouch, and look bored. Occasionally she would rise out of her passive-aggressive stance and shout, "That's not true" or "Liar" in response to a comment someone else made. Both these responses had the power to draw attention to her and disrupt whatever was occurring in the session.

Outside the sessions, Cindy continued to violate any limits her stepmother tried to set. More often than not, following a weekend, the session would begin with Mr. or Mrs. Martin complaining about what Cindy had done or not done. The sessions began to mirror the family's home life, which was dominated by Cindy's behavior. The therapist's attempts to explore the triangle were continually short-circuited as Cindy demanded attention.

If this pattern continued, the therapy sessions would merely repeat the family patterns, with the therapist serving as one more adult trying to control Cindy. She knew how to make the veins stand out in adults' necks and would be fully capable of countering the therapist's attempts to control her. Moreover, other issues—the marital relationship, attempts to form a stepfamily, relationships with Cindy's mother and extended family—would never have a chance to come up. Thus, as a resistance, her hostile, passive-aggressive, and acting-out behavior would deflect all other issues. For therapy to progress, her behavior demanded a therapeutic response.

In such a situation, a therapist is walking a fine line between addressing an adolescent's hostility or passive-aggressiveness and being sidetracked by it. A key, therefore, is not to pursue the obvious. For example, it was not the therapist's job to draw Cindy out or reduce her hostility but rather to change family patterns. Consequently, for him to go head to head with Cindy would have been akin to flying into the teeth of the family's resistance to change. To avoid being triangled into the basic patterns, several options existed for the therapist:

> **Therapist** (in response to Cindy's passive-aggressive, silent withdrawal): Well, Cindy, something must have happened recently for you to withdraw like this. I assume you must be angry or hurt by something but can't talk about it right now. I would love to hear what it is, but whether you tell me or not is your choice, and I can't make you talk. Unfortunately, you leave me no choice but to talk about you with your parents.

In this response, the therapist is acknowledging Cindy's behavior, speculating on the reasons for it, and inviting her to participate, but he is also clearly communicating that the session would proceed and Cindy would not be the center of it.

With Cindy, this type of reaction from the therapist typically challenged her. She could not just sit back and have people talk about her. More often than not, she would pick her spot and shout "Liar!" to counter what another family member had said. Again, this would serve to disrupt the session and refocus the attention on her.

> **Therapist** (following one of Cindy's angry interruptions): Cindy, in this office, you don't yell, and in particular, you don't yell "Liar!" If you have something to say, I would love to hear it. In fact, I think you have a lot of opinions of what's going on here, but I can't make you say them. When you want to say them, let me know.

Here, the therapist was drawing a therapeutic boundary and addressing Cindy's hostility. In drawing the boundary, the therapist was stating what was and was not permitted in the sessions. In addition, he was modeling firm behavior for the parents.

This therapeutic boundary serves as a prototype for future exchanges with Cindy.

The therapist reinforces what is and is not permitted in the therapy sessions. Family members, and Cindy in particular, are allowed to disagree without provoking and to state opinions without insulting others. That said, if Cindy continues to interrupt angrily, the therapist directly confronts her:

> **Therapist:** Cindy, now I know you have something to say because you are clearly objecting to something. I think the problem is you do not have any other way to say it, or you may not believe you will be heard anyway. So I'll tell you what: Explain to me what you are reacting to and what you want to say.

At this point, the therapist engages Cindy in a dialogue and gives her ample opportunity to express her opinions directly. In doing so, the therapist serves as a temporary communication bridge between Cindy and the rest of the family members.

Acting-out behavior between sessions typically sets the agenda for the next session and serves to derail the focus of the therapy. In these situations, the challenge for the therapist is to address the behavior but also to maintain the therapeutic focus. Cindy, for example, would chronically fail to follow rules established by her stepmother, which would lead to a series of arguments. By the next session, if a phone call had not already been made, the family members were eager to discuss the event:

> **Therapist** (following a heated exchange to begin the session): Cindy, I guess you decided to test your parents again. What did you discover?

With this comment, the therapist is placing Cindy's behavior in a therapeutic context: She was testing the capacity of her parents to draw a firm boundary.

> **Therapist:** I know this weekend must have been upsetting for both of you (the parents) and that it feels like nothing is getting better. But this was no different from what Cindy has done previously. So how did you handle it differently this time? What were your options?

The therapist is acknowledging the parents' frustration but also avoiding being caught up in the emotionality of the event. Instead, the blow-up is used as a learning experience for the parents. The therapeutic message to the parents was clear and consistent: You have been here before, there is nothing new, so how do you want to handle it, what are your choices? Thus, rather than be derailed, the therapist uses the acting-out to further the therapeutic goals.

2. Triangle of Cindy and Her Parents

It was clear in the early phase of treatment that the relationship between Mr. Martin and his ex-wife (Cindy's mother) was a key to understanding Cindy's behavior. There was a sense that their divorce had been a bitter one and that Cindy, as the only child, had been triangled into her parents' lingering conflict. Each parent would ask Cindy questions about the other parent, and each parent would complain about the other to Cindy. The hardest struggles occurred over finances. In a typical scenario, Cindy requested money for something; her mother told her to ask her father because he had all the money; her father told Cindy that he gave her mother ample child support and that she was a poor money manager; and Cindy went back and forth between both parents while becoming angrier and angrier.

Furthermore, the three of them for years had played a game of Where Will Cindy Live'? In a heated argument, Cindy's mother would yell, "Well, if you don't like it here, then move in with your father." Not to be outdone, Cindy would likewise threaten her mother, "I can't stand living with you; I want to live with Dad." Unfortunately, until she came to live permanently with her father, she bounced back and forth between the two households. As soon as conflicts arose at one household, she spent the night or weekend at the other.

Therapeutically, no matter how much Peter and Susan changed, if Cindy was continually trapped in the triangle with her parents or could play one household off against the other, few therapeutic gains would be made. Thus, the relationship between Mr. Martin and his ex-wife had to be addressed. Because of the resentment and anxiety involved, however, he was resistant to involving Cindy's mother.

> **Therapist:** In trying to understand Cindy's actions, it's clear to me that her mother plays a central role. Because of this, I'd like to involve her in our therapy sessions. How to do this, I am not sure, and I need your guidance.

> **Mr. Martin:** Wait a minute! We're here because of Cindy and what's happening in our family. I don't see any reason to involve Cindy's mother.

Here, the therapist is at a crucial point. Mr. Martin was sending a clear message that his ex-wife was a threatening issue and that he did not welcome her involvement. Consequently, the therapist could respect the resistance and back off the issue. This would be a conservative position. In this case, the therapist saw Cindy's mother's involvement as crucial for change; therefore, he confronted the resistance:

> **Therapist:** I am sorry. I didn't realize involving Cindy's mother would pose a problem. Maybe I don't fully understand the relationships among Cindy, her mother, and you. Would you tell me some of the history of your feelings?

Rather than backing off the issue or insisting on Mr. Martin's ex-wife's involvement and raising the family's anxiety level, the therapist begins to work through the past to the present. History is sometimes less threatening to talk about than the present, and in focusing on the past, Mr. Martin started to reveal his feelings.

To summarize briefly, Mr. Martin spoke of his continuing frustration in dealing with his ex-wife, particularly when it involved Cindy. The therapist asked him to speculate on how this conflict had affected Cindy. Building on Mr. Martin's concern, the therapist gave his own interpretation of the triangular relationships and persistently emphasized the importance of involving everyone. Having been reassured that the therapist would be in charge of such sessions and that the past would not be dragged up, Mr. Martin agreed to involve Cindy's mother.

3. Marital Relationship

At the time of referral, both Mr. and Mrs. Martin were disillusioned and frustrated in their attempts to create a stepfamily. Financial concerns and the demands of children and extended family had begun to take their toll on the marriage. However, the marital issues remained dormant as the problems with Cindy superseded other concerns. More to the point, the conflicts with Cindy served as an escape valve for the family pressures.

After several sessions, the marital tension was clearly evident. Mr. and Mrs. Martin were quick to interrupt and contradict one another. If the tension became too pointed between them, however, Mrs. Martin would bring up a problem with Cindy, or Mr. Martin would withdraw. Each pattern diffused the marital tension but at the cost of not developing more effective problem-solving styles. They loved one another and desperately wanted the marriage and stepfamily to be successful. Consequently, they feared conflict between them and preferred to avoid it rather than threaten the marriage. Over time, unfortunately, more and more hurt was being swept under the carpet.

The therapeutic question, therefore, was how to address the marital issues without raising anxiety past manageable limits and provoking strong resistance. This was accomplished by exploring the differences between the Martins in parenting Cindy and tying these differences into the marital relationship. After relating another crisis with Cindy, for example, the therapist asked them the following questions:

"You each seem to react to Cindy in different ways. What are some of these differences?"

"Are these differences reflected in parenting Robert and Karen?"

"Are these differences evident in the ways you deal with each other?"

"What has surprised each of you about the other's style of managing problems?"

"What are some problems that have developed between the two of you because of the differences in your styles?"

Notice the flow of these questions. They begin by focusing on the presenting problem and move to the marital relationship. The emphasis is on the differences in style and not on who is right and who is wrong.

4. Influence of the Extended Family

Theoretical models differ on the importance of extended family issues. For instance, Bowen adherents would extensively employ the genogram to understand, depict, and work through issues such as those influencing family dynamics. But because the Martins were in a state of crisis at the time of referral and help was needed in building the new stepfamily, pushing extended family issues would probably have provoked unnecessary resistance. They wanted immediate help with Cindy, and extended family issues were far from their concern. Thus, exploring extended family issues was low on the list of intervention priorities.

Still, the therapist was not blind to these issues and used current events to explore the extended family's influence:

Therapist: Mr. Martin, when we were constructing the genogram, you mentioned that Cindy reminded you of your brother. Would you tell me a little about him so that I can understand Cindy better?

Therapist: Mrs. Martin, you said you raised Robert and Karen just as you had been reared and that was what made Cindy's behavior so difficult for you. Would you tell me how you were reared and how your parents influence you today?

Rather than systematically exploring the extended family issues, the therapist was probing these issues as they spontaneously occurred in the session. In doing so, he was responding to the family's initiative and pursuing the issue until he met with resistance. For example, Mr. Martin readily talked about his brother and his concern that Cindy might have many of Sean's personality traits. However, when the therapist asked him the state of the relationship now between him and his brother, Mr. Martin became defensive:

> **Mr. Martin:** Is this (the discussion of Sean) really relevant to our problems with Cindy?

> **Therapist:** Perhaps and perhaps not; I am honestly not sure. But if it's making you uncomfortable, please tell me because we can talk about other things.

In this exchange, the therapist honestly answered the question and also communicated that this might be a relevant topic but that he respects Mr. Martin's discomfort.

Although it did not occur with the Martins, with some families, after the initial complaint has been addressed and their anxiety has been reduced, extended family issues rapidly emerge to broaden the focus of therapy. Typically, the family members, with the therapist's guidance, begin to see and make their own connections between current and extended family issues. Again, the key is that both the therapist and the family logically move in this direction.

Treatment Notes

Frequent Resistance Patterns

Resistances That Challenge the Therapist's Credibility

Venturing into the family therapy waters is unsettling for a therapist in and of itself: "What am I doing? What am I looking for? Have I missed anything?" A beginning therapist is frequently more concerned with managing his or her own anxiety and getting through the session than anything else. Add in a family that is ambivalent and perhaps hostile about being there in the first place, and resistance will quickly arise. In these situations, particularly in the engagement phase, early challenges test the therapist's mettle.

Sometimes, the family seems to sense the novice therapist's anxiety, asking such questions as these:

"How long have you been doing this?"

"What does your degree mean?"

"Are you married?"

"Do you have children?"

On the surface, and in all fairness, family members may be merely seeking information with these questions. On the other hand, if the inquiries are persistently pursued—"I am afraid you would not understand because you do not have children"—and stand as an impediment to therapeutic progression, they can be characterized as the first signs of resistance.

In these situations, the resistance message is very clear: "We are ambivalent about beginning therapy and wish to first test the waters." The questions, furthermore, serve the purpose of deflecting the therapist's focus from the family and permitting the family to take the measure of the therapist: "Will the therapist be defensive? Will the therapist be straightforward? Will the therapist answer our questions?"

It is unreasonable to expect a new family therapist to overflow with confidence. That will come with time. In fact, as a therapist seasons, the types of questions mentioned earlier will rarely be asked. In the meantime, however, these challenges to the therapist's credibility can be unsettling. More specifically, the challenges that create the most anxiety are those that the therapist has already entertained: "How can I counsel someone 20 years older than I? How can I discuss marital problems when I am not married (or, worse yet, divorced)? How can I advise parents when I don't have children of my own?"

The following list outlines a series of responses to these and similar challenges to the therapist's credibility:

1. *Answer directly.* When a therapist gives a simple, straightforward answer and avoids reading more into a question than is intended, he or she begins to establish a working relationship with the family. In this simple act, the therapist is communicating directness and honesty in dealing with the family. Frequently, this is a more important communication than the answer. How the therapist handles the challenge speaks volumes to the family.

2. *Avoid defensiveness.* Immediate defensive comments (that avoid an answer)— "Why do you ask that question?"—only increase the family's defensiveness.

3. *Question only after answering.* After answering the family's questions, the therapist is then in a reciprocal position to ask the family questions: "You asked me several questions about my background. That information must be important to you. Could you tell me why?" Again, the answer to these questions is more often than not unimportant compared with the process of the exchange. The family is ambivalent (fearful) about entering therapy and needs to test the therapist. Their resistance is evidence of their uncertainty. By testing the waters, they are seeking reassurance that they will be dealt with fairly and that therapy will be a safe environment.

Equally important, in the reciprocal exchange of questions, the therapist begins to establish therapeutic norms: "I will be direct and honest with all of you, and I expect the same in return."

4. *Be aware of your own vulnerabilities.* All therapists have vulnerabilities and doubts about their ability to be effective. Consequently, recognizing these goes a long way toward addressing them honestly in therapy sessions. Rather than hoping not to be challenged by the family, for example, the therapist should expect the challenge. Knowing how to respond to these challenges will help to eliminate the anxiety. When a therapist is tentative, families have an amazing ability to sense this anxiety and move right toward it. Conversely, when the therapist is fully and comfortably prepared to answer questions, his or her anxiety is decreased and, surprisingly, the families don't even ask questions.

Resistances Co-Opting the Therapist

A therapist's desire to help can be an Achilles' heel. Sometimes the therapist becomes enmeshed with the family system and loses sight of the overall goals. Worse yet, in

Responses when therapist credibility is challenged.

this entanglement, the therapist becomes part of the resistance. Two examples of this are the triangulation of the therapist and a family's pseudocompliance.

As mentioned in Chapter 2, triangulation occurs when the stress between two people becomes so great that a third party is needed to siphon off the unmanageable conflict. The third party is a detour from the conflict; for example, parents argue over their child's behavior instead of addressing their marital conflict. In other cases, the third person forms a coalition with one party against the other.

In the process of therapy, both these patterns invite the therapist into the system. For example, Mr. and Mrs. Martin can each turn to the therapist and argue their view of what needs to be done with Cindy. In this situation, the therapist is invited to choose a side or to negotiate their differences. Studiously avoiding choosing a side, the therapist begins to negotiate.

Unfortunately, once on the negotiation path, the therapist is likely to be triangled into the system and unknowingly support the dysfunctional status quo. Mr. and Mrs. Martin, for example, avoided one on one conversations. Their communication always involved talking about or going through a third person: Cindy. When the negotiation path is chosen, the therapist replaces Cindy and assumes her point in the triangle.

In the short run, by being Cindy's replacement, the therapist relieves the pressure on her and, predictably, Cindy's behavior will begin to improve. As an initial intervention, this is very sound. However, if the therapist persists in being the mediator between Mr. and Mrs. Martin and not fostering their ability to communicate directly, the family's basic patterns are maintained: The parents do not learn how to deal with each other constructively. Worse yet, Cindy's behavioral change will persist only as long as the therapist is involved with the parents. If therapy terminates at this point, Cindy will be reenlisted into the parental triangle.

A more insidious form of triangulation involves seducing the therapist into a coalition. For example, depending on the therapist's predilections, more empathy could exist for one parent than for the other. Mr. Martin, for instance, could be seen as a caring husband and father who is trying to balance the demands of his daughter and his wife. Consequently, the therapist could begin to agree with Mr. Martin's position and attempt to seek Mrs. Martin's compliance with her husband's strategy for dealing with Cindy.

On the other hand, Mrs. Martin could be seen as a woman stuck in the impossible situation of trying to parent a new stepdaughter without the support of her husband. Here, the therapist might seek to persuade Mr. Martin to support his wife.

Finally, Cindy could be seen as the victim of the adults' conflicts. The therapist might defend or excuse her behavior and subtly put the blame on the parents.

As these examples show, once the therapist is triangled into the conflicts, the basic system has not changed and new patterns have not emerged. Instead, the therapist has become an additional player in the family's preexisting drama. As a result, the therapist becomes part of the resistance to change.

The second co-opting resistance is a family's pseudocompliance. Pseudocompliance is an even more difficult resistance to detect because it occurs to the therapist only after a period of time has elapsed. Pseudocompliance is an illusion that the family members are cooperative and engaged in the therapeutic process. The members come to the sessions regularly and on time. They politely nod in agreement with the therapist's observations or listen attentively. The therapist, in turn, looks forward to meeting with the family because of the comfort level that has been established.

In some cases, the family is flattering—"What you said last session was very helpful"—further confirming the therapist's choice of the profession. The parents, in particular, are sincere and pleasant.

What begins to dawn on the therapist, however, is the family's passivity. As the therapist has become more involved in solving the family's problems, the family has become less active. Suggestions by the therapist are met with the family members' commenting, "Well, we tried what you suggested, but it did not work." Rather than confronting such statements as one would do with clear, noncompliant resistance (described below), the therapist is led by the family's basic cooperativeness to increase his or her activity.

In these cases, a therapist has inadvertently assumed the major responsibility for change. As a result, the family's basic patterns are not confronted or challenged. The therapist has acted on the assumption that this is a pleasant, nice, cooperative family who will follow directions. The family colludes by encouraging the therapist in these efforts. Again, the therapist has become part of the resistance to change.

With co-opting resistances, therapy does not progress and appears at an impasse. The lack of progress is a signal for the therapist to take a step back and reevaluate:

1. *Reevaluate the definition of the problem.* Sometimes the problem the family presents is unsolvable. For example, parents who want their teenage son to "have a better attitude" about his future are presenting an impossible goal because it is couched in terms of subjective judgment: What is a good and bad attitude? Also, the goal of alleviating a bad attitude leaves the therapy sessions open to point/counterpoint discussions: "You have a bad attitude." "No, I don't!" "Yes, you do!" In such debates, family members inevitably ask the therapist to choose a side.

2. *Ask yourself what makes working with this family so comfortable or frustrating.* As mentioned, co-opting resistances seduce the therapist into playing a role in the family drama, which enhances the drama instead of rewriting it. Ironically, many times that therapy sessions progress smoothly, particularly from the beginning of treatment, the therapist is playing a role that supports the existing patterns. For example, if the Martins' therapist agreed to "cure" Cindy, the parents would have comfortably sat back and waited for this to happen. Existing patterns would not have been challenged, and the parents would have waited to see what the therapist would do. Of course, without a change in the existing patterns, Cindy's behavior is highly unlikely to improve on any lasting basis. Consequently, the initial sessions would go smoothly until a vague dissatisfaction would begin to settle over treatment because Cindy would continue to act out.

3. *Reassess goals with the family.* A straightforward response to a treatment impasse is to open the issue up for discussion:

> "I don't know about anybody else in the room, but I have a funny feeling we are not getting anywhere. Does anyone else think that?"
>
> "I would like to check out with you how far we've come and where we should go from here."
>
> "Maybe I am missing something here. Do other people have some ideas?"
>
> "Boy, this is really frustrating, isn't it? I am open to some ideas."

Again, in emphasizing the importance of process, the answer to these questions is not nearly as important as the process in which they are answered: Do members participate in the discussion? Will they assume responsibility for change? Is a cooperative effort being established between the therapist and family (some indication of the success of the engagement process)? Moreover, by inviting the family members to participate in identifying the impasse and devising the solution, new patterns will be established within the therapeutic alliance (therapist + family).

Resistance of Noncompliance

Between resistance that overtly challenges the therapist and the subtle resistance that co-opts the therapist is resistance of noncompliance. Noncompliant resistance brings progress to a halt. It communicates that the family members' anxiety is increasing and that it threatens to overwhelm them. As a strategy, noncompliance is the family's refusal to go any further.

As with the types of resistance discussed earlier, the kinds of noncompliant resistance range from blatantly overt to quietly covert. Although many types could be added to this list, four occur frequently: helplessness, pseudohostility, silence, and refusal to do assigned tasks.

Occurring in the beginning stages of treatment and likely to reappear throughout the sessions, *helplessness* is a plea from the family members to the therapist to save the family. This plea frequently accompanies a crisis. As such, the family moves from the collaborative effort with the therapist to a dependent position. The message is direct: "Help us! Not only are we powerless to change anything, but the pain is rapidly building. Do something!"

As a type of resistance, helplessness is very effective. The family pleads helplessness, the therapist becomes motivated by a sense of responsibility, and the tenor of therapy shifts so that the therapist is doing all the work.

At these points, a therapist becomes increasingly direct with the family, offering advice or giving the family assigned tasks. For their part, the family members eagerly absorb the therapist's suggestions but return for the next session in much the same condition, whereupon the therapist offers more suggestions that, unfortunately, result in more of the same helplessness.

A variation of this theme is the issue of *pseudohostility*. Pseudohostility is the family's capacity to argue over trivial events while avoiding the underlying issues. The "hostility" may be viewed as the family's fear of intimacy; that is, the arguing is heightened when the family members move emotionally closer together. In these situations, the arguing is a smoke screen that is more easily dealt with than the basic conflicts.

Pseudohostility is evidenced when family fights are evoked with the least provocation. Simply choosing seats in the therapist's office results in conflict as two of the children both go for the same chair, wedging themselves between the arms. At this point, the children whine, "Mom, I had this seat first." In turn, the parents become angry and intervene by shaking fingers at each child, "You, sit in this chair now before you really catch it!"

Likewise, pseudohostility is readily apparent with recalcitrant adolescents who beg for confrontations. In these cases, anger explodes at the drop of a hat. The parents are lamenting their frustration with their sullen son when a single comment—for example, "And we don't like the friends he hangs out with"—launches the boy into a defensive tirade.

Occurring during the therapy session, pseudohostility has the power to rivet the therapist's attention. Whatever issue was being pursued is quickly forgotten in the heat of battle. Worse yet, the arguments invite the therapist to intervene as a mediator.

For pseudohostility to be successful as a resistance, the therapist must participate equally. As petty arguments absorb more and more of the therapist's attention and he or she spends more and more time attempting to negotiate a settlement, the underlying issues will recede deeper into the background, remaining unaddressed. Unfortunately, the same patterns are played out session after session until both the family and the therapist become frustrated with the whole experience.

Equally powerful in diverting the therapist's attention and raising anxiety are silences. Silences are usually much louder to the therapist's ears than pseudohostility. At least with pseudohostility, there is something to work with; silences are akin to pulling teeth.

As a resistance, silence reflects the basic defensive maneuver of the young child or early adolescent. For a family to employ such a defensive posture, therefore, clearly indicates that the threatening material—for example, anger, hurt, pain, disappointment, fear—is just below the surface and that the family fears an eruption.

Again, for silence to be an effective resistance, the therapist must collude in the process. The family members exert tremendous pressure on the therapist by simply staring at the floor or at the therapist without speaking, and by answering questions in one word or a single sentence. For beginning therapists, in particular, any number of thoughts run through their heads: "Oh, this is really going poorly; no one is talking." "I must do something; this is a complete failure." "What should I do? What should I do?"

Again, just as with pseudohostility, in these situations the therapist is likely to become more and more energized in an attempt to have members speak. What typically occurs then is a series of dyadic conversations between the therapist and individual family members. The family interactions have ceased as the therapist works harder and harder, but to little avail.

Finally, the fourth common resistance is the *family's failure to follow the therapist's assigned task*. As discussed in the following chapter, therapeutic interventions are frequently assigned for the family to perform at home between sessions; these assignments are made to further the therapeutic goals. Even with the most thorough planning and preparation, however, the family returns for the next session with a halfhearted excuse: "Well, we tried to do what you suggested, but then our daughter got sick, and my mother came over, and the kids were off from school."

Giving the family the benefit of the doubt, the therapist assigns another homework task. If the family returns with additional excuses, however, he or she should assume that resistance is operating and take a step back to consider.

The worst thing for a therapist to do is to take the family's noncompliance with assignments personally. Once the noncompliance is personalized, the therapist has engaged the family in a power struggle: "The family needs to do this assignment, and I *will* get them to do it!" Here again, the therapist has colluded in the resistance by making the resistance the issue. In fact, one could argue that in this power struggle, the therapist has now also become resistant to change.

Much more productive for the therapist is to change his or her tack and approach the family from another direction. As a means of addressing noncompliant resistance, the following steps are offered. First, stop and evaluate what is threatening the family at this time. When resistance appears, ask yourself, "Have I been pushing a theme that the family is too uncomfortable with at this time? Has a sufficient level of trust been built up to go into this area of family conflict? Which family member is most threatened?"

Second, use judo (figuratively) to work with the resistance. As a martial art, judo uses the weight and movement of the opponent to one's advantage. So too, therapeutic judo uses resistance to enhance growth. Here are examples for dealing with the four types of noncompliant resistance:

> **Therapist** (in response to a plea of helplessness): I see what you mean; these problems seem to reappear no matter what you do. You must feel terribly defeated. I must admit this is one of the most difficult situations I have had to deal with. What do you think we should do about it?

Notice that in this brief paragraph, the therapist is accomplishing several things. First, the family reality is acknowledged—yes, this is difficult. Second, feelings are hinted at or stated—the family must feel "defeated." Third, the therapist aligns himself with the family—this is difficult for me also. And finally, the therapeutic alliance is reinforced—What will we do?

> **Therapist** (in response to a family's pseudohostility): Boy, all of you are amazing. You are some of the best fighters I've come across in a long time. How did you get so good at this?

> (Or:) How will this fight end? Is someone supposed to give up, or is someone else supposed to jump in? I was just wondering because I wanted to bring up something else.

The obvious key to these interventions is that the therapist acknowledges the argument but does not get caught up in the conflict and attempt to negotiate a settlement. Because of this, the pseudohostility is rendered ineffective in disrupting or distracting the session's focus.

> **Therapist** (in response to silences): I think we have hit a point where it is best not to say anything to one another. I respect everyone's judgment on this point so please take my silence as a sign of respect.

> (Or:) From everyone's silence, I am assuming that it is very hard for you to talk to one another. My guess is that you have a great deal to say but find the words difficult. Please know that I won't make anyone talk in these sessions and that your silence is your own choice. I believe each of you will decide when you will talk.

Again, the resistance is being acknowledged in each of these cases, but the therapist does not oppose the resistance. Instead, he gives permission for the family members to act in ways they choose and communicates that they will have the responsibility for change.

Therapist (in response to the family's uncompleted task): I guess I blew it by asking you to do that task. It was probably more than you could accomplish at this time. Please, in the future, if I come up with another idea like that, let me know.

Here the therapist accepts responsibility for the uncompleted task and subtly challenges the family—it was more than you could do. Also, the therapist invites the family members to criticize future ideas he might present; resistance is thus made much more overt. As a result of this intervention, future tasks have a much greater chance to be completed successfully because the family has been challenged and the task has been discussed.

Therapist: You know the last task I assigned was not a very good one; any objections to this one?

With this preparation, the therapist is in a win-win position. If the family members perform the task, all is well and good. If they do not, the responsibility clearly falls on their shoulders, and the agenda for the next session is set: What went wrong in trying to accomplish the task?

Summary

The dance of change involves the therapist's capacity to promote change while not overwhelming the family's morphostatic/morphogenetic balance. Families are thought to enter therapy when the disequilibrium accompanying their need for change is more than they can assimilate or accommodate to. They seek therapy to break this impasse. The therapist, in turn, relying on the tension produced by the disequilibrium as the motivation for treatment, assesses the family's existing patterns and helps them develop more effective ones.

Because change threatens the family's status quo but is required, a family enters therapy with a tenuous internal balance between forces for change and forces to maintain the existing state. As the family and therapist begin to collaborate and form a therapeutic alliance, this tenuous balance is threatened. Consequently, resistance to change may emerge within the treatment process in the interaction between the therapist and the family.

Ironically, resistance can signify that change is occurring or that the system is recognizing the pull toward change (Anderson & Stewart, 1983). This is not to say, however, that the family is completely resisting therapy; rather, it is assumed that at any given point in the treatment process, the anxiety level in response to threatening change can rise past manageable limits.

In summary, the therapeutic dance of change is the rhythmic movement between the therapist and family. From the therapist's perspective, the dance requires the ability to assess patterns and discern when to push for change, when not to push, when to challenge, when to avoid issues, and so on. The treatment process, thus, has an air of creative tension. The underlying question in the therapist's mind is two-pronged: Is the therapeutic intervention promoting more change than the family can manage at this time, or is the intervention merely supporting the status quo and resulting in no change? Successful interventions, therefore, are based on appreciating the existing family patterns and working with the tension of disequilibrium to promote growth.

Glossary

First-order change Quantitative change that is continuous but remains within the parameters of existing patterns; the structure of the system does not alter.

Problem focus A strategy for therapy that focuses on the problems or symptoms that are a consequence of dysfunctional family patterns.

Resistance Any aspect (family, therapist, situation) of the therapeutic system that interferes with the process of therapeutic change.

Second-order change Qualitative change that is discontinuous and creates new structures and patterns.

Solution focus A strategy for therapy that focuses on family members' attempts to solve their problems. Interventions focus on creating alternative solutions.

7

Change Techniques

Conceptually, the therapist intervenes in the family's interactive patterns from the beginning of the first interview or even the first telephone contact. As the therapist and family form a collaborative therapeutic alliance, new patterns are evolving from the beginning moments of treatment. This chapter, however, focuses specifically on designed interventions that the therapist can employ to further the treatment goals by requiring a response from family members. These designed interventions are referred to as **techniques**.

The field of family therapy has embraced numerous techniques, and each school of thought has evolved a series of interventions to further its defined therapeutic goals. Family therapists flock to conferences and workshops hoping to find a new technique that will work wonders with those recalcitrant families back home. Techniques are wonderful tools that enhance a therapist's skill, but they are merely that—tools. They are only as good as the person using them. They are no substitute for understanding the family: its norms, motivations, hopes, and fears.

Techniques are not ends in and of themselves, and families do not change because of them. Instead, they are effective because the therapist matches the appropriate one with the family system at a time in treatment that presents an opening for change. Thus, techniques can be used to facilitate the therapeutic process, but their effectiveness is based on the therapist's understanding of the family and the strength of the therapeutic alliance.

The techniques presented in this chapter make up a basic repertoire of interventions with which most family therapists are familiar. They are not representative of one model but instead introduce a variety of possibilities. Where applicable, the theoretical model for the technique is identified.

A number of writers have reviewed many of the techniques used by family therapists; among these are L'Abate, Ganahl, and Hansen (1986); Minuchin and Fishman (1981); Nelson and Trepper (1992); and Sherman and Fredman (1986). Whereas their books describe a variety of techniques, this one attempts to place the use of the techniques within the ebb and flow of the therapy session.

The techniques are illustrated by applying them to the Martin family's treatment goals. Although all these would not be used with the same family—that would be technique overkill!—their application to the Martin family serves an instructional purpose. Finally, in integrating the process of the Martin family's therapy with a discussion of techniques, this chapter highlights the relationship between techniques and specific treatment goals. To refresh your memory, here are the intervention priorities established for the Martin family (Chapter 5):

1. Address the dysfunctional triangular patterns among Cindy, her father, and her stepmother.
2. Clarify the relationship between Mr. Martin and his ex-wife, Susan Waters, particularly as it affects Cindy's behavior.
3. Explore interaction among the three parents (Mr. Martin, Mrs. Martin, and Cindy's mother) and the consequences for Cindy's behavior.
4. Focus on the marital relationship—specifically, how Cindy's behavior has affected the couple and what other issues generate conflict.
5. Identify the extended family's influence on the Martins—in particular, Mr. Martin's estranged relationship with his brother and Mrs. Martin's allegiance to her parents.
6. Assist the family in building on their strengths and developing a narrative that better suits a new blended family.

To bring order to these various techniques, they are classified as first- or second-order interventions. Seeking change through the family's existing patterns is the essence of first-order change. This means a family does more or less of established behaviors. For example, Peter needs to renegotiate parental boundaries involving Cindy with Susan, his ex-wife. At other times, first-order change refines existing patterns: Peter and Donna need to improve their communication skills. Sometimes, first-order change helps the family members better understand their dilemmas: Peter and Donna believed they were failing as parents because of the conflicts in the family. Helping them realize that most blended families go through similar growing pains normalizes their experience and raises their hopes for the future.

Although first-order techniques appear to be commonsense interventions, they can be quite helpful for many families. For example, from the perspective of an outsider, the therapist suggests a change in behavior that has not occurred to the family members. Or, as a result of the therapist's support and encouragement, they do more or less of their existing patterns of behavior and greatly enhance the quality of their relationships.

Many families enter therapy having already tried their own first-order interventions. Donna insisted repeatedly that Cindy clean her room, but it was still a mess. Donna bit her tongue and said nothing, and Cindy's room was still a mess. Donna asked Peter to talk to Cindy about cleaning her room; he did, and it was still a mess. Unfortunately, as each of Donna's commonsense interventions failed to obtain the desired results, her anger grew. Entering therapy, Donna looked directly at the therapist and said, "I have tried everything."

Second-order change involves not quantitative but qualitative shifts (Watzlawick et al., 1974). These techniques challenge the structure and rules governing the family. For example, Donna needed to realize that she would not be able to parent Cindy as she did her own two children. Adjusting her parenting style would be a substantial shift for Donna. Likewise, Peter and Donna needed to evolve new parenting patterns to cope with the challenges of adolescence.

In prioritizing the intervention sequence, first-order interventions are tried first. These build on existing family patterns and support the family's commonsense solutions; consequently, they meet with less resistance than second-order techniques. Because the family's basic view of the world is unchallenged, the absence of resistance speeds the therapeutic process.

For many families, however, by the time they enter therapy, they have exhausted their attempts at change. In the initial stages of therapy, these families meet each therapist's suggestion with a repetitive, "We tried that, but it did not work." Likewise, each first-order intervention attempted produces minimal or no change. It is here that second-order interventions are most applicable—when the resistance to change outweighs the need for change.

This sequential pattern of change offers an orderly progression to the levels of intervention. Following the assessment phase of treatment, first-order interventions build on and expand existing family strengths. If therapy is falling short of the established goals, second-order interventions challenge the family to change.

An underlying bias in many techniques is the influence of social constructionism and the solution-focused approach. These influences are chosen because they reflect current thinking in the field. Specifically, they represent a shift from viewing the therapist as a family expert who does something to a dysfunctional system to seeing the therapist as a collaborator in developing the family's strengths to meet continuing stressors.

First-Order Techniques

People enter therapy with a variety of motivations and a certain amount of ambivalence. Sometimes the mother has pushed, pulled, and cajoled the family into therapy. Sometimes both parents are anxious for any advice concerning their children. For a family, entering therapy is akin to being adrift in uncharted waters. They have never been there before and do not know what to expect.

The family enters therapy, however, when their pain outweighs their reservations. First-order interventions assume that the majority or at least the most powerful of the family members are motivated to make the family better. Entering therapy is a statement of their commitment. Collaborating with the family in seeking solutions, the therapist employs first-order techniques to give structure and direction to the sessions.

Existing Solutions

Before entering therapy, a family has attempted a number of solutions to their difficulties. Some have met with moderate success; some have met with limited success; and some have made things worse. Regardless of their effectiveness, these solutions guide a therapist's approach.

Sometimes a solution might have worked if only it had been attempted longer. Peter and Donna had drawn up clear consequences for Cindy's behavior: If she skipped school, she was grounded the following weekend. Unfortunately, the rule was inconsistently applied. If a special event was scheduled, Peter would let Cindy go out in hopes of bringing peace to the household. As a result, Cindy never took any of her parents' threats of grounding seriously.

Likewise, Donna's solution for dealing with Cindy's behavior was to increase her control efforts. Cindy resented Donna's assuming an authority role with her and fought back through acting out and passive-aggressive tactics. When this happened, Donna increased her control efforts and Cindy's behavior escalated.

As a first step, the family's existing solutions are identified through a series of questions:

1. What have you tried already?
2. What worked? Why?
3. What did not work? Why?

The answers to these questions guide potential interventions. For example, existing solutions might need to be supported. The consequence for Cindy's skipping school was a good idea that needed consistent follow-through.

Therapist: The consequence to skipping school seems fair to me, but you say it has not worked. What happens? Would you give me an example of the most recent event?

The therapist encourages the solution while exploring why it falls apart. Within the explanation of the failed solution is frequently the point of intervention for the therapist.

Therapist: Peter, as I understand it, you agree with Donna that Cindy needs to be grounded, but then you change your mind. Something tells me that at those times, you feel stuck in the middle. Would you tell me what goes through your mind at those moments?

Instead of criticizing Peter for his inconsistency, which Donna has already done, the therapist acknowledges Peter's inconsistency but empathizes with his position and asks for his story of the events.

At other times, the persistency of the failed solution is challenged:

Therapist (to Donna and Cindy): This feels like a tug-of-war between the two of you. Is this the only way you believe you must deal with one another?

On one level, the therapist is asking Donna to reflect on her solution, particularly its lack of success, but the therapist is also laying the groundwork for potential second-order change: Donna might need to change her parenting style with Cindy.

As a first step, exploring existing solutions reveals both the behavior patterns and the meanings behind these patterns. The patterns and meanings are guideposts for future interventions.

Psychoeducation

Another strategy that is sometimes effective with families is psychoeducation, which originated as a therapeutic approach for families with a schizophrenic member. Viewing the family as a system struggling with a chronic, genetically inherited illness, the psychoeducational model seeks to provide the information, support, structure, and sense of control that these families need when they are in crisis (Anderson, Reiss, & Hogarty, 1986). Instead of blaming the family for causing or contributing to the illness, the therapist collaborates with the family members to mobilize and maximize their strengths.

Although best articulated in work with families of which one member has schizophrenia, the basic principles apply to other families either dealing with a chronic illness or experiencing a normal developmental crisis. The Martins are an example of the latter.

First, many of the themes the Martins present are characteristic of newly blended families, particularly those with teenagers. There could be a reservoir of anger in one or more family members left from the divorce or resentment of a stepparent, resulting in the angry teenager's retort, "I don't have to listen to you! You are not my real mother!" At the very least, the blended family struggles to combine two families with distinct histories, norms, and values. They are indeed starting from scratch in establishing lines of communication, authority hierarchy, and even basic household chores.

The Martin family was also trying to adjust to two teenagers/young adults. Like any family with adolescents, the parents found their limits tested as the teenagers pushed for more freedom and the parents struggled with how to allow this freedom and still protect and guide the young people. For the Martins, these normal predictable transitions were crises. Blaming one another for the family stress, the family members created multiple scapegoats.

To free the Martins of their guilt and blame, the therapist was in a position to share information regarding normal patterns in blending families and raising adolescents. In doing so, he helped the family see that what they were experiencing was normal. Peter and Donna are not failing but instead are taking on a difficult challenge. Their hope can be rekindled when they see their present situation as a normal variation of blending two separate families with adolescents and not as a sign of looming disaster.

Besides reducing the family's resistance to therapy, psychoeducational interventions place the therapist in a collaborative position. From this position, he or she can guide the family into more productive patterns, such as reinforcing generational boundaries, strengthening the marital and parental dyad, and shaping family norms.

Communication and Negotiation Skills

As a newly blended family, the Martins had not yet developed their communication and negotiation skills. Donna and Peter, in particular, had not foreseen the difficulties they were now experiencing. They were just learning to solve problems together when the crisis with Cindy erupted. Unfortunately, communication concerning Cindy was full of hurts and misunderstandings.

The Martins' difficulties were exacerbated by their poorly developed communication skills. To encourage development of these skills, the therapist structured and monitored their process.

Structuring and Monitoring Communication

Communication is a cyclical process in which person A sends a message to B who needs to listen actively to receive the entire message. As feedback, B acknowledges receiving the message and offers his or her response. At any point in the cycle, communication may break down. For example, A sends a confusing message, or B does not fully listen to A's message and cuts short the exchange by saying, "I know what you are going to say before you say it!" or B's response has nothing to do with A's initial message.

The following techniques offer a way of structuring and monitoring family communication. This is not an inclusive listing but provides basic guidelines:

> **Therapist:** Peter, we just heard what Donna would like from you. She, however, frequently wonders if you have heard her. Would you please look at her and tell her what you just heard her say?

Asking Peter to paraphrase what he just heard ensures that the message was heard. Also, by looking at his wife, Peter increases the couple's contact and listening skills.

> **Therapist**: Donna, Peter just paraphrased what you said. Was that an accurate restatement? If you do not believe you were fully heard, please say it again.

The therapist stays on the point until a clear message is being sent and received, and feedback has been returned.

At other times, a more active stance is needed in establishing communication rules:

> **Therapist**: To improve your communication, I would like everyone to follow two simple rules: (1) Begin sentences with "I" and (2) turn every question into a statement.

Family members obsessed with blame frequently begin messages with or include the word *you* in their messages: "You don't listen to me!" "We would not be sitting here if it were not for you." Within these contexts, the word *you* is an accusation that puts the receiver on the defensive. To counterattack, the receiver typically responds with his or her own you-blaming message.

Beginning sentences with *I* forces the sender not only to send a clearer message but also to disclose something of his or her own thoughts and feelings. Initially, this rule is confusing and frustrating to the family members. They have been blaming one another for so long that the movement to I is initially resisted. As they are encouraged to persevere, they frequently remark how difficult this is to do, but also in their voices is a recognition of the destructiveness of you-messages.

Likewise, families who specialize in indirect communication conceal their thoughts and feelings in questions instead of statements. "Do you want to talk to

Cindy about last night?" can be Donna's legitimate question of Peter, but it can imply a statement, "I want you to talk to Cindy about last night," or "You'd better talk to Cindy about last night!" Sometimes the receiver knows the request or statement behind the question, but if the receiver hears it only as a question, a misunderstanding results. For example, later that night, Donna is boiling mad because Peter did not speak to Cindy. He, however, is incredulous and says, "I did not know you wanted me to speak to Cindy."

Questions from one family member to another are misleading. A question can be a request, an implied statement, or a means of testing receptivity. For example, there are multiple possible interpretations of the question, "Would you like to go to my mother's house this weekend?" Encouraging the speaker to turn the question into a statement—"I would like to go to my mother's house this weekend"—facilitates direct communication between family members.

As a further way of structuring and monitoring communication, a very effective technique is censoring interruptions. In emotionally charged exchanges, family members fail to hear and understand because they are too busy interrupting one another. Therapy sessions can also be marked by frequent interruptions, leaving the communication dominated by the family members who interrupt the most and in the loudest voices.

> **Therapist:** I don't know whether any of you have noticed, but all of you are quick to interrupt while someone else is speaking. I think these interruptions stop all of you from hearing one another. With your permission, I will block the interruptions and encourage the speaker to continue.

The therapist establishes a new norm for the therapy session: Interruptions will not be permitted. With luck, that rule will generalize to other situations—in particular, the home.

In summary, the principles discussed here are applicable to all families. Employing first-order communication interventions, the therapist (1) encourages active listening; (2) asks family members to paraphrase what they just heard; (3) requests the use of I-messages and the rephrasing of questions as statements, thus facilitating the expression of feelings and thoughts directly and succinctly; and (4) prohibits interruptions and blaming. To build on these interventions and to improve their negotiating skills, clients do homework assignments that continue the work of therapy between sessions.

Homework Assignments

Family therapy does not have to be limited to the treatment sessions. In reality, a great deal of spontaneous family therapy occurs on the family's ride to and from the therapist's office. Depending on the stage of treatment, some families begin the session long before they arrive. Consciously or unconsciously, the anticipated anxiety of the upcoming session frequently sets the family's patterns in motion. The adolescent "forgets" to come home on time, so that the family is running late. A husband and wife increase the tension between themselves on the day of their appointment.

The ride home is usually more interesting because it is marked by silence, animated conversation continuing where the session left off, or possible angry accusations and denials: "How could you say that about me in front of him?" Because of this, it can be enlightening for the therapist to ask at the next session: "At the end of our last meeting, several important things were said. I was wondering what the ride home was like."

Rather than leaving the time between therapy sessions to the family's own devices, the therapist can attempt to continue the work of therapy in the home environment. Homework assignments are very specific demands that more often than not detail precise behaviors to be performed and attempt to build skills within the family (L'Abate et al., 1986). As such, they have a strong behavioral orientation. With Donna and Peter, the therapist asks them to return home and during the week, draw up a list of household responsibilities for all the family members: doing the dishes, doing the laundry, cleaning, grocery shopping. Then they are to negotiate on their own and come up with a division of labor or bring in the list for the next session and negotiate then.

Homework assignments are effective if they are consistent with the therapeutic goals, are clearly defined to the family, and are followed up. If therapeutic goals have been established and agreed on by both the therapist and the family, homework assignments are a natural outgrowth furthering those goals; for example, Peter and Donna wanted to learn to negotiate in better ways.

Another important point in homework is clarity. Clearly defined homework assignments are more likely to be carried out. For instance, in the earlier example, if the therapist had only, seemingly in passing, asked the couple to "decide who should do what around the house," the purpose of the assignment would not have been placed within the therapeutic context. Too much would have been left to the discretion of the family—if they could negotiate successfully, they would not be in therapy in the first place—and the path to the goal would be unclear. If the therapist had not taken the time to plan the intervention thoroughly and explain it carefully to the couple, how could they be expected to take it seriously?

Finally, follow-up not only highlights strengths to build on and weaknesses to address in treatment, but also serves as the content for the next session:

> **Therapist:** In the last session, I asked the two of you to negotiate a list of responsibilities. How did it go? What was easy? What was hard?

In other words, the follow-up process serves as a diagnostic tool by identifying what the family can and cannot do and underlines the areas for future interventions.

For example, if Donna and Peter successfully negotiated a list of household responsibilities, they could next be asked to negotiate the number and time of visits (boundaries) with their extended families. In contrast, if the negotiation was a complete failure and broke down into an argument, the point of breakdown becomes the focus of therapy.

Historical Interventions

Historical interventions address the past and, in particular, family-of-origin issues. Certainly, of all the family therapy approaches, Bowen's Family Systems Model best captures the richness of the influential extended family system (Bowen, 1976, 1978;

Kerr & Bowen, 1988). (For a more personal account of Murray Bowen's life and theory, see Wylie, 1991.)

It would be a disservice to briefly summarize Bowen's theory and its implications for the process of family therapy. However, the genogram, which evolved directly from Bowen's theory, can serve as a highly useful intervention. Detailed in Chapter 4, the genogram is a nonthreatening intervention that explores family patterns. As an objective task, constructing the genogram allows all family members to participate. In so doing, each family member begins to express his or her point of view; the differences can be highlighted in a nontoxic way. More important, the problematic behavior is then placed in the context of larger family interactions.

The genogram is a formal, structured means for intervening historically; for the observant therapist, the past might reappear at any time during the treatment process. The question, therefore, is not how to elicit the material but rather when and in what ways to use it. This section provides several guidelines for exploring historical issues.

1. Explore When the Door Is Opened

Peter (in response to his wife's urging that he must be tougher with Cindy): You sound just like my ex-wife.

Donna: How dare you accuse me of that!

At this point, the therapist is presented with an option of whether to pursue the ongoing disagreement between Donna and Peter or to explore the historical issue just opened up. Believing that the disagreement may be reopened at any time, the therapist builds on Peter's remark to explore historical themes:

Therapist: Peter, I am not sure what you meant when you said Donna sounds like your ex-wife. What were some of the issues in your first marriage?

In this example, the therapist is pursuing an issue not previously mentioned in therapy. Jumping on the spontaneity of the moment, he explores the issue's ramifications for the current marital interaction:

Therapist: Peter, in looking back, what were some of the issues of disagreement in your first marriage, and which ones have recurred with Donna?

As he builds on spontaneity to explore historical issues, the therapist can create his own openings:

Therapist: Because your differences in parenting are so obvious, I wonder if you would each tell me what growing up in your families was like? What were your parents' styles?

As an alternative,

Therapist: What do you each want to repeat and avoid from your earlier marriages?

2. Respect the Closed Door

As quickly as a door to the past opens, it can close. For example,

> **Peter:** I don't know what my relationship with my ex-wife has to do with Donna's and my arguments.

> **Therapist:** Perhaps absolutely nothing or perhaps something. What matters is what makes sense to you, so let's stay with resolving these arguments.

Here, the therapist leaves open the possibility that there was a correlation between Peter's past and his current relationship with his wife, but does not push the issue.

At this point, the basic therapeutic assumption is that if and when Peter's patterns in the first marriage become central to treatment, this theme would resurface. Peter's response clearly indicated that his first marriage is currently too threatening an issue. Consequently, underlining the point, the therapist backs away.

3. Present Options for Family Members to Pursue

With historical issues, the therapist is increasing the family's awareness of patterns, tying these issues into current dynamics, and exploring options with the family members.

> **Therapist:** Peter, you do not have to respond to Donna as you did to your ex-wife. You have choices! For example, what are other ways of reacting to Donna?

The therapist was building on Peter's earlier answers and challenging his patterns by asking him to brainstorm alternatives.

4. Respect the Family Members' Decisions

Ultimately, the family members' decisions concerning therapeutic focus need to be respected. Historical issues can be a gold mine of insights and motivations for change, or they can rapidly raise the resistance in the room and result in premature termination. A therapist lowers the risk of error by explaining the therapeutic options to the family members and then respecting their judgment:

> **Therapist:** Donna and Peter, it is clear to me that a key element in your disagreements is the relationships you each have with your family of origins and the patterns you both carry from your first marriages. If you'd like, focusing on these issues for a while may prove quite fruitful. What does each of you think of that?

Second-Order Techniques

First-order techniques work quickly and rapidly with families who are well motivated and with whom an adequate therapeutic alliance has formed. The therapist serves as a valued consultant who underlines and builds on the family's strengths by encouraging the family members to do more or less of existing behavioral patterns. Working with these families is gratifying and reassures the therapist in his or her career choice.

However, the majority of families will not be so straightforward. Family members will differ in their degree of motivation and their level of pain. Someone desperately wants another person to change, but is unwilling to change himself or herself. Sometimes the hidden agenda in therapy is the hope that the therapist will change the other person. In other situations, family members fear change because of the threat to their fragile self-esteem: "I do not need to change. I am fine. It is her fault."

Power struggles dominate other families; for them, therapy sessions resemble a painful tug-of-war: "I will not change until you change the way I want you to change." These conflicts may contain secondary gains for one or all participants. Cindy, for example, did not like being "hassled" by her stepmother but was secretly pleased that Donna was so upset. Not only did Cindy feel more powerful, but she was also acting out her anger at the divorce and her fear that Donna had taken her place with her father.

Likewise, although he wanted the arguments between his wife and daughter to end, Peter feared getting in the middle. He did not want to incur the wrath of his wife or of his daughter. Unfortunately, his passive withdrawal only exacerbated the situation.

The power struggles and fear of change left the Martin family at a standstill. First-order techniques facilitated an initial change, but soon therapy was at a standstill. Negotiations between the family members frequently broke down and arguments occurred with little provocation. Homework assignments were not completed or were not tried because one family member would say, "We have tried that and it did not work." Second-order techniques were called for at this point in treatment.

Process Interventions

Process interventions are techniques that the therapist can employ with most families in response to the here-and-now dynamics of interactions in the therapy sessions. They are particularly useful for patterns that continually repeat in the sessions and reflect the family patterns at home.

A frequently overlooked technique is the well-timed and well-phrased question. Questions can challenge existing perspectives, provoke new ways of thinking about an issue, and guide the family members into new, alternative behaviors. Questions employed as change techniques can be strategic or reflexive. Furthermore, brief, solution-oriented approaches have evolved a number of specific change-oriented questions.

Strategic and Reflexive Questions

In Chapter 5, a distinction was made between statements and questions. Statements set forth positions or views, whereas questions call forth positions or views. Accordingly, each school of family therapy varies in terms of the balance struck between the therapist's direct statements to the family and questions asked of the family (Tomm, 1988).

Tomm defines four types of questions used in the treatment process: linear, circular, strategic, and reflexive. Linear and circular questions were discussed within the assessment process (see Chapter 5). Strategic and reflexive questions, however, have direct relevance to process interventions.

The therapist asks strategic questions to influence the family in a specific manner. Such questions are based on the assumption that the therapist determines how the family should change. These questions, therefore, challenge and confront the family patterns:

> "Peter, are you aware that you turn away from Donna when she asks for your help with Cindy?"
>
> "Donna, you meet with continual frustration in trying to parent Cindy. Why do you continue trying in the same ways?"
>
> "Cindy, you appear to challenge your stepmother at every opportunity. Are you aware of doing this? What do you hope to accomplish?"
>
> "Peter, when you talk about Cindy's mother, there is an edge to your voice. I was wondering, what is that all about?"

These questions not only contain the therapist's assumptions of existing difficulties, but also focus the discussion on these behaviors.

Reflexive questions, in contrast, influence the family members by asking them to reflect on their patterns. The therapist endeavors to interact with the family in ways that help them see new possibilities in their patterns:

> "Peter, what do you think it is like for Donna as the mother in this family?"
>
> "Donna, what are the dilemmas Peter is struggling with?"
>
> "Cindy, what changes have you had to go through in the last year? How well have you managed them?"

Reflexive questions presuppose that the therapist is co-constructing the therapeutic reality with the family members who are "experts" in their problem and that the therapist is simply an expert in maintaining conversations about it (Goolishian & Anderson, 1987). Accordingly, the therapist is a conversational expert asking questions from a position of "not-knowing" (reflexive) rather than asking questions that demand specific answers (strategic) (Goolishian & Anderson, 1990). Within this constructivist framework, change occurs as family members have new conversations with each other rather than the same problem-oriented conversations over and over.

From my perspective, however, when a therapist is promoting the resources of the family to solve their own problems, he or she is never asking a question from a position of purely "not-knowing." If this were the case, there would be little reason for the questions. Instead, every question is guided by what the therapist considers important in forming clinical hypotheses. Even a reflexive question directs the family's and therapist's attention by focusing the session on a particular aspect of family functioning.

Consequently, although the distinction is important—strategic questions directly try to change the system, whereas reflexive questions facilitate the family's own self-discovery—both lines of questioning have their place within the therapeutic process. Strategic questions pointedly call attention to an aspect of the interactive patterns and challenge the rigid, entrenched patterns. Reflexive questions invite the family to speculate and become aware of their own patterns.

Specific Change-Oriented Questions

1. Exception-oriented questions Looking at times when the problem is not happening can be a productive strategy (DeShazer, 1991; O'Hanlon & Weiner-Davis, 1989). Presenting problems can dominate the therapy sessions. If these problems are left unchallenged, the family members increasingly view their interactions through a narrow, problem-oriented window. Instead of focusing on the problematic interactions, the therapist can ask for exceptions to the problem.

> **Therapist:** I have a pretty good picture of the problems, but to fill in the gaps, I need to know when these arguments are not occurring, what's happening instead?

After identifying exceptions, the therapist builds on these to expand the problem-free functioning of the family:

> **Therapist:** I am glad to know that there are times when all of you are not fighting. But I am curious, what are you each doing during those times that is different from the arguing moments?

> **Therapist:** How can we create more of those problem-free times?

2. Presuppositional questions Presuppositional questions (O'Hanlon & Weiner-Davis, 1989) highlight the distinction between "problem" talk and "solution" talk. These questions assume and imply change will take place and that it is only a matter of how and when.

> **Therapist:** How will you know when you do not have to come here anymore? What will be occurring at that time?

> **Therapist:** What will I need to look for to know we are on the right track?

> **Therapist:** Imagine the family the way you want it to be. What is going on and what are you thinking and feeling?

This consistent use of "solution/change" talk serves almost as a subtle form of hypnosis. Instead of adopting the family's pessimistic and stuck definitions of the problems, the therapist, through solution talk, is introducing a new language of change.

3. Miracle questions Designed to move clients rapidly into a future reality without problems, miracle questions (DeShazer, 1991) bypass the family's problem-saturated conversation.

> **Therapist:** Suppose you wake up tomorrow and a miracle has occurred. Things are as you hoped they would be. What would be different from today? How would you be different?

> **Therapist** (following each family member's description): How can that begin today?

Miracle questions ask the family members to move into a future without problems. In doing so, the present interactions and individual motivations are challenged: How can tomorrow be today?

4. Coping questions Coping questions (Selekman, 1993) can often show families strengths they are unaware of. Some families are quite pessimistic and resist seeing any positive future. All they see is more of the same arguments and disappointments. They are skeptical and view the therapist as a Pollyanna or one who does not fully understand the depths of their problem. Coping questions shift away from solution/change talk and mirror the family members' pessimistic stances—but in a way that helps the family see its strength.

> **Therapist:** I realize things are very difficult at home, but it has left me wondering why things aren't worse? What are you doing to prevent it from getting worse?

By asking what each member is doing to prevent further deterioration, the therapist uncovers ways in which the family members are acting to preserve the family. Thus, even in the worst of times, individuals are knowingly or unknowingly acting to maintain the family. Identifying these initiatives highlights the members' efforts that are preventing the situation from getting worse. Not only are these behaviors praised for their effectiveness, but they can also be built on to improve the family's strengths.

5. Externalizing questions Externalizing questions (White & Epston, 1990; White, 1991) build on the belief that people feel oppressed by their problems and subsequently develop "problem-saturated" stories that dominate the family's life. Donna has constructed her story of Cindy as a rebellious, destructive teenager who is bent on destroying the new blended family. Cindy's story is of an evil stepmother. Their arguments are a by-product of the perceived personality traits in each other.

Externalizing questions seek to separate people from their problem-saturated stories. In the Martin family, the arguments are the problem, not any particular family member or relationship. Consequently, the therapist seeks to redefine the presenting problem as an objectified external tyrant oppressing the family. Externalizing questions are particularly useful with highly rigid and resistant families (Selekman, 1993).

> **Therapist:** These arguments have a life of their own. How long have they dominated the family?

> **Therapist:** These arguments stop the family from growing. What specifically do these arguments prevent?

The family's "problem" is shifted from personality traits—Cindy is rebellious; Donna is controlling—to something objectified as outside the individual family members. Externalizing the problem separates a family member from internalized guilt and shame while avoiding the blame game. The arguments, not individuals, are the focus of the change. The family members are thus united in seeking solutions to their externalized arguments and are not in the business of changing each other.

After externalizing the problem and examining the influence of the problem over the family, a second set of questions explores the influence family members have had over the problem.

> **Therapist:** Have there been times when an argument could have erupted but you did not give in to that? On those occasions, what enabled you to defeat the argument?

These questions reinforce the externalization of the problem and begin to introduce a new story to the family by highlighting the control they do have over the problem. White (1991) refers to this as exploring unique outcomes—exceptions to the family's problem-saturated story.

Increasing Family Awareness and Introducing Choice

Family awareness, akin to the concept of interpretation and insight in individual psychotherapy, means that the family members become increasingly conscious of the function and circularity of their interactions (Byng-Hall & Campbell, 1981). This is not to say that the therapist presents his or her analysis to the family—"Cindy, I believe you are hurt and angry over your parents' divorce and your father's remarriage"—but rather asks reflexive questions to lead the family members into their own awareness.

Direct interpretations might be satisfying to the therapist, but they frequently inhibit rather than facilitate treatment. First, direct interpretations imply that the therapist knows what is wrong far better than the family does. Second, the therapist might create resistance where none existed. Cindy might reject the therapist's analysis, which she finds threatening: "I don't have any feelings about my parents' divorce." Third, interpretations refocus the flow of interaction from between family members to a dyadic interaction between therapist and individual family member. The following techniques, in contrast, highlight the family's interactive patterns and introduce the option of choice to the family (Worden, 1991). Any one or a combination can be used.

1. Identifying Patterns

> **Therapist:** There seems to me to be a consistent pattern occurring here. Cindy refuses to do something, an argument breaks out between Cindy and Donna, Donna asks Peter for help, Peter feels caught in the middle, and the argument escalates. When this occurs at home, what happens next? How does it die down?

By asking the family at the time the argument is occurring in the session what the next step is in their fights, the therapist was exploring each person's level of awareness of his or her patterns. Not only is this diagnostic—determining who is most attuned to the patterns and at what level—but it also plants a seed of awareness that their fights have predictable patterns.

2. Predicting the Next Step

> **Therapist** (following Cindy's irritation at Donna's complaint): Cindy, it looked like you just stiffened in your chair when your stepmother described what happened last weekend. You seem very sensitive to her remarks, and I have a feeling you are ready to come back at her. How do you want to reply? What do you hope to accomplish?

While predicting the next step in the sequence—Cindy's retaliation toward her stepmother—the therapist was also asking Cindy to develop alternative responses. Moreover, with these comments, the therapist was stating an opinion about Cindy.

At this point she could deny her sensitivity or admit it. If she denied it, she would be reluctant in future conversations to retaliate quickly against her stepmother in order to prove the therapist wrong. If she admitted it, the therapist could discuss her anger at her stepmother with her.

> **Therapist** (following Cindy's denial): Well, I guess I misread your reaction. If you weren't angry, what were you feeling just now?

> **Therapist** (following Cindy's acknowledgment of her anger at her stepmother): Cindy, how long have you felt this anger? Sometimes, anger is a consequence of being hurt. In what ways have you been hurt?

3. Encouraging the Next Step Before Its Turn

> **Therapist:** Peter, Cindy just called your wife a liar. What's going to be your next response?

Rather than waiting for the next step in the sequence to occur—Peter chastising his daughter—the therapist encouraged Peter to act and to think about what he wanted to say. With this intervention, not only is the dysfunctional pattern interrupted, but Peter is also presented with a choice of how he wishes to respond, a choice that in the previous heat of battle he did not fully realize he had.

4. Stopping the Sequence and Then Giving Permission to Continue

> **Therapist:** Excuse me, Donna, I think that if you keep talking about Cindy's faults, she'll soon jump in to defend herself. If that's what you want, please continue.

Again, the therapist is in a win-win position. If Donna decided that was not what she wanted, she would shift approaches, and the dysfunctional pattern would be interrupted. If she chose to continue, she would be acknowledging the pattern and making a conscious choice to carry on with the discussion and accept Cindy's reaction.

5. Speculating on the Motives of Others

> **Therapist:** Peter, Donna has frequently mentioned your relationship with Cindy's mother. Why do you think she raises that issue?

> **Therapist:** Donna, how does Peter try to balance the perceived demands from Cindy, Susan, and you? Is he successful?

Speculating on the motives of others offers several avenues to change: (1) Underlying motives are challenged; (2) perceptions are opened up for discussion; and (3) underlying issues—Peter's attempt to pacify three different people—surface.

All these interventions focus the discussion in the here-and-now of the therapy sessions, are reactions of the therapist to the dysfunctional process, and lead the participants into awareness of and insight into their patterns. The focus is not the therapist's interpretations but the family's own discovery. A basic assumption with these types of techniques is that awareness has greater meaning when discovered by the family (Worden, 1991).

Moreover, many of the above interventions possess a paradoxical flavor (the use of paradox is discussed later in the chapter). The dysfunctional pattern is interrupted, and the family is then given permission to continue it. However, permission is contingent on the family's making a choice to continue. The message from the therapist is simple: "Here are the points where you get into trouble; if you choose to continue, please do so."

Avoiding Triangulation

As discussed in Chapter 2, triangulation is the attempt of a conflicted dyad to involve a third person in the dispute. Within the therapeutic context, a therapist is vulnerable to the family's emotional whirlpool. The family might ask the therapist to judge who is right and who is wrong, to ally with one side against the other, to absorb the family's anxiety, and so forth. When Donna's and Peter's anger had risen to the boiling point and they had reached an impasse in dealing with each other, they would turn to the therapist for a decision on who was right and who was wrong.

More to the point, when Donna and Peter were at home and a similar disagreement erupted, they would isolate themselves in silence. Therapeutically, the impasse needed to be breached. To do so, the therapist employed each of the following strategies.

1. Pushing the Sequence One Step Further

Therapist: Donna, you looked frustrated when you just turned to me. Keep talking to Peter until you clear up your frustration.

In directing the sequence of interaction one step further, the therapist was pushing the couple to break through the impasse. This intervention might not break the impasse but, at the very least, the therapist disrupted the dysfunctional pattern and asked the participants to generate new behavior. Also, triangulation was avoided as the therapist redirected the conflict back to the dyad.

2. Directing the Message to the Appropriate Recipient

Therapist: Peter, you look at me when you talk about your dilemma in balancing the different demands you feel. Don't you want Donna to understand more than you want me to? Tell her how you see things.

Peter: It's no use. She feels I give in too much to Cindy and jump when Susan calls.

Therapist: Maybe that is exactly what she thinks, but try to explain it to her.

Frequently, in the course of a therapy session, family members will look to the therapist to plead their case or to tell the therapist what another family member is like. This subtle movement is an invitation for the therapist to join the dysfunctional dance. If the therapist colludes in this, the interactions between family members become fewer and fewer, and more and more comments are directed toward the clinician. In response, as a powerful therapeutic intervention, the therapist acts like a switchboard operator, directing messages to the appropriate recipient.

This role can be accomplished in a number of ways. The therapist can use verbal comments: "Would you please speak directly to your wife?" Or the therapist can send nonverbal messages. Instead of looking toward and thus acknowledging the speaker, he or she looks at the person to whom the message should be addressed. In cases where good rapport has been established, the therapist simply looks at the speaker and points a finger in the direction of the person to whom the speaker should send the message.

Directing the message to the appropriate recipient is simple but powerful and is often different from what the family does on its own. At home, the family's interactive patterns break down into a series of triangles and truncated conversations, or the family members break off contact before any message is fully sent or acknowledged. By simply having the family complete their messages, the therapist is building the family's repertoire of behavior and changing the system's interactions.

Structural Interventions

The family's structure refers to its organizational norms: roles, power hierarchy, boundaries among the subsystems. Minuchin (1974) says, "Family structure is the invisible set of functional demands that organizes the ways in which family members interact" (p. 51). **Structural interventions**, in turn, are designed to change these organizational patterns in which the problem behavior is embedded.

This section is a brief introduction to these structural techniques. They are covered extensively in the writings of structural family therapists such as Minuchin (1974), Minuchin and Fishman (1981), and Stanton and Todd (1979).

Challenging the Family Norms

In most cases, by the time a family visits a therapist, rigid, entrenched, chronic dysfunctional patterns of interaction have become embedded in the family norms that maintain the family's structure. Consequently, Minuchin and Fishman (1981) observe that all family therapists are alike in challenging the dysfunctional aspects of the family homeostasis but differ in their methods and targets, depending on their theoretical positions.

With the Martin family, several dysfunctional norms were clearly in evidence. First, the family's ability to solve problems effectively had rapidly deteriorated into a series of mutual accusations. It was easier for them to attack each other than to acknowledge the pain behind their attacks. Second, problem solving was further inhibited because the family members broke off contact with one another before resolution could be reached. Ironically, they all felt the fragility of the new stepfamily and feared the consequences of their continual disagreements. Only when things became intolerable would disagreements be voiced. Finally, the personal feelings surrounding change and loss were not spoken. The family acted as if feelings about the past would threaten the present. (Visher and Visher [1988] identify coping with loss and change as a first task in building a stepfamily.) The following are various ways of challenging these family norms (Worden, 1991).

1. Exploring the Function of Norms

Therapist: In this family, people frequently accuse one another of some misdeed or another. I was wondering, what do you gain from that?

Therapist: It seems important when two of you are arguing to break off contact at some point. I assume you are doing this for some reason. Would you tell me what that might be?

Therapist: There has been a great deal of change and loss for each of you in the past few years. Donna, you lost a husband and Robert and Karen a father. Peter, you have gone through a difficult divorce, and Cindy, you had to watch your parents break up. But what amazes me is that I have a sense all of you never talk about these things. Is there some reason for that?

Therapist: On top of the losses, all of you are trying to build a stepfamily with all the changes that entails. Do you ever talk about the difficulties you have each experienced in building this new family?

2. Questioning How Things Are Done

Therapist: I am beginning to think that all you two (Cindy and her step-mother) do is argue. Would you tell me some of the things both of you have successfully talked through?

Therapist: Do you two (Donna and Peter) believe you are saving your marriage by not finishing a disagreement?

3. Challenging Each Member's Desire for Change

Therapist: If the three of you (Donna, Peter, and Cindy) don't start solving your disagreements, I'm afraid they'll tear the family apart. Are you really interested in change or in deciding who's wrong?

4. Search for Alternatives

Therapist: Cindy, can you imagine telling your father how he hurt you without first attacking your stepmother?

Therapist: Peter, is there anything else you can do besides pulling away during these arguments?

A note of caution: Challenging the family's norms has the inherent risk of directly threatening the family and increasing resistance. Because of this risk, the therapist needs to first establish a solid therapeutic alliance with the family. Challenges are much more accepted and entertained by the family if the members believe the therapist cares for and is honest with them.

Boundary Marking

Family boundaries include the interpersonal boundaries between individual family members; subsystem generational boundaries involving the sibling subsystem, parental subsystem, extended family subsystem (grandparents, uncles, and aunts); and the entire family's boundary with the larger community. Ideally, the boundaries are permeable but at the same time protect the individual and the various subsystems.

Boundaries are determined by "the rules defining who participates (in the family or subsystem), and how" (Minuchin, 1974, p. 53). They differentiate the family's subsystems. In a stepfamily, however, the boundaries are being newly formed and dramatically increase in number.

For example, what will be the roles in parenting Cindy? How much will her mother be involved? How much will her stepmother be involved? How will Mr. and Mrs. Martin evolve co-parenting responsibilities for their three children? What will be the relationship between Mr. Martin and his ex-wife? What will be the relationship between the new stepfamily and Mrs. Martin's extended family? How much time will Cindy spend at each household?

In a traditional family, boundaries evolve with time and as individual developmental needs require. A stepfamily rarely has the luxury of time. Two families come together with each member at a particular developmental stage and attempt to create boundaries agreeable for all members—a difficult task indeed!

Visher and Visher (1988) point out that a fundamental source of stress in stepfamilies is boundary ambiguity. Boundary ambiguity refers to the lack of clarity in these new structures and particularly to who is in and who is out of the family (Boss & Greenberg, 1984). Cindy, for instance, would not accept Mrs. Martin's parents as her grandparents. She rejected going to their home for Sunday dinners. Robert and Karen felt that with their mother, they were a family unit distinct from Mr. Martin and Cindy. Mr. Martin wanted one big family. Cindy, unfortunately, did not feel a part of any family unit.

Clearly, the boundary ambiguity alone would contribute to the great stress the Martins were experiencing. Consequently, a chief therapeutic intervention was **boundary marking** to clarify and delineate as many boundaries as possible. Following are the boundaries addressed and the techniques employed.

1. Clarifying the Boundary Between the Households

Before Mr. Martin remarried, Cindy had a pattern of bouncing back and forth between her father's and her mother's households. After one parent attempted to draw a firm limit with her, an argument would ensue, and she would pack her bags and stay with the other parent for several days. This was exacerbated by the lingering bitterness between Peter and Susan.

Mr. Martin was highly resistant to involving his ex-wife in therapy and agreed only after the therapist was fairly insistent:

Therapist: Peter, there's little if any chance of changing Cindy's behavior as long as she can leave a situation before the limits have a chance to work. If some agreement isn't reached between you and Cindy's mother, you can only expect more of the same from Cindy.

Following Peter's reluctant agreement, the therapist contacted Susan, and two sessions were held with Cindy's biological parents. (The therapist decided to exclude Donna because her presence might have threatened Susan and distracted from the session agenda. Additionally, excluding Donna underlined the boundary of Cindy's biological parents.) The focus of the sessions was to reach an agreement whereby Cindy would not be able to move back and forth between her parents whenever she disagreed with their restrictions.

Although the sessions were tense at times because of bitterness, the parents reached an agreement that allowed Cindy to stay with her mother every other weekend but only by prearrangement.

2. Clarifying the Boundary Between the Former Spouses

The unresolved issues and truncated relationship between Peter and Susan were viscerally evident in the conjoint sessions. Each was quick to accuse the other of "messing up" Cindy. Each was quick to elicit the therapist's alliance. In this setting, the therapist struggled with maintaining a constructive focus on Cindy and co-parenting issues.

> **Therapist:** The anger and bitterness between the two of you is quite clear.
> How long has this been going on? And what have you done about it?

In response, each acknowledged that the anger was the reason for the divorce in the first place, despite marital counseling, and that things were better when they avoided each other.

> **Therapist:** It may be fine for the two of you to avoid each other, but you
> have a daughter to rear. And from what I can see, she is going to force
> the two of you to deal with each other. Now if you cannot put aside your
> anger for Cindy, there's little hope. Your anger will feed Cindy's anger.

Here, the therapist was challenging the parents and making a connection between their behavior and Cindy's. The responsibility for change was placed on their shoulders, not on Cindy's.

Although it would be unrealistic to expect the former spouses to resolve their differences—after previous marital counseling, divorce had been their solution—they could be expected to cooperate as parents. To further the co-parenting and to keep an eye on their underlying bitterness, the therapist agreed to serve as a mediator and offered conjoint sessions whenever issues with Cindy needed to be discussed.

3. Delineating Parenting and the Children's Subsystems

In the glow of love and the hopes of beginning anew, Mr. and Mrs. Martin had given little initial thought to how they would co-parent their children and stepchildren. Difficulties soon arose in several areas.

First, Peter and Donna had been reared quite differently. Her emotionally involved and structured childhood contrasted sharply with his low involvement and loosely structured upbringing. Although these differences were not a problem for them as a couple, they loomed very large when the two of them attempted to co-parent. She complained that her husband was too laid back and needed to take a more active hand with the children. He, on the other hand, felt his wife was too strict and overcontrolling.

These differences were minimal concerning Mrs. Martin's children, Robert and Karen. She was quite comfortable parenting them as she always had, and Mr. Martin felt no need to interfere. Cindy, however, was a different matter. Mrs. Martin strongly believed Cindy needed a tighter structure and that if Mr. Martin did not exert some authority, her authority with her own children would be undermined: "How can we have a family if Cindy gets away with things my children can't do?"

To address these issues the therapist took three steps. First, he attempted to build parental boundaries by establishing a list of priorities:

> **Therapist** (addressing Mr. and Mrs. Martin in a session without the children): It is becoming clear to me that the parenting style differences are tearing the family apart. It would be unrealistic to think the two of you will agree on everything, but I'd like to establish some priorities in your parenting. For example, what are your expectations of each other and the children?

In establishing a priority list, rather than dealing with vague generalities, the parents were encouraged to talk out their differences and reach some agreement on what was important. The list, furthermore, served as a guide for therapy: "What are we working on now, and have we reached our goal?"

As a second step, the therapist encouraged the couple to make decisions jointly:

> **Therapist** (again, to Mr. and Mrs. Martin in a private session): Because we can't begin to anticipate all the eventualities that will come up with the children, I'd like both of you to follow one basic rule for the next month: Any decision involving the children will be discussed and decided jointly.

By asking the parents to follow this basic rule, the therapist was again encouraging them to confront their differences but also to act as co-parents. Thus, the parenting boundary was being strengthened. Also, the consequences of following this basic rule were grist for the therapy sessions:

> **Therapist** (the session has just started, and Mrs. Martin is relating an event whereby her husband made a unilateral decision regarding Cindy): Well, it appears that our basic rule (joint decision making) wasn't a very good idea. I did not realize it would be so hard to follow. What made it so difficult?

Notice that the therapist was taking responsibility for the poor idea and its lack of success. This was done for two reasons: (1) Already chastised by Donna for his slip, Peter fully expected the same from the therapist. If the therapist had followed Donna's lead, the triangle would have been joined; Peter would have assumed the role of the bad little boy who needed to make excuses: "Well, Donna wasn't home; what was I supposed to do?" This, of course, would have been more of the same dysfunctional pattern the couple had initially presented. (2) In accepting the blame for the lack of success and not undermining Peter's defenses, the therapist opened the door to a deeper understanding of Peter's dilemma.

> **Therapist** (moving the discussion from one of blame to one of collaboration): Peter, is this the type of situation where you feel torn between

being a good father and being a good husband? If so, is there any way out of it?

The therapist's third step was to encourage the family to delineate roles and responsibilities. Who is responsible for what? Who will take care of what? How will they divide the tasks? As in any organization, the clearer the roles, the smoother the organization runs:

> **Therapist** (with all family members present): I am not clear who is responsible for what around the home. I would like to go around to each of you and have you tell me what your responsibilities are and what other people's are.

Even though disagreements would probably quickly emerge, the therapist was encouraging the family members to look at their individual roles and the roles of others. In this process, individual boundaries are highlighted.

4. Delineating Extended Family Boundaries

An issue just below the surface with the family was Mrs. Martin's involvement with her extended family. Although not a factor in bringing the family into treatment, it was beginning to be divisive.

> **Therapist:** It has occurred to me that in building this stepfamily, grandparents and other extended family must play an important role. How have the extended families been integrated?

Opening the door to the issue of extended family, the therapist was allowing the family members to first paint the picture. When the family minimized the boundary, the therapist pushed further:

> **Therapist:** I'm glad to hear it has gone so smoothly. How do you decide when to visit your parents or have them over?

Again, as with most interventions, timing is important. If this is a point the family is willing to deal with, conversation readily ensues. If it is resisted, however, the therapist retreats from the issue but remains ready to bring it up at another time.

Reframing

As a technique, reframing is the stock-in-trade of many family therapists (Alexander & Parsons, 1982; DeShazer, 1982; L'Abate et al., 1986; Selevini Palazzoli, Cecchin, Boscolo, & Prata, 1978). Moreover, positive reframing is to family therapy what interpretation is to individual therapy (L'Abate et al., 1986).

Briefly, **reframing** is changing "the conceptual and/or emotional setting or viewpoint in relation to which a situation is experienced and to place it in another frame which fits the 'facts' of the same concrete situation equally well or even better, and thereby changes its entire meaning" (Watzlawick, Weakland, & Fisch, 1974, p. 95). In other words, the therapist takes the family's presentation, or *negative frame*, of the "facts" and presents an alternative, *positive frame*. In so doing, the therapist attempts to change the meaning of what is going on without changing the facts. If he or she is successful, the problematic behavior is seen in a different, more positive light, and new, more functional patterns can then evolve.

For example, Donna's "complaints" (as Peter has framed them) can be reframed as attempts on Donna's part to improve their marriage and family because she loves Peter and wants to have a better marriage and family. Likewise, his ambivalence in supporting his wife can be seen as arising out of his desire to be fair to both her and Cindy. Finally, Cindy's acting out is an attempt on her part to discover what the rules are in the new stepfamily.

Although simple in concept, reframing is a powerful technique in freeing families from repeating dysfunctional patterns. Alexander and Parsons (1982) argue that interactions cannot shift until family members change their view of themselves and other family members. Furthermore, L'Abate and his colleagues (1986) argue that reframing is the basis of much of psychotherapy in that changing a client's worldview allows for more alternative behaviors. For instance, as long as Cindy views her stepmother as acting alone in trying to control her, she will resist Donna's "control" in her characteristic ways. Likewise, as long as Donna sees Cindy in active defiance, she must respond by trying to control Cindy. The following are possible reframings to promote change in the Martin family.

> **Therapist** (reframing the couple's arguments): This marriage must be very important to each of you because you are willing to fight for it.

> **Therapist** (reframing Peter's protection of his daughter and lack of support for his wife): Peter, it sounds as if you're determined to make up to Cindy for the past. Your love for her is powerful. But, just like eating a gallon of ice cream, does it ever feel like too much of a good thing?

> **Therapist** (addressing the couple's mutual frustration): I know I am meeting the two of you at a difficult time, but there must be a lot of strength in your relationship for both of you to be here today.

> **Therapist** (reframing the couple's withdrawal pattern): I think each of you must pull away from one another during these fights because the hurt is so great and not getting through to the other person is so painful.

> **Therapist** (commenting on Cindy's acting-out behavior): Cindy, I think you are determined to make this family stronger by testing the limits.

> **Therapist** (in response to Peter and Donna's argument over Cindy's behavior): Sometimes when the two of you are arguing over Cindy's actions, I get the sense that this is the only way you can disagree and express anger.

> **Therapist** (reacting to Donna's complaint of trying to juggle the demands of the family with the needs of her parents): Donna, it looks to me that you are trying very hard to be a good wife, mother, and daughter. Your loyalty and sense of duty are admirable. Somehow though, I wonder if this is too much for you and if Peter feels your commitment to him.

The therapist's search for positive perspectives and motivations is at the heart of the reframing technique. If the therapist is also "stuck" on the negatives—Cindy is an acting-out teenager who is angry at her stepmother; Peter is too passive and does not support his wife; Donna is rejecting Cindy and is too controlling; Cindy's mother, Susan, constantly undermines Donna and Peter's attempts to parent Cindy—then change is based on eliminating those negatives.

Positive reframing focuses the therapy on developing strengths and redirecting those strengths in more productive pathways. Cindy is hurt and overwhelmed by the changes in her family and her emergence into adolescence; she needs firm limits but also a forum to voice her hurt. Peter wants to please everyone but needs to recognize that this is not always possible and that his ambivalent behavior makes the situation worse. Donna is doing the best she can in a difficult situation but needs to understand the limits of her role as stepmother. Susan has lost her only daughter and is confused about what her role should be. She needs assistance in forming this new role.

As important as it is for the therapist to see the positive side and reframe everyone's behavior accordingly, the reframing will fall on deaf ears if the alternative viewpoints are presented in ways that the individual or family cannot assimilate. For example, Mrs. Martin is so angry at Cindy for what she perceives as her disrespect that to be told Cindy is testing the limits simply does not fit with her beliefs. The therapist's comments appear ludicrous and naive. However, another reframing might be readily accepted: "Donna, I think Cindy acts out when she is hurt and scared." With this reframing, the therapist could hit a responsive chord; Donna can understand being hurt and frightened.

Also, success in using reframing lies in the timing of the intervention. If, in the first interview, the therapist had said that Cindy is testing the limits in the new stepfamily, Donna would probably have rejected this view. Donna is trying to tell the therapist how she views the world, and she is not ready for the therapist to suggest subtly that she is not looking at it correctly. At this point, Donna will feel misunderstood and reject the therapist's reframing. The therapist's skill, therefore, lies in the ability to look for openings and to time the intervention when it will most likely be heard.

Finally, reframing is successful not because the therapist is clever but because the family accepts it. A therapist convinced of his or her perceptions may be just as rigid as the family patterns and, in the attempt to "sell" the reframing, may endanger the engagement process and raise unnecessary resistance in the family. When a reframing is effective, a therapist typically senses immediate recognition from the family— "I never thought of it that way"—or facial expressions that communicate pleasant surprise. Thus, in the ongoing process of treatment, when the family does not accept the reframed perspective, the therapist should quietly drop it.

Paradoxical Prescriptions

Strategic family therapists have devoted the most attention to both the theory of paradox and paradoxical techniques (Frankl, 1975; Haley, 1976; Mandanes, 1981; Papp, 1983; Selvini Palazzoli et al., 1978; Sherman & Fredman, 1986; Watzlawick et al., 1974). Referring to the previous chapter's discussion of resistance, strategic family therapists would argue that a symptom evolves in a family in an attempt to maintain the family's threatened homeostasis. Consequently, removal of the symptom— a goal of therapy—would threaten to disrupt the family's homeostasis and is resisted.

(This is particularly true with families dominated by rigid, morphostatic forces; to them change is threatening.) Therapists should therefore expect oppositional behavior from family members rather than cooperation. **Paradoxical techniques** assume oppositional behavior from the family and are based on a therapeutic paradox whereby family members are exposed to contradictory instructions from the therapist. Confronted with these contradictory instructions, family members change by either accepting or rejecting the therapist's prescriptions.

Briefly, a paradox is a contradiction that follows from logical premises and deductions. For example, to tell someone to "be spontaneous" is a paradoxical contradiction. A frequent paradox in therapy is a family's stated desire to change one member's behavior but not any other patterns, as if that member can be changed in isolation from the rest of the system. Another is for family members to request help, only to ignore the therapist's directions: "We're here because you are the expert, but we will not follow your advice."

Likewise, a therapeutic paradox (a paradoxical situation initiated by the therapist) occurs when the family expects, and is ready to reject, therapeutic direction but none is forthcoming. For example, the family members have presented their problems and wait for the therapist to offer suggestions that they will then reject. In these situations, the therapist employs therapeutic judo on the family's resistance:

> **Therapist:** Because these patterns have been going on for so long, I really don't see any way of changing them. I think they will be with you a long time. If you like, we could talk about how to try to live with them.

With this statement, the therapist has hit the ball back into the family's court. The family's symptom is untenable, but threatening the status quo is more frightening to the family members. Change, therefore, is forged in this therapeutic double bind: For the family to continue to resist the therapist—to reject the notion that they must live with their patterns—the family members must change their patterns.

As was discussed earlier, argumentative families have the capacity to resist and reject the therapist's attempts to negotiate a settlement. Thus, in a paradoxical approach, the therapist intervenes by saying:

> **Therapist:** I don't fully understand these arguments yet, so would you please continue them until I figure them out?

In this double bind, the family members can resist the intervention only by stopping their fights. If the fighting does continue, then the therapist thanks the family members for their cooperation; if the fighting stops, then change has occurred.

Steps in Paradoxical Interventions

Papp (1983) describes three steps in paradoxical interventions: (1) redefining, (2) prescribing, and (3) restraining. Redefining is analogous to the reframing technique described earlier. Prescribing asks the family to do more of the same behavior. Restraining occurs when the family shows signs of change and the therapist cautions against it.

The following are examples of paradoxical interventions employed with the Martins to disrupt the recurrent dysfunctional patterns and to facilitate the development of more productive interactions.

1. Redefining

> **Therapist:** I know that each of you has tried to make things better and that you feel frustrated. I've been thinking about this, and I've decided these arguments protect you. The fighting keeps all of you interacting but maintains a safe distance between you at the same time. It's as if all of you share ambivalence about this whole stepfamily thing and move to protect one another.

> **Therapist:** Cindy, I guess you don't want your dad to get too close to Donna. You must have seen how hurt he was in the divorce and don't want him to experience that type of hurt again. Also, if you can keep them apart, maybe you won't lose your dad.

> **Therapist:** Peter, it looks to me as if you want to protect Donna from Cindy. Your hope is that if Cindy is allowed to do what she wants, she'll be happy and won't fight with Donna.

> **Therapist:** Donna, by continuing to fight with Cindy, you must want to protect Peter from these disagreements. It looks as though you take on the tough parenting jobs to protect Peter from being hurt by Cindy.

The arguments were redefined as serving valuable functions within the family. The therapist implied that each person was colluding in this pattern and that they should continue to protect one another.

2. Prescribing

> **Therapist:** During the next week, whenever it looks as though someone requires protection, I'd like one of you to start an argument and create a little distance between you. The argument will signal that you need distance and that someone needs protection, right now!

Building on the redefinition of the arguments, the therapist encouraged the behavior. He prescribed the arguments to serve as signals that one or both parties wanted emotional distance and were seeking to protect someone. Moreover, the fights would not be spontaneous expressions of frustrations but would be planned. He implied that if family members can start the arguments when they choose, they will have more control over them than they initially believed.

3. Restraining

If the intervention is well timed and the family accepts the reframing, behavior changes. In the earlier examples, the pattern could continue as long as someone believed he or she was the aggrieved party. If a family member were seeking distance, however, or protecting someone, the anger behind the conflict would dissipate.

> **Peter** (at the next session): I don't know what happened, but we fought a great deal less this week. In fact, we got along pretty well.

> **Therapist:** Oh, oh! This makes me a little uneasy. I think this is too quick a change for people who are as good at fighting as all of you. Look, don't

stop the fighting entirely. At least have several arguments between now and the next session.

With this remark, the therapist was not only staying consistent with the paradoxical approach but was also reinforcing the earlier prescription. Restraining change, again, anticipates the family's resistance. Paradoxically, by resisting the therapist's admonishments to fight more, the family members were fighting less.

Candidates for Paradoxical Techniques

Paradoxical techniques have a great deal of appeal. Powerful when successful, they would appear to offer rapid change. In the world of changing people, however, nothing is ever so straightforward. As a word of caution, resistance, and thus the expected oppositional behavior, implies that a stable homeostasis is operating within the family and that long-term, rigid, repeating patterns of behavior dominate the interactions. Diagnostically, the family's rigid resistance patterns would recur in the initial therapy sessions. Paradoxical techniques are designed specifically for these types of families.

In contrast, families that require increased structure and controls (disorganized and chaotic) are not candidates for paradox (Sherman & Fredman, 1986). These families present a lack of consistent patterns and internal structure. Examples are families experiencing divorce or death of a parent, in which the remaining spouse is attempting to reorganize the family, or families wracked by the effects of poverty and trying to meet basic survival needs. These families are not struggling with rigid patterns but are suffering because of their lack of stability.

Paradoxical techniques should also not be attempted unless a strong rapport exists between the therapist and the family. Without the rapport, the family will greet the paradoxical intervention with quizzical looks and a sense that the therapist has not heard one word they have said. Worse yet, the family might believe the therapist is making fun of them. In these situations, the therapist feels quite clever, but the family might never return for another session.

A Variation on a Theme: Paradox and Awareness

Rather than risking a full-blown paradoxical approach and its accompanying liabilities, the therapist can combine the power of paradox with increasing the family members' awareness of their patterns through reflexive questions.

Therapist: Cindy, if I told you to start a fight with your stepmother by 10 o'clock tonight, what would you do?

Cindy: Well, I would probably start by blasting my radio and keeping Karen awake.

Therapist: Why would she fall for that?

Cindy: She hates it when I mess with her precious Karen.

Therapist: Donna, would you really fall for that?

Paradoxically, in these examples, the therapist is not focusing on stopping the arguments or negotiating their settlements, as the family expected, but instead explores how to start them. In the process, the therapist has asked Cindy to reveal her strategy and has hinted that Donna would take the bait. By interrupting the fight sequence, the therapist forces the family to evolve new responses to one another.

In summary, not a "cure" in and of itself, a paradoxical intervention can help loosen rigid, entrenched behavioral patterns and open the way to change. Again, paradoxical interventions are most productive (1) with rigid, resistant patterns, (2) when the therapist has successfully assessed the dysfunctional patterns, and (3) when a trusting relationship has been established with the family.

Techniques with Young Children

Young children offer unique challenges to the family therapist. Sometimes they are essential players in the family drama, offering unique insights into family patterns and themes. At other times, they serve as a defensive distraction when the focus of a treatment session is lost because the parents are busy managing their young children's behavior. In these situations, thoughts and sentences are left partially completed as the parents attempt to stop their 2-year-old from pulling the books off a shelf.

The younger the children, the more play is their medium of communication. It is a way of expressing underlying thoughts and feelings with the therapist and family. Consequently, play can be an essential element of therapy in work with these families.

Play offers you an opportunity to observe family interactions and to intervene by modeling or helping to shape new behaviors and new ways for family members to connect. Gil (1994) observes that "therapists can teach parents to observe, decode, and participate in their children's play in such a way that their understanding of their child's experience is enhanced, and the possibility for deeper emotional contact with children becomes available" (p. 39).

Play does not readily fit into specific, planned techniques nor is it easily classified as first- or second-order change. Instead, play by definition is spontaneous. The therapist can, however, create and encourage opportunities for play. For example, the therapist can make play materials readily available to the family members. A side table with paper, magic markers, crayons, modeling clay, puppets, family figurines, and toys is inviting to young children. With these materials at hand, young children can play quietly or involve family members.

For the observant therapist, a young child's play reveals a wealth of information. For example:

Is the young child able to leave the parents' sides and play in the corner?

Do the parents hover over the child's play?

Does the child produce something he or she eagerly shows to the parents?

How do the parents respond to their child's request for approval?

Does the child approach the therapist with his or her drawing?

Does the child invite other family members to play? Who?

Does a parent spontaneously join in the play?

Does the child demand attention while playing?

Who goes to soothe the child?

The therapist's participation in play can also enhance the therapeutic alliance and offers new avenues for change. With all techniques, however, play needs to fit the family's style and to be introduced at the appropriate time in therapy. Moreover, the therapist must be comfortable with the spontaneous nature of play in the therapy sessions. The following guidelines are offered as initial steps in integrating play into family therapy sessions:

1. Play can be threatening and inappropriate for rigid, highly controlled families. Diagnostically, in these families, the young children may not spontaneously approach the play table without first being given permission. For the therapist to encourage play without the parents' permission risks threatening the family norms and is an affront to the family.

2. Play can be inappropriate, at least initially, with depressed families. By encouraging play, the therapist is blatantly misreading the family's emotional state. There is sadness in these families that first needs to be addressed.

3. Play might be inappropriate to the theme of the session. For example, playing would be inappropriate in a session for which the parents are discussing a loss, separation, or impending divorce. Not only would the therapist be missing the emotional tone, but the family members might feel their problems were misunderstood, belittled, or minimized by the therapist.

4. A conservative approach for the therapist is to present the opportunity for play and follow the child's or family's lead.

5. Finally, for more detailed guidelines to the use of play in family therapy, Zilbach (1986) presents a history of play therapy and Gil (1994) applies play to family therapy by a series of techniques and clinical examples.

A more structured and systematic approach to working with young children is Behavioral Family Therapy (Taylor & Biglan, 1998). Behavioral Family Therapy assumes that children's behavior is reinforced and maintained by environmental factors. Directed specifically at parents, the focus of treatment is to increase their use of positive reinforcements, reduce punishments, clarify limits, and increase consistency. This approach is particularly helpful for families with children who exhibit aggressiveness, conduct problems, oppositional behavior, and hyperactivity (Taylor & Biglan, 1998).

Summary

Some might argue that the distinction made in this chapter between first- and second-order techniques is arbitrary at best. For example, historical interventions can produce profound shifts in individual family members' perceptions of themselves, which can also lead to significant behavioral changes. Still, when a therapist thinks first order, then second order, intervention techniques assume a logical sequence: First-order techniques build on existing behavior patterns or strengths, while second-order techniques provide a sharp shift when therapy has reached an impasse and the rules of the game are challenged.

The techniques outlined in this chapter are just a few of many that have evolved in the field of family therapy. They were selected because of their broad appeal and ready application to a variety of clinical situations. With experience, therapists find certain techniques that blend well with their personalities and theoretical perspectives, but for beginners, a wise course is to develop skill with a few techniques initially and then build a repertoire.

Although techniques are frequently seductive in their appeal, particularly when presented in a workshop by an experienced therapist, they are only as good as the person using them. Minuchin and Fishman (1981) note that a technique is a pathway to change, but the therapist gives it direction by his or her conceptualization of the family dynamics and the process of change. Likewise, Sherman and Fredman (1986) argue that the value in any technique is how it is used and with what skill. Clearly, the therapist's ability to engage the family and to make an accurate assessment of the problem behavior precedes any technique.

Moreover, there is a danger in becoming too technique oriented. Nichols (1987) warns that the indiscriminate use of techniques might serve the therapist more than the family. For example, the therapist working with the Martin family might begin to feel overwhelmed by the volatile, emotionally charged conflicts. In the face of the family's anxiety and his own, he might move rapidly through a series of techniques in an attempt to contain the mutual anxiety. Nichols (1987) points out that this rush to "techniquism" detaches the therapist from the family's pain and serves as a quick fix, which rarely holds up over the long term.

Still, if techniques are not viewed as ends in themselves, they have great utilitarian value to assist therapeutic movement. They can be extremely helpful in shifting perspectives within the family, increasing awareness, reorganizing the family, providing structured guidelines, and promoting change. Used judiciously, techniques are tools of the craft.

Glossary

Boundary marking A structural technique employed to clarify and delineate boundaries within the family.

Paradoxical techniques Therapy strategies based in therapeutic paradox whereby family members are exposed to contradictory instructions and change by either accepting or rejecting the therapist's prescriptions.

Process interventions Techniques employed during a therapy session in response to here-and-now dynamics of the interactions.

Reframing Relabeling individual or interpersonal behavior from a negative perception to a positive viewpoint and thus making the system more amenable to therapeutic change.

Structural interventions Techniques designed to change the family's organizational patterns: that is, challenging norms, reframing, and boundary marking.

Technique Planned therapeutic intervention requiring a reaction from the family members.

8

Termination

Treatment Summary

Termination Process

Premature Termination

Dropouts

Summary

The word *termination* is perhaps a misnomer in family therapy. From a family systems perspective, the therapist-family therapeutic system has reached an end point, but the family system certainly continues. From a broader view, the therapist intervenes at a moment in the family's ongoing history, helps correct the dysfunctioning patterns, and then exits. The therapist's mission, therefore, is to become obsolete as soon as possible as the family continues on its unique developmental path.

Termination also implies completion, but completion is a meaningless word in life cycle development. The family members had problems before they entered therapy and will have problems after they leave therapy; this is called life. If the therapy is successful, however, their approach to problems will be quite different from what it was before.

Still, ending the therapeutic alliance is the final phase of treatment proper. This chapter addresses the decisions concerning termination: When is termination indicated? How should this step be accomplished? How can gains made in therapy be consolidated?

As neat and tidy as termination—and, for that matter, family therapy in general—appears in books, it is rarely so in real life. More often, a clinician's caseload contains as many dropouts or cases that terminate prematurely as it does cases that move to a logical stopping point. Managing these cases is therefore a necessary skill for a therapist and is discussed below. Before directing attention specifically to the termination process, a treatment summary is in order.

Treatment Summary

The Martins entered therapy after one year as a stepfamily. Their chief complaint was the conflict in the home surrounding Cindy, Mr. Martin's 14-year-old daughter from his first marriage. Cindy had recently come to live with her father and his new wife following several years with her mother after her parents' divorce. The escalating conflicts between Cindy and her mother, Susan Waters, precipitated Cindy's move to her father's home.

After a short time in the Martins' home, Cindy began to experience escalating conflicts with her stepmother. Perceiving her father as more "laid back" than her mother, Cindy was surprised and angered when her stepmother attempted to enforce limits on her behavior. The dysfunctional triangle involving Cindy, her father, and her stepmother dominated the assessment process.

Three evaluation sessions were held with all family members present (Mr. Martin, Cindy, Mrs. Martin, and her two children from her first marriage, Karen and Robert). Initially, both parents wanted the therapist to "fix" Cindy, giving a linear definition of the problem. Following the evaluation sessions, however, the systemic goal established between the therapist and family was to reduce the conflict in the home and, in so doing, improve the family relationships.

In terms of the priority of intervention, the dysfunctional triangle involving Cindy, her father, and her stepmother was the first element to be addressed. This triangle had brought the family into treatment and was their major concern. At the same time, the functioning of this triangle underlined several dynamics operating within the family:

1. As a newly formed stepfamily, the boundaries, particularly the parental roles, were very much in flux.

2. Mr. Martin's guilt over his divorce hampered his effectiveness as a father.

3. The marital dyad was still in the forming stage (family life cycle), and the couple had not yet evolved effective problem-solving skills, particularly in the face of the challenges Cindy presented.

4. Cindy was able to exploit the lingering bitterness between her biological parents and to play each against the other. However, her acting-out behavior also reflected the pain caused by her parents' divorce and her father's remarriage.

5. Culture differences between Mr. and Mrs. Martin underlay differences in their parenting styles.

6. The culture differences were most noticeable in Donna's anger at Cindy's "disrespectful" behavior.

7. Extended family pressures amplified the tension between Mr. and Mrs. Martin and surfaced in their interactions with Cindy: It was easier to argue about Cindy than about Donna's relationship with her parents.

In the middle phase of treatment, the sessions focused on disrupting the dysfunctional triangular patterns and facilitating the development of more functional patterns. (The specific intervention techniques are discussed in Chapter 7.) Despite this focus, the dysfunctional patterns were highly resistant to change. First, Cindy's acting-out behavior frequently demanded attention. Predictably, when the treatment focus began to broaden to include marital and extended family issues, Cindy would be at the center of a family crisis.

To combat this syndrome, the therapist focused on developing and reinforcing the parental subsystem. He did this by establishing clear goals and guidelines for Mr. and Mrs. Martin as parents but also by exploring the underlying dynamics—that is, Mr. Martin's guilt, cultural differences in marital and parenting styles, and Mrs. Martin's hurt in reaction to Cindy's testing behavior. Nevertheless, when marital issues surfaced, the parents were quick to minimize them. Clearly, the marital bond was still too fragile to absorb much scrutiny.

As Mr. and Mrs. Martin became more consistent and mutually supportive of one another in parenting, Cindy's mother was triangled into the conflict. Specifically, Cindy would complain to Susan, who would then call Peter and complain about his new wife. Peter's passivity only exacerbated the situation, as everyone demanded that he do something. Additionally, Cindy would threaten to return to live with her mother.

Despite Peter's reluctance, two sessions were held with him and Susan, Cindy's mother. An agreement was reached whereby Cindy, despite her protests, would remain living with her father for a period of six months and would visit her mother on a regular, prescribed basis. At the end of six months, the living arrangement was to be reevaluated. A third session was held with Peter, Susan, and Cindy. The purpose of this meeting was to discuss the guidelines and to make sure everyone was in agreement.

As these dynamics were addressed and Mr. and Mrs. Martin became stronger as parents and as a couple, Cindy's acting-out behavior began to diminish greatly. There were still occasions when the old patterns would reemerge, but Mr. and Mrs. Martin were much more comfortable in managing them. Consequently, with the tension in the family lessened, the issue of termination was first raised.

Termination Process

Who Raises the Issue, and When?

Frequently, one or more family members first bring up the issue of termination:

Peter: I was wondering what the purpose was in continuing these sessions.

Before replying, the therapist questions the timing of this comment and who made it. For instance, the question might be raised at a particularly difficult time in therapy, as a strong reflection of the family's resistance. A family member who has been consistently defensive and resistant might also raise the question.

If the Martins' therapist believed that the question of termination was premature, he would see Peter's statement as resistance and as an expression of Peter's discomfort with the focus of treatment.

> **Therapist:** Peter, I think the question of termination is a legitimate issue and needs to be discussed, particularly in light of how far all of you have come as a family. However, I think we are right in the middle of something and not at the end of it.

Peter's introducing the issue of termination was both resistance and an acknowledgment that therapy had accomplished the initial goals. Cindy's behavior had improved significantly; but from the therapist's perspective, the underlying marital and extended family issues potentially threatened the stepfamily's evolution. In addition, the unaddressed marital conflict had the potential to triangle Cindy into future covert disagreements. Nevertheless, when the therapist began to probe the covert marital issues, both Peter and Donna quickly united to seal over any differences. They believed they could now function better as parents and were pleased with the progress they had made with Cindy. The marital differences the therapist was pointing out were not a problem.

In this situation, having accomplished the initial, specific goals of therapy and in the face of Peter's and Donna's satisfaction with what had occurred and their reluctance to go further, the therapist began consolidating the gains made in therapy (a process detailed below) and terminated with the family.

Have Specific Goals Been Met?

On the most basic level, the question of termination is very simple: Has the chief complaint been resolved, and have the initial goals established for treatment been met? If this is the case, the treatment process has come full cycle, and the initial goals have led to a clear termination point.

Clearly established goals serve as a beacon throughout treatment, but they are invaluable at termination. The question of whether to end the sessions becomes straightforward: Are the family members satisfied with the progress they have made toward their goals?

Another guide is the therapist's theoretical model. For strategic and behavior-oriented family therapists, problem resolution is the end in and of itself and signals termination. Structural family therapists emphasize the reorganization of the family's structure and its ability to nurture and support its members. Psychoanalytic family therapists would be concerned with the emergence and resolution of unconscious processes. Bowenian family therapists would assess the increase in differentiation within the family and the changes in family-of-origin relationships.

As always, the therapist's agenda might conflict with the family's goals. The family might reach a point at which further sessions are not warranted, whereas the therapist, staying within a conceptual model, sees much more work to be done. Certainly, the therapist needs to raise concerns and point out the areas where additional therapy is needed, but the family makes the final decision.

In taking this position, the therapist not only communicates respect for the family but also leaves the door open for future contacts. The fastest way to burn any future bridges between the therapist and the family is for the therapist to "resist" the family's request for termination and to doggedly point out all the additional work needed. This not only diminishes the family's work to this point but also pushes the family into an oppositional stance: The family members must demonstrate that they are ready to terminate by sealing off problems. Worse yet, the family might be very reluctant to return to the therapist in the future because of the therapist's implied, "I told you so."

With the Martins, the therapist clearly saw a need for additional therapeutic work pertaining to the marital dynamics and extended family issues. Nevertheless, the initial goals were accomplished, and the family did not wish to go any further. Of course, the therapist could have pushed for further sessions and confronted the family with their resistance, but this would have served only to damage the therapeutic alliance. From another perspective, perhaps Peter and Donna were wise not to go into their marital dynamics at this time. Perhaps they needed first to experience more success as a parental team, which in turn would reduce the pressure on their marriage. As always, the element of timing must be respected.

Thus, rather than staying within a theoretical position to determine the timing of termination, therapists can take a broader view and ask the following questions:

1. Is there a reduction in the symptom behavior?
2. Has the family made basic changes in their interactions concerning the symptom area?
3. Do they possess some knowledge of the circularity of their interactions?
4. Is the family on its way to new rules for problem solving?

How Can Gains Be Consolidated?

Deciding that termination is the next logical step in the treatment process, the therapist proceeds through a termination sequence designed to consolidate the gains made in therapy and to leave the door open for future contacts.

1. Taking Inventory

The first step in this sequence is much like taking inventory. Each family member is asked what has changed, and then he or she is asked to comment on what others have said:

Therapist: As a way of ending our sessions, I would like to go around the room and ask each of you what changes you see in the family.

At this point, the Martins' therapist engaged all family members individually, drawing them out and asking clarifying questions. His purpose was to explore the various points of view and to highlight similarities and differences between the participants:

Therapist: Peter, you agree with Donna that the two of you are more effective parents. Would you give me some examples of this?

Therapist (addressing Peter and Donna): What has helped you become more effective as parents?

After each family member had spoken, the therapist asked that each one comment on what the others had said. On a diagnostic level, the therapist observed how difficult or easy this was to do: Did the family members readily and easily interact with one another? How were differences managed? On a process level, the family members were consolidating their gains by exploring one another's perspectives.

2. Providing Explanations

The therapist is now in a position to share with the family his or her own impressions of the changes that have taken place. Here, the therapist might offer his conceptual understanding of the changes in the family:

> **Therapist:** I believe that as parents, you have drawn a clearer boundary between yourselves and the children and the in-laws.

Or a more concrete explanation:

> **Therapist:** You two have really begun to act like effective parents, and I think it shows throughout the family.

> **Therapist:** Peter, I know it has been difficult drawing a firmer line with Cindy, but I think you've succeeded wonderfully. What has helped you do this? How has Donna helped with this, and what can she do in the future?

> **Therapist:** As the two of you have become more consistent with Cindy, I believe she has come to see that she can rely on both of you to be firm and fair. In the process, you have made her world a more secure place.

> **Therapist:** Cindy, I give you a world of credit. It has not been easy for you given all that you've been through over the past several years. I must say how impressed I've been at your ability to express your hurt and anger in more productive ways.

In this exchange of impressions, the therapist was in a position to consolidate change by highlighting the key elements and providing the family with an understanding of those changes. This cognitive labeling enabled the family to take something concrete from therapy, which could serve as a reminder and guideline in future situations. As Bandler, Grinder, and Satir (1976) point out, the outcome of family therapy is not simply an experience that the family can use but also an understanding of that experience and specific tools the family can use to enhance their own growth.

3. Speculating on the Future

The next step combines termination and a therapeutic intervention whereby the therapist and family outline future pitfalls facing the family:

> **Therapist:** I think we have a sense of where we have been, but I was wondering if we could look into the future. What in the future might happen that would test the changes you've made? What do you think will be next in your development as a stepfamily?

> **Therapist:** Can the two of you (Donna and Peter) imagine any issue that could arise in parenting your children where you might disagree?

Therapist: What would keep the two of you from reaching an agreement? If you were in a marital argument, would this interfere with your being parents?

Therapist: Cindy, can you imagine anything in the future that you and your stepmother might argue about?

As a prophylactic measure, the therapist explores the possible pitfalls that await the family. Playing devil's advocate, the therapist challenges the family's ability to manage future conflicts:

Therapist: I hope none of these events (the future pitfalls) occur, but I'm a strong believer in preparing for the worst.

Paradoxically, by challenging the changes made so far in the family and predicting future pitfalls, the therapist was cementing the change to this point and stiffening the family's resolve to maintain those changes. Thus, he was not only building in a prophylactic trip wire but also intervening in a paradoxical fashion.

4. Eliciting Feedback

Termination offers the therapist an opportunity to learn. By asking the family members what was helpful and what was not helpful during treatment, the therapist builds a personal database. Sometimes, hearing what each family member has found helpful is quite surprising. What the therapist had intended and what the family found helpful might be quite different. There are, furthermore, as many different responses as there are family members. Regardless, each will have something unique to add.

Also, by asking the family members for feedback, the therapist gains an appreciation of his or her personal style. Although they may have the same theoretical position, no two therapists conduct therapy in quite the same way. Knowingly or unknowingly, each therapist develops a unique style. Fortunately, for the therapist who is open to it, the family's feedback offers the opportunity to learn what is effective and what is not effective in one's style.

5. Leaving the Door Open for Future Contacts

As mentioned above, from a system, life cycle perspective, families are in constant evolution. Thus, problems will continually present themselves. Ideally, what they have learned in therapy can be applied to future situations, but the unexpected will always occur. Consequently, the therapist leaves the door open for future contacts.

Therapist: Before we close, I just want to say that I would be happy to meet with any or all of you in the future. Please feel free to contact me.

It is not uncommon for a therapist to be recontacted by a family later. Sometimes it is because old patterns have reemerged. Sometimes the next developmental stage presents challenges that appear overwhelming to the family. Sometimes it is a simple one-session checkup. Whatever the reason, termination sets the stage and extends the invitation for future contact.

Premature Termination

In many situations, the family raises the issue of termination in the middle of the treatment process (as the therapist perceives it). Frequently, the issue is raised as a complaint. The therapist's first response is to address it as resistance and weigh the family's reaction.

> **Peter** (after four sessions and after Cindy has begun an intense testing of the parents' new limits): Things have become worse, not better, since we've been coming here! I don't know if we should keep coming.

> **Therapist:** Whether or not you come has always been your decision, but your frustration could be a result of trying to learn something new. Cindy is certainly going to test these new limits, and I think she's wondering which way you'll go.

At other times, however, the threat of premature termination raises the therapist's anxiety. Instead of addressing the complaint as resistance, the therapist fears losing the case and therefore colludes in the resistance. For instance, in the above example, the therapist could have backed off the therapeutic focus on the couple and returned to focusing solely on Cindy. In the short run, this would have reduced Peter's anxiety, and he would have continued the sessions. However, he probably would have continued only as long as the therapist focused on Cindy and asked little of him. Thus, the eventual shift to the broader system would probably have again raised Peter's anxiety.

At these points in treatment, the therapist's art and intuition enter the picture in determining whether the therapeutic focus is too threatening to the family: "Should I continue to push the parental and marital issues, or shift back to the initial focus on Cindy? Will the family be able to absorb an increase in anxiety, or am I pushing them to drop out? Is there a way of reframing the shift to the parental issues that will be more acceptable to Peter?"

As outlined above, the most straightforward means of addressing premature termination is to respect the family's opinion but also to identify the future pitfalls and further obstacles to change and to leave an open door for the family. Rather than judging these families as resistant and confronting their resistance, the therapist views them from a developmental perspective and considers the element of timing. Although Peter and Donna were reluctant to discuss their covert marital conflict at this time, they were more likely to resume therapy at a later date if the therapist planted the seed (the marital relationship) and terminated, even though prematurely, on good terms.

Dropouts

Several missed appointments explained by questionable excuses hint that the family is ready to drop out of treatment. At the close of a session, a family member explains to the therapist, "I don't know our plans for next week, so I'll give you a call to schedule the next appointment." The phone call never comes, or the family simply fails to come to a scheduled appointment and does not bother to call. Each of these signals a dropout.

Dropouts can occur in any phase of treatment. Sometimes they occur in the early part of treatment because of a lack of engagement between the family and the therapist. This might be because of an initially low level of motivation on the family's part, the therapist's inability to engage the family, or both. Sometimes dropping out occurs in the middle phases of treatment, as the family's anxiety is pushed past manageable limits and withdrawal is their last defense.

Dropouts are a fact of life for even the most experienced family therapist. Masters (1978) reports on a family therapy study in which only highly motivated families were selected for treatment. Despite the rigid screening procedures, 40% of the families dropped out after six to 10 sessions. Thus, even when maximizing the possibilities for success by controlling for motivation, dropouts still occurred—a humbling thought!

Of course, the rest of us do not have the luxury of a controlled study to screen out our clients. Families come into our offices with a wide variety of problems and motivations. To believe we will engage every family and terminate their sessions only after successful therapy borders on hubris. Still, dropouts can be minimized.

First, a thorough assessment phase in and of itself not only tests the family's motivation for therapy but also enhances the engagement process. In the assessment phase, how open the family is to the therapist's questions is an initial indication of motivation: Does the family readily respond to the questions? Are the family members honest and straightforward in their responses? Are family members guarded or suspicious? Are family members apathetic or indifferent?

Sometimes a family's poor motivation can be overcome by a successful engagement between the family and the therapist. In these cases, a therapeutic alliance forms when the family members believe the therapist understands them and appreciates their struggles. In an empirical study on families that drop out of therapy after one or two sessions, a disconnection between the therapist and family was a major factor (Lever & Gmeiner, 2000). The disconnection occurred when a family was not clear on the process and purpose of family therapy and when the therapist imposed his or her view on the family.

When engagement is difficult and the family appears reluctant or ambivalent concerning therapy, however, it is best for the therapist to put the issue on the table:

Therapist: Through our conversations, I have a good sense of the problems you face as a family, but I also have a sense that some of you are not sure about this therapy business. I believe it would be helpful if we could discuss some of these concerns.

The therapist is not only addressing the family's ambivalence but is also developing a therapeutic alliance. Paradoxically, as the family members honestly discuss their ambivalence and reluctance to begin therapy, they are developing a therapeutic bond with the therapist: "We agree to disagree and will be honest in the process" (Worden, 1991).

Of course, this works only as long as the therapist is open to hearing the family's reluctance and is not afraid of the family's dropping out. With this stance, the therapist communicates respect for the family members' concerns and willingness to accept their decision about beginning therapy, whatever it might be. In particular, this is a vital message to families struggling with control issues. When they are experiencing internal control battles, the last thing they need is a control battle with the therapist over whether to begin therapy.

If the family has canceled or not shown up for several appointments, a follow-up call is in order. Although, with a follow-up call, the therapist walks a fine line between chasing a reluctant family and encouraging the engagement process, he or she is communicating concern and willingness to work with the family. Consequently, rather than asking the family member why he or she has canceled the appointments or has not called, and possibly putting that person on the defensive, the therapist wants to make sure he or she is understood:

> **Therapist** (in a follow-up call): I am calling because you have canceled several of our appointments. I was wondering if some difficulties have come up, and I was also wondering if I was unclear about the purpose of our meetings.

The therapist is expressing concern for the family and asking if he or she has been clear in explaining the purpose of therapy. Moreover, the therapist has expressed a desire to meet the family halfway and to open a dialogue with the family members.

Dropouts, however, raise a therapist's anxiety. In some cases, pathology is so prevalent—severe acting-out, suicide potential, substance abuse—and the family's defensive denial is so powerful that engaging the family is quite difficult. This is particularly true with families who are not self-referred but have been coerced into therapy by an external authority (for example, by school or legal authorities). These families sometimes go through the motions of attending several sessions (usually until they believe they have satisfied the external authority) and then they drop out. The therapist is left feeling helpless and in a quandary. "Do I bother calling the family? Do I notify the referral source? Do I try to contact the family and convince them of the severity of their problems?"

As an aside, with families coerced into treatment by an external authority, it is important (and saves needless worry) to address the issue of coercion in the first session. Clarifying the role of the therapist in relationship to the referring authority—for example, having the family sign the necessary release of information forms—is part of the contract with the family. Thus, if the family does drop out, the therapist has a clear direction on whether to involve the referral source according to the agreement:

> **Therapist** (to the family members): What is the agreement you have with the school (or probation officer) about being in therapy? For example, how many sessions are you supposed to attend? What is the problem you were referred for?

> **Therapist:** Also, before we begin any meetings, I would like to call the person who referred you and be clear on my responsibilities in working with you.

If the therapist is unable to telephone the family that has missed appointments, a letter to the family might be in order. Not only is a letter a formal means of contacting the family; it is also an official record terminating therapy. In the letter, the therapist documents the length of contact and expresses specific concerns for the family or individual family members. For example, if the therapist is concerned about suicidal tendencies with one of the family members, this is spelled out. The letter concludes by inviting the family to contact the therapist again at any point.

Finally, although having families unexpectedly drop out of treatment is an occupational hazard, it behooves the therapist to identify any possible patterns in his or her caseload. For example, are many cases lost in the engagement phase? Do most dropouts occur in the middle phase of treatment? Are certain types of families more likely to drop out than others? Alcoholic families? Depressed families? Chaotic, acting-out families?

Consistent dropout patterns are feedback to observant therapists who are open to learning and improving their style. When such patterns are identified, constructive supervision serves as an invaluable aid for enhancing a therapist's skill and benefiting the families with whom he or she works.

Summary

Termination is more like closing a chapter than a book. From a life cycle, developmental perspective, families do not reach an end point. They continually evolve from one generation to the next. The therapist enters a family to facilitate the unlocking of patterns that are inhibiting a whole family as well as its individual members from growing; then, the therapist exits as soon as possible.

Certainly, the therapist's involvement—the creation of a therapeutic alliance—has a beginning, middle, and end, but it is an end for that specific time only. In fact, most family therapists' caseloads have their share of families who are being seen for the second or third time. This does not mean the first go-around in therapy was unsuccessful or incomplete. Rather, it indicates that the family members highly valued their first experience with the therapist; if they did not, they would find a new therapist. It shows they are seeking assistance with another obstacle they have found difficult to hurdle. Lebow (1995) refers to this as open-ended family therapy.

From this longitudinal perspective, a therapist terminates with a family by consolidating the gains made in treatment, providing problem-solving skills for the future, and encouraging additional contacts.

9

Epilogue

While I was teaching an introductory course in family counseling, I was approached by a student who said, "I'll be graduating with my master's in counseling in May and opening a private practice in marital and family therapy. How do I go about getting referrals?" Standing with my mouth open, I was undecided whether to burst out in laughter or hit the student over the head. After one introductory course in family counseling, he barely knew the appropriate questions, much less the answers.

What struck me even more was his seemingly cavalier attitude toward working with people, particularly families. Working with people in the intimacy of therapy is a sacred trust, a responsibility one assumes in becoming a therapist. As a therapist, you will be seen as an "expert" by the people with whom you work, and your words will be weighed heavily. You are in a position to do a great deal of good or a great deal of harm. Consequently, you owe your clients the best you can offer; therefore, you can never get enough experience, training, and supervision.

If you will permit more soapbox statements, the following is a list of do's and don'ts regarding family therapy:

- Ask of family members only what you ask of yourself. Therapists can be notorious for asking clients to do the very behavior they themselves find difficult to do. For example, pushing a spouse to confront the other spouse carries more authority if the therapist is also capable of such behavior.

- Similarly, don't rework your own family-of-origin issues with the families that come to you; do that in your own personal therapy.

- Don't attempt to remake families toward an ideal goal. Ideal families exist in psychological theories and on television! Realistic treatment goals are much more likely to be reached than utopian heights.

- Let families teach and guide you. Each family has its own style, and understanding how each family functions expands your own knowledge base.

- Be flexible and appreciate the value of diverse approaches. Research does not show the value of one theory or method to family issues over another; rather, there is value in tailoring an approach to fit a specific family and problem (Lebow, 2000).

Your development as a family therapist and your professional reputation will emerge from your ability to respect families and their individual members. This respect entails being direct and honest with the family members and doing your utmost to assist them with their difficulties. Research has shown that the effectiveness of any given therapy can vary considerably depending on what therapist is providing the treatment, because the major agent of effective psychotherapy is the personality of the therapist (Luborsky, McLellan, Woody, O'Brien, & Auerbach, 1985). Remember, your most valuable resource in developing your professional skill will not be techniques or theories but yourself.

References

Alexander, J., & Parsons, B. (1982). *Functional family therapy.* Monterey, CA: Brooks/Cole.

Andersen, T. (1993). See and hear, and be seen and heard. In S. Friedman (Ed.), *The new language of change: Constructive collaboration in psychotherapy.* New York: Guilford Press.

Anderson, C. M., Reiss, D., & Horgarty, G. E. (1986). *Schizophrenia and the family: A practitioner's guide to psychoeducation and management.* New York: Guilford Press.

Anderson, C. M., & Stewart, S. (1983). *Mastering resistance: A practical guide to family therapy.* New York: Guilford Press.

Anderson, H., & Goolishian, H. (1992). The client is the expert: A not-knowing approach to therapy. In S. McNamee & K. J. Gergen (Eds.), *Constructing therapy: Social construction and the therapeutic process.* London: Sage.

Aries, E. (1996). *Men and women in interaction: Reconsidering the differences.* New York: Oxford University Press.

Bandler, R., Grinder, J., & Satir, V. (1976). *Changing with families.* Palo Alto, CA: Science and Behavior Books.

Beall, A. E. (1993). A social constructionist view of gender. In A. E. Beall & R. J. Sternberg (Eds.), *The psychology of gender.* New York: Guilford Press.

Beavers, W. R. (1977). *Psychotherapy and growth: A family systems perspective.* New York: Brunner/Mazel.

Beavers, W. R., & Hampson, R. B. (1990). *Successful families: Assessment and intervention.* New York: W. W. Norton.

Beavers, W. R., & Hampson, R. B. (2000). The Beavers Systems Model of Family Functioning. *Journal of Family Therapy, 22,* 128–143.

Berg, I. K., & DeShazer, S. (1993). Making numbers talk: Language in therapy. In S. Friedman (Ed.), *The new language of change: Constructive collaboration in psychotherapy.* New York: Guilford Press.

Bergman, J. S. (1985). *Fishing for barracuda: Pragmatics of brief systemic therapy.* New York: W. W. Norton.

Bertrando, P. (2000). Text and context: Narrative, postmodernism and cybernetics. *Journal of Family Therapy, 22,* 83–103.

Best, D. L., & Williams, J. E. (1993). Cross-cultural viewpoint. In A. E. Beall & R. J. Sternberg (Eds.), *The psychology of gender.* New York: Guilford Press.

Bishop, D., Epstein, N., Keitner, B., Miller, I., & Zlotnick, C. (1980). *The McMaster Structural Interview for Family Functioning.* Providence, RI: Brown University Family Research Program.

Blumstein, P., & Schwartz, P. (1983). *American couples: Money, work, sex.* New York: William Morrow.

Blumstein, P., & Schwartz, P. (1991). Money and ideology: Their impact on power and the division of household labor. In R. L. Blumberg (Ed.), *Gender, family, and economy: The triple overlap.* Newbury Park, CA: Sage.

Bogard, M. (1990). Women treating men. *The Family Therapy Networker, 14*(3), 54–58.

Bordin, E. S. (1982). A working alliance based model of supervision. *The Counseling Psychologist, 11,* 35–42.

Boss, P., & Greenberg, J. (1984). Family boundary ambiguity: A new variable in family stress theory. *Family Process, 23,* 535–546.

Boszormenyi-Nagy, I., & Spark, G. M. (1973). *Invisible loyalties: Reciprocity in intergenerational family therapy.* New York: Harper & Row.

Bowen, M. (1976). Theory in the practice of psychotherapy. In P. J. Guerin, Jr. (Ed.), *Family therapy: Theory and practice.* New York: Gardner Press.

Bowen, M. (1978). Family therapy in clinical practice. New York: Jason Aronson.

Boyd-Franklin, N. (1987). The contribution of family therapy models to the treatment of black families. *Psychotherapy, 24*(35), 621–629.

Boyd-Franklin, N. (1989). *Black family in therapy: A multisystem approach.* New York: Guilford Press.

Bray, J. H. (1995). Systems-oriented therapy with stepfamilies. In R. H. Mikesell, D. D. Lusterman, & S. H. McDaniels (Eds.), *Integrating family therapy: Handbook of family psychology and systems theory.* Washington, DC: American Psychological Association.

Burns, R. C. (1982). *Self-growth in families: Kinetic family drawings (K-F-D): Research and application.* New York: Brunner/Mazel.

Burns, R. C., & Kaufman, S. H. (1970). *Kinetic family drawings (K-F-D): An introduction to understanding children through kinetic drawings.* New York: Brunner/Mazel.

Burns, R. C., & Kaufman, S. H. (1972). *Actions, styles and symbols in kinetic family drawings (K-F-D): An interpretative manual.* New York: Brunner/ Mazel.

Byng-Hall, J., & Campbell, D. (1981). Resolving conflicts in family distance regulation: An integrative approach. *Journal of Marital and Family Therapy, 7*(3), 321–330.

Cancian, F. M. (1989). Love and the rise of capitalism. In B. J. Risman & P. Schwartz (Eds.), *Gender in intimate relationships: A microstructural approach.* Belmont, CA: Wadsworth.

Carli, L. L. (1990). Gender, language, and influence. *Journal of Personality and Social Psychology, 59,* 941–951.

Carr, A. (2000). Empirical approaches to family assessment. *Journal of Family Therapy, 22,* 121–127.

Carter, E. (1988). Remarried families: Creating a new paradigm. In M. Walters, E. Carter, P. Papp, & O. Silverstein (Eds.), *The invisible web: Gender patterns in family relationships.* New York: Guilford Press.

Carter, E., & McGoldrick, M. (Eds.). (1988). *The changing family life cycle: A framework for family therapy* (2nd ed.). Boston: Allyn & Bacon.

Celano, M. P., & Kaslow, N. J. (2000). Culturally competent family interventions: Review and case illustrations. *American Journal of Family Therapy, 28*(3), 217–228.

Chodorow, N. (1978). *The reproduction of mothering.* Berkeley: University of California Press.

Clingempeel, W. G., Grand, E., & Ievoli, R. (1984). Stepparent-stepchild relationships in stepmother and stepfather families: A multimethod study. *Family Relations, 33,* 465–473.

Cohn, L. D. (1991). Sex differences in the course of personality development: A meta-analysis. *Psychological Bulletin, 109,* 252–266.

Combrinck- Graham, L. (1985). A developmental model for family systems. *Family Process, 24*(2), 139–150.

Cross, S. E., & Markus, H. R. (1993). Gender in thought, belief, and action: A cognitive approach. In A. E. Beall & R. J. Sternberg (Eds.), *The psychology of gender.* New York: Guilford Press.

DeShazer, S. (1982). *Patterns of brief family therapy: An ecosystemic approach.* New York: Guilford Press.

DeShazer, S. (1991). *Putting difference to work.* New York: W. W. Norton.

DeShazer, S. (1994). *Words were originally magic.* New York: W. W. Norton.

Drumm, M., Carr, A., & Fitzgerald, M. (2000). The Beavers, McMaster and Circumplex clinical rating scales: A study of their sensitivity, specificity and discriminant validity. *Journal of Family Therapy, 22,* 225–238.

Efran, J. S., Lukens, M. D., & Lukens, R. J. (1990). *Language, structure, and change: Frameworks of meaning in psychotherapy.* New York: W. W. Norton.

Epstein, N., Baldwin, L., & Bishop, D. (1983). The McMaster Family Assessment Device. *Journal of Marital and Family Therapy, 9,* 171–180.

Epstein, N., Bishop, D., Keitner, G. & Miller, I. (1990). A systems therapy: Problem-centered systems therapy of the family. In R. Wells & V. Giannetti (Eds.), *Handbook of brief psychotherapies.* New York: Plenum.

Etchison, M., & Kleist, D. M. (2000). Review of

narrative therapy: Research and utility. *The Family Journal: Counseling and Therapy for Couples and Families, 8*(1), 61–66.

Falbo, T., & Peplau, L. A. (1980). Power strategies in intimate relationships. *Journal of Personality and Social Psychology, 38,* 618–628.

Falloon, I. R. (Ed.). (1986). *Handbook of behavioral family therapy.* New York: Guilford Press.

Fanger, M. T. (1993). After the shift: Time effective treatment in the possibility frame. In S. Friedman (Ed.), *The new language of change: Constructive collaboration in psychotherapy.* New York: Guilford Press.

Fisch, F., Weakland, J. H., & Segal, L. (1982). *The tactics of change: Doing therapy briefly.* San Francisco: Jossey-Bass.

Friedman, S., & Fanger, M. T. (1991). *Expanding therapeutic possibilities.* New York: Lexington Books.

Garmezy, N. (1985). Stress resistant children: The search for protective factors. In J. E. Stevenson (Ed.), Recent research in developmental psychopathology. *Journal of Child Psychology and Psychiatry Book Suppl.* No. 4. Oxford: Pergamon Press.

Geis, F. (1993). Self-fulfilling prophecies: A social psychological view of gender. In A. E. Beall & R. J. Sternberg (Eds.), *The psychology of gender.* New York: Guilford Press.

Gergen, K. J. (1985). The social constructionist movement in modern psychology. *American Psychologist, 40,* 266–275.

Gerson, R. (1995). The family life cycle: Phases, stages, and crises. In R. H. Mikesell, D. D. Lusterman, & S. H. McDaniels (Eds.), *Integrating family therapy: Handbook of family psychology and systems theory.* Washington, DC: American Psychological Association.

Gil, E. (1994). *Play in family therapy.* New York: Guilford Press.

Glick, P. C., & Lin, Sung-Lin. (1986). Recent changes in divorce and remarriage. *Journal of Marriage and the Family, 48,* 737–747.

Goldenberg, I., & Goldenberg, H. (1985). *Family therapy: An overview.* Monterey, CA: Brooks/Cole.

Goolishian, H., & Anderson, H. (1987). Language systems and therapy: An evolving idea. *Psychotherapy, 24*(35), 529–538.

Goolishian, H., & Anderson, H. (1990). Understanding the therapeutic process: From individuals and families to systems language. In F. W. Kaslow (Ed.), *Voices in family psychology.* Newbury Park, CA: Sage.

Gottman, J. M. (1994). *Why marriages succeed or fail.* New York: Simon & Schuster.

Gottman, J. M., & Levenson, R. W. (1992). Marital processes predictive of later dissolution: Behavior, physiology and health. *Journal of Personality and Social Psychology, 63,* 221–233.

Green, R., & Herget, M. (1991). Outcomes of systemic/strategic team consultation: III. The importance of therapist warmth and active structuring. *Family Process, 30,* 321–336.

Green, R. J., & Werner, P. D. (1996). Intrusiveness and closeness-caregiving: Rethinking the concept of family "enmeshment." *Family Process, 35*(2), 115–136.

Guerin, P. J., Jr., & Pendagast, M. A. (1976). Evaluation of family system and genogram. In P. J. Guerin, Jr. (Ed.), *Family therapy: Theory and practice.* New York: Gardner Press.

Gurman, A. S., & Kniskern, D. P. (1978). Deterioration in marital and family therapy: Empirical, clinical, and conceptual issues. *Family Process, 17,* 5.

Gurman, A. S., & Kniskern, D. P. (1991). *Handbook of family therapy* (Vol. 2). New York: Brunner/Mazel.

Gurman, A. S., Kniskern, D. P., & Pinsof, W. M. (1986). Research on the process and outcome of marital and family therapy. In S. L. Garfield & A. E. Bergin (Eds.), *Handbook of psychotherapy and behavior change.* New York: John Wiley.

Haley, J. (1976). *Problem-solving therapy.* San Francisco: Jossey-Bass.

Hampson, R. B., & Beavers, W. R. (1996a). Family therapy and outcome: Relationships between therapist and family styles. *Contemporary Family Therapy, 18,* 345–370.

Hampson, R. B., & Beavers, W. R. (1996b). Measuring family therapy outcome in a clinical setting. *Family Process, 35,* 347–360.

Hare-Mustin, R. T. (1989). The problems of gender in family therapy theory. In M. McGoldrick, C. M. Anderson, & F. Walsh

(Eds.), *Women in families: A framework for family therapy.* New York: W. W. Norton.

Hatfield, E., & Rapson, R. L. (1993). *Love, sex, and intimacy.* New York: HarperCollins.

Hawley, D. R., & DeHaan, L. (1996). Toward a definition of family resilience: Integrating life-span and family perspectives. *Family Process, 35*(3), 283–298.

Hetherington, E. M., Bridges, M., & Glendessa, M. I. (1998). What matters? What does not? Five perspectives on the association between marital transitions and children's adjustment. *American Psychologist, 53*(2), 167–184.

Hoffman, L. (1981). *Foundations of family therapy: A conceptual framework for systems change.* New York: Basic Books.

Hyde, J. S. (1981). How large are cognitive gender differences? A meta-analysis using w and d. *American Psychologist, 36,* 892–901.

Kagan, J. (1984). *The nature of the child.* New York: Basic Books.

Keeney, F. P., & Ross, J. M. (1985). *Mind in therapy: Constructing systemic family therapies.* New York: Basic Books.

Kerr, M., & Bowen, M. (1988). *Family evaluation.* New York: W. W. Norton.

Keshet, J. K., & Mirkin, M. P. (1985). Troubled adolescents in divorced and remarried families. In M. P. Mirkin & S. L. Koman (Eds.), *Handbook of adolescent and family therapy.* New York: Gardner Press.

L'Abate, L., Ganahl, G., & Hansen, J. C. (1986). *Methods of family therapy.* Englewood Cliffs, NJ: Prentice Hall.

Lebow, J. (1995). Open-ended therapy: Termination in marital and family therapy. In R. H. Mikesell, D. D. Lusterman, & S. H. McDaniels (Eds.), *Integrating family therapy: Handbook of family psychology and systems theory.* Washington, DC: American Psychological Association.

Lebow, J. (2000). What does research tell us about couple and family therapies? *Journal of Clinical Psychology, 56*(8), 1083–1094.

Lever, H., & Gmeiner, A. (2000). Families leaving family therapy after one or two sessions: A multiple descriptive case study. *Contemporary Family Therapy: An International Journal, 22*(1), 39–65.

Levine L. B., & Fish, L. S. (1999). The integration of constructivism and social constructionist theory in family therapy: A delphi study. *Journal of Systemic Therapies 18*(1), 58–84.

Liddle, H. A. (1983). Diagnosis and assessment in family therapy: A comparative analysis of six schools of thought. In J. C. Hansen & B. P. Keeney (Eds.), *Diagnosis and assessment in family therapy.* Rockville, MD: Aspen.

Liddle, H. A., Rowe, C., Dakof, G., & Lyke, J. (1998). Translating parenting research into clinical interventions for families of adolescents. *Clinical Child Psychology and Psychiatry, 3*(3), 419–443.

Low, N. S. (1990). Women in couples: How their experience of relationships differs from men's. In R. Chasin, H. Grunebaum, & M. Herzig (Eds.), *One couple, four realities: Multiple perspectives on couple therapy.* New York: Guilford Press.

Luborsky, L., McLellan, T., Woody, G. E., O'Brien, C. P., & Auerbach, A. (1985). Therapist success and its determinants. *Archives of General Psychiatry, 42,* 602–611.

Luepnitz, D. A. (1988). *The family interpreted: Feminist theory in clinical practice.* New York: Basic Books.

Lutz, P. (1983). The stepfamily: An adolescent perspective. *Family Relations, 32,* 367–375.

Mandanes, C. (1981). *Strategic family therapy.* San Francisco: Jossey-Bass.

Masters, R. S. (1978). Family therapy in child and adolescent psychiatry: A review of 35 families. *Child Psychiatry Quarterly, 11*(3), 70–82.

McGoldrick, M. (1982). Irish families. In M. McGoldrick, J. K. Pearce, & J. Giordano (Eds.), *Ethnicity and family therapy.* New York: Guilford Press.

McGoldrick, M., & Gerson, R. (1985). *Genograms in family assessment.* New York: W. W. Norton.

McGoldrick, M., Pearce, J. K., & Giordano, J. (1996). *Ethnicity and family therapy* (2nd ed.). New York: Guilford Press.

McGoldrick, M., Preto, N. G., Hines, P. M., & Lee, E. (1991). Ethnicity and family therapy. In A. S. Gurman & D. P. Kniskern (Eds.), *Handbook of family therapy* (Vol. 2). New York: Brunner/Mazel.

Miller, I., Kabacoff, R., Bishop, D., Epstein, N., & Keitner, G. (1994). The development of the McMaster Clinical Rating Scale. *Family Process, 33,* 53–69.

Miller, I. W., Ryan, C. E., Keitner, G. I., Bishop, D. S., & Epstein, N. B. (2000). The McMaster Approach to Families: Theory, assessment, treatment and research. *Journal of Family Therapy, 22,* 168–189.

Minuchin, S. (1974). *Families and family therapy.* Cambridge, MA: Harvard University Press.

Minuchin, S., & Fishman, H. C. (1981). *Family therapy techniques.* Cambridge, MA: Harvard University Press.

Mishne, J. M. (1986). *Clinical work with adolescents.* New York: The Free Press.

Nelson, T. S., & Trepper, T. S. (1992). *101 interventions in family therapy.* Binghamton, NY: Haworth Press.

Newberry, A. M., Alexander, J. F., & Turner, C. W. (1991). Gender as a process variable in family therapy. *Journal of Family Psychology, 5*(2), 158–175.

Nichols, M. P. (1987). *The self in the system: Expanding the limits of family therapy.* New York: Brunner/ Mazel.

Nichols, M. P., & Schwartz, R. C. (1991). *Family therapy: Concepts and methods* (2nd ed.). Boston: Allyn & Bacon.

Norum, D. (2000). The family has the solution. *Journal of Systemic Therapies, 19*(1), 3–15.

O'Hanlon, W. H., & Weiner-Davis, M. (1989). *In search of solutions: A new direction in psychotherapy.* New York: W. W. Norton.

Olson, D. H. (2000). Circumplex Model of Marital and Family Systems. *Journal of Family Therapy, 22,* 144–167.

Olson, D. H. (1991). Three dimensional (3–D) Circumplex Model and revised scoring of FACES. *Family Process, 30,* 74–79.

Olson, D. H., Russell, C. S., & Sprenkle, D. H. (1989). *Circumplex Model: Systemic assessment and treatment of families.* New York: Haworth Press.

Olson, D. H., Russell, C. S., & Sprenkle, D. H. (1983). Circumplex Model of Marital and Family Systems: VI. Theoretical update. *Family Process, 22,* 69–83.

Olson, D. H., Russell, C. S., & Sprenkle, D. H. (1979). Circumplex Model of Marital and Family Systems I: Cohesion and adaptability dimensions, family types, and clinical applications. *Family Process, 18,* 3–28.

Orlinsky, D., & Howard, K. (1986). Process and outcome in psychotherapy. In S. L. Garfield & A. E. Bergin (Eds.), *Handbook of psychotherapy and behavior change.* New York: John Wiley.

Papp, P. (1983). *The process of change.* New York: Guilford Press.

Pare, D. A. (1995). Of families and other cultures: The shifting paradigm of family therapy. *Family Process, 34,* 1–19.

Piercy, F. P., & Sprenkle, D. H. (1986). *Family therapy sourcebook.* New York: Guilford Press.

Pilgrim, D. (2000). The real problem for postmodernism. *Journal of Family Therapy, 22*(1), 6–23.

Preto, N. G., & Travis, N. (1985). The adolescent phase of the family life cycle. In M. P. Mirkin & S. L. Koman (Eds.), *Handbook of adolescents and family therapy.* New York: Gardner Press.

Reiss, D. (1981). *The family's construction of reality.* Cambridge, MA: Harvard University Press.

Rotunno, M., & McGoldrick, M. (1982). Italian families. In M. McGoldrick, J. K. Pearce, & J. Giordano (Eds.), *Ethnicity and family therapy.* New York: Guilford Press.

Rutter, M. (1999). Resilience concepts and findings implications for family therapy. *Journal of Family Therapy, 21,* 119–144.

Saleebey, D. (1994). Culture, theory, and narrative: The intersection of meanings in practice. *Social Work, 39*(4), 351–359.

Schwartz, S. (2000). *Abnormal psychology.* Mountain View, CA: Mayfield.

Selekman, M. D. (1993). *Pathways to change: Brief therapy solutions with difficult adolescents.* New York: Guilford Press.

Selevini Palazzoli, M. S., Cecchin, G., Boscolo, L., & Prata, G. (1978). *Paradox and counterparadox.* New York: Jason Aronson.

Shapiro, R. (1981). Countertransference reactions in family therapy. In A. S. Gurman (Ed.), *Questions and answers in the practice of family therapy.* New York: Brunner/Mazel.

Sherman, J. A. (1980). Therapists' attitudes and sex role stereotyping. In A. Brodsky & R. T. Hare-Mustin (Eds.), *Women and psychotherapy: An assessment of research and practice.* New York: Guilford Press.

Sherman, R., & Fredman, N. (1986). *Handbook of structured techniques in marriage and family therapy.* New York: Brunner/Mazel.

Simon, R. M. (1989). Family life cycle issues in the therapy system. In B. Carter & M. McGoldrick (Eds.), *The changing family life cycle* (2nd ed.). Boston: Allyn & Bacon.

Skynner, A. C. (1981). An open-systems, group-analytic approach to family therapy. In A. S. Gurman & D. P. Kniskern (Eds.), *Handbook of family therapy.* New York: Brunner/Mazel.

Spiegel, J. (1982). An ecological model of ethnic families. In M. McGoldrick, J. K. Pearce, & J. Giordano (Eds.), *Ethnicity and family therapy.* New York: Guilford Press.

Sprenkel, D. H., & Fisher, B. (1980). An empirical assessment of the goals of family therapy. *Journal of Marital and Family Therapy, 6,* 131–139.

Stanton, M. D., & Todd, T. C. (1979). Structural family therapy with drug addicts. In E. Kaufman & P. Kaufmann (Eds.), *The family therapy of drug and alcohol abuse.* New York: Gardner Press.

Steinglass, P., Bennett, L., Wolin, S., & Reiss, D. (1987). *The alcoholic family.* New York: Basic Books.

Stiver, I. P. (1991). The meanings of "dependency" in female-male relationships. In J. V. Jordan, A. G. Kaplan, J. B. Miller, I. P. Stiver, & J. L. Surrey (Eds.), *Women's growth in connection: Writings from the Stone Center.* New York: Guilford Press.

Tannen, D. (1990). *You just don't understand: Women and men in conversation.* New York: Ballantine Books.

Tavris, C. (1992). *The mismeasure of woman.* New York: Touchstone Books.

Taylor, T. K., & Biglan, A. (1998). Behavioral family interventions for improving child rearing: A review of the literature for clinicians and policy makers. *Clinical Child and Family Psychology Review, 1*(1), 41–60.

Titleman, P. (1987). *The therapist's own family: Toward the differentiation of self.* Northvale, NJ: Jason Aronson.

Tomm, K. (1987a). Interventive interviewing: I. Strategizing as a fourth guideline for the therapist. *Family Process, 26*(1), 3–13.

Tomm, K. (1987b). Interventive interviewing: II. Reflexive questioning as a means to enable self-healing. *Family Process, 26*(2), 167–183.

Tomm, K. (1988). Interventive interviewing: III. Intending to ask lineal, circular, strategic, or reflexive questions? *Family Process, 27*(1), 1–15.

Visher, E., & Visher, J. (1988). *Old loyalties, new ties: Therapeutic strategies with stepfamilies.* New York: Brunner/Mazel.

Wallerstein, J. S., & Kelly, J. B. (1980). *Surviving the break up: How children and parents cope with divorce.* New York: Basic Books.

Walsh, F. (1995). From family damage to family challenge. In R. H. Mikesell, D. D. Lusterman, & S. H. McDaniels (Eds.), *Integrating family therapy: Handbook of family psychology and systems theory.* Washington, DC: American Psychological Association.

Walsh, F., & Scheinkman, M. (1989). (Fe)male: The hidden gender dimension in models of family therapy. In M. McGoldrick, C. M. Anderson, & F. Walsh (Eds.), *Women in families: A framework for family therapy.* New York: W. W. Norton.

Walters, M., Carter, R., Papp, P., & Silverstein, O. (1988). *The invisible web: Gender patterns in family relationships.* New York: Guilford Press.

Watzlawick, P. (Ed.). (1984). The invented reality: How do we know what we believe we know? *Contributions to constructionism.* New York: W. W. Norton.

Watzlawick, P., Weakland, J., & Fisch, R. (1974). *Change: Principles of problem formation and problem resolution.* New York: W. W. Norton.

Werner, E. E. (1993). Risk, resilience, and recovery: Perspectives from the Kauai Longitudinal Study. *Development and Psychopathology, 5,* 503–515.

Whitaker, C. A., & Bumberry, W. M. (1988). *Dancing with the family: A symbolic-experiential approach.* New York: Brunner/Mazel.

Whitaker, C. A., & Keith, D. V. (1981). Symbolic-experiential family therapy. In A. S. Gurman & D. P. Kniskern (Eds.), *Handbook of family therapy.* New York: Brunner/ Mazel.

White, B. B. (1989). Gender differences in marital communication patterns. *Family Process, 28*(1), 89–106.

White, M. (1991). Deconstruction and therapy. *Dulwich Centre Newsletter, 3,* 21–40.

White, M., & Epston, D. (1990). *Narrative means to therapeutic ends.* New York: W. W. Norton.

Widiger, T. A., & Clark, L. A. (2001). Toward DSM-V and the classification of psychopathology. *Psychological Bulletin, 126*(6), 946–963.

Will, D. (1983). Some techniques for working with resistant families of adolescents. *Journal of Adolescence, 6*(1), 13–26.

Williams, J. E., & Best, D. L. (1990a). *Measuring sex stereotypes: A multination study.* Newbury Park, CA: Sage.

Williams, J. E., & Best, D. L. (1990b). *Sex and psyche: Gender and self viewed cross-culturally.* Newbury Park, CA: Sage.

Worden, M. (1991). *Adolescents and their families: An introduction to assessment and intervention.* Binghamton, NY: Haworth Press.

Worden, M., & Worden, B. D. (1998). *The gender dance in couples therapy.* Pacific Grove, CA: Brooks/Cole.

Wylie, M. S. (1991). Family therapy's neglected prophet. *The Family Therapy Networker, 15*(2), 24–46.

Zilbach, J. J. (1986). *Young children in family therapy.* New York: Brunner/Mazel.

Index